Killer Woman Blues

Books by Benjamin DeMott

THE BODY'S CAGE

HELLS & BENEFITS

YOU DON'T SAY

A MARRIED MAN

SUPERGROW

SURVIVING THE SEVENTIES

THE IMPERIAL MIDDLE

THE TROUBLE WITH FRIENDSHIP

KILLER WOMAN BLUES

Books edited by Benjamin DeMott

SCHOLARSHIP FOR SOCIETY

AMERICA IN LITERATURE

CLOSE IMAGINING

CREATED EQUAL

Benjamin DeMott

Killer Woman Blues

··

Why Americans can't think straight about gender and power

HOUGHTON MIFFLIN COMPANY

BOSTON · NEW YORK   2000

For information about permission to reproduce selections from
this book, write to Permissions, Houghton Mifflin Company,
215 Park Avenue South, New York, New York 10003.

Visit our Web site: www.houghtonmifflinbooks.com

Library of Congress Cataloging-in-Publication Data
DeMott, Benjamin, date.
    Killer woman blues : why Americans can't think straight
about gender and power / Benjamin DeMott.
        p.   cm.
    Includes bibliographical references.
    ISBN 0-395-84366-9
    1. Sex role — United States.   2. Power (Social sciences) —
United States.   I. Title.
HQ1075.5.U6 D45 2000
305.3'.0973 — dc21   00-056711

Printed in the United States of America

Book design by Robert Overholtzer

QUM 10 9 8 7 6 5 4 3 2 1

The author is grateful for permission to quote from the following works:

Iron John: A Book About Men by Robert Bly. Copyright © 1990 by Robert Bly. Reprinted
by permission of Perseus Book Publishers, a member of Perseus Books, L.L.C.

The Oppositional Imagination: Feminism, Critique, and Political Theory by Joan Cocks.
Copyright © 1989 by Joan Cocks. Reprinted by permission of the author.

In a Different Voice by Carol Gilligan. Copyright © 1982, 1993 by Carol Gilligan.
Reprinted by permission of Harvard University Press.

Feminism Unmodified: Discourses on Life and Law by Catharine A. MacKinnon.
Copyright © 1987 by the President and Fellows of Harvard College. Reprinted by
permission of Harvard University Press.

"New York Is Assailed for Welfare Delays," *New York Times*, Nov. 24, 1998. Copyright ©
New York Times. Reprinted by permission of the New York Times.

To Jamie, Billie, Nathaniel, and Tyrone
with love

Contents

Introduction ix

O N E "For This We Chained Ourselves to Fences?"

1. Women-Becoming-Men: Voices of Kickbutt Culture 3
2. Anatomy of Gender Shift (1): Politics and Personae 19
3. Anatomy of Gender Shift (2): Hardening Processes 31
4. The Media's Love-Hate Relationship with Women-Becoming-Men 50
5. Killer Women and Corporate Kindness 73

T W O A Vision of Variousness

6. Gender Flexibility: The Front Line 83
7. The Pursuit of Compositives 95
8. Spies in the House of Love 108
9. A Community of Beings in a Single Self 121

T H R E E Whiplash Injuries

10. Positivity Lost 133
11. The Detachment Trap 142
12. Self-Censorship and Double Binds 150
13. Shades of Darkness 159

FOUR Traducing History vs. Growing Capital

14. Three Styles of Nostalgia 173
15. Achievements in Variousness: A Conclusion 194

Notes 211
Acknowledgments 237

Introduction

M Y SUBJECT IS the demise of an ideal: the betrayal, largely
for profit, of the concepts of justice, sexual openness, and
full human development for both sexes which once
shaped this country's politics of liberation and equality.

Everywhere in the culture—from Cadillac, Heineken, Coors,
and Gatorade commercials to Jim Beam print ads, from *Vanity Fair*
to *Leg Show*—smart, career-minded, theoretically liberated women
are depicted as driven by rage to scorn and humiliate men. The
multiplex and the tube choke with stories of women of ambition
who rape and murder—announcements to tens of millions that
equal justice means free expression of violent hatred of the other
sex. Night after night Sitcom America's working mothers, single
and married, display remoteness from and indifference to their
young, as though the key project of liberation was to place cynical
detachment high above steadiness of concern for the helpless on
the scale of human virtues. The entire culture industry appears obsessed with reducing feminism itself to a venture in wish fulfillment, an expression of the presumably universal desire of women
to think, feel, and behave like stereotypical men.

And there is little or no counterattack by women—and some
mindlessly ardent participation by them in the slander. Women

who have held national attention for decades—and women with swiftly rising reputations as well—appear undisturbed by reductive versions of liberationist politics. That politics was once admired for both its programmatic goals and its underlying values, and the admiration was deserved. Liberationist politics taught that the achievement of gender equality would curb autocratic impulses across the board. It taught that ending hypocritical elevation of the "purer sex" would launch an era of unprecedented good faith and truthfulness between the sexes. It taught that releasing the sexes from imprisonment in fixed gender roles would mean richer, more amply imagined lives for all. The broad embrace of these and related teachings actually effected, for a time, a significant transformation of public and private life.

But in turn-of-the-millennium America that transformation seems under siege. A new enlightenment affirms that the point of gender equality is simply to extend the formerly males-only experience of bullying and exploiting to females. It proposes that descending from the pedestal makes sense for women because of the exemption gained—resembling men's—from exacting codes of conduct. It hints that release from fixed gender roles is good because it enables women to develop "masculine" tastes for coarseness, coercion, and violence.

And the new enlightenment appears to be having large impact. Tough-guy feminism legitimizes ever higher levels of corporate callousness and arrogance, and worsens the effect of labor's continued decline. Many factors figure in recent American draconianism: boomlets for capital punishment, profit-fixated managed care, harsh dealing with society's poorest and weakest—and for awarding, in every conflict between market values and their alternatives, preferential treatment to market values. But it's unlikely that any factor matters more than the dogmas set under examination in the pages ahead. The assault on the liberationist vision and the devitalization of the instinct for decency are, by my reckoning, two sides of a single coin.

. . .

At the center of the dogmas I speak of lies the phenomenon of gender shift: a debased version of the feminist ideal of gender flexibility.

In its modern incarnation the ideal of gender flexibility emerged roughly four to five decades ago—almost a half century after the constitutional amendment broadening the vote—during the struggle to liberate women from sex-role stereotypes and end public and private sexism. Enthusiasm for the ideal was spurred by women's awakening to the lie of their "natural" submissiveness and by men's awakening to the lie of their "natural" peerlessness— by rejection, in other words, of ascribed inferiority and superiority. Real-world events swiftly demonstrated that the ideal was more than a figment. For long decades the only vocabulary appropriate for women's progress had been that of slow molecular advance—hard-won gains and long-anticipated breakthroughs. But overnight the pace of change quickened. Well-publicized ascent by women to the top of managerial and other hierarchies, triumphs in the arts and sciences, incontrovertible evidence that women were making it as commercial pilots, physicians, combat engineers, clerics, geneticists, city editors, Supreme Court justices: these induced confidence that occupational interchangeability between the sexes was entirely conceivable.

Social and intellectual history alike supported the confidence. Social upheavals had transformed public and private manners, class relationships, recreation and entertainment, installing openness as a cardinal virtue. Intellectual upheavals had erased boundaries between a raft of formerly noncommunicating disciplines—anthropology and literature, chemistry and biology, many more. Among the challenges to convention that bristled in the new thought, few were clearer than the challenge lodged against orthodox views of the human sexes: views holding that human maleness and femaleness were fixed, timeless, contextless universals separable from human will and interest and preceding organized social existence.

Feminism brought this challenge onto the public stage, now in blunt anger, now with sophistication and nuance. It argued that the status and character of men and women—the separate strengths, weaknesses, competencies, and failings perceived at any particular moment as proof of "natural differences"—were ordained neither by nature nor by gods; they were, instead, cultural constructions. Behind the constructions lay centuries of caste dementia—false pride and false abjectness grown in the soil of presumed male superiority and female inferiority and fed by the same unreason that sustained belief in the divinity of kings, the justness of slavery, and the evil of impugning power and authority.

Bent on overturning caste dementia, feminism introduced audiences to the elementary but underrecognized truth that biological differences between the human sexes were one thing, cultural differences quite another. It proposed *gender* as the right name for the accumulated bodies of opinion, superstition, and law regarding "masculinity" and "femininity": decrees about proper relationships between the sexes and rituals and practices translating the decrees into daily behavior. It accompanied its explanation of gender with avowals that no culture's version of gender differences can be "absolute or true" (as one scholar put it) or "separable from [or prior to] social organization."

And in the process it brought to life an extraordinary new vision centered on the ideal—gender flexibility—that soon ranked as a principal influence on late twentieth-century changes in male-female relationships. That ideal animated belief in possibility, pointing new paths for the development of both sexes, instilling the conviction that the structures and forms blocking development should be—could be—transformed. Gender flexibility became the core of thinking about a new kind of society inhabited by men and women educated to different aspirations from those that ruled the past and embodying in themselves new understandings of each other. The vision asked of both sexes a certain height; it required of both sexes readiness to explore fresh concepts of human identity; it markedly transformed millions of lives.

Today's mania for gender shift—for women-becoming-men—is in process of undoing the advance.

Most Americans are introduced to gender shift by narrative entertainment and commercials; both regularly raid and pillage gender identity territory—to amuse or excite or shock. And both traduce or travesty—mock and parody—the substance of gender history. The story lines floating up at the touch of a remote focus on familiar opposites: toughness and tenderness, aggression and sensitivity. The situations clothe in weird glamour a cluster of obnoxious behaviors: boorish, mean, cruel, or absurd on one hand, enervated, feckless, and self-indulgent on the other. The talk and laugh tracks celebrate a paradise of instant, doltish role reversal. Women gluttonize at meals, lather their cheeks and shave, physically punish weaker members of their own sex, rape male underlings. (Males respond—in a variety of mediums, including "literary" fiction—by taking up effeminacy or ditsiness as modes of charm or "style," or by adopting the sulky manners of the cunt-tease.) Moral inversion—vices redefined as virtues, stupidity preening as sophistication—serves as the norm. Corruption is dignified, and arrogance and abuse—violence as well—are established as values. The past, particularly gender history itself, is stripped of the capital resources that alone can generate morally positive visions of the human future. *No* morally positive vision of human variousness is allowed even momentarily to breathe.

The ascendant ethos is, moreover, no mere affair of story lines, pop or literary; it's a force in family life and in workplaces high and low, a prompter and inhibitor claiming that this or that vexing reality could be better controlled or managed if one shed femaleness, rid oneself of "sentimentality," concentrated on the bottom line, struck a macho pose. Most centrally, gender shift is a new attitude toward self and others, and a new tone of voice. The sound is easily recognized. Listen to the voice behind you on the bus, someone opining to a friend: "Guys have needs. I have needs—hey, forget 'relationships,' let's deal." Listen to an amusing scribble in the mail, a letter from a friend who's a new mother: "Sometimes the only thing that stops Susie crying is a CD of old Johnny Cash songs. She bobs her head at the part where he sings, 'I shot a man in Reno just to watch him die.' A good sign." Listen to a successful magazine editor appearing to claim, in the *New York Observer*, that she has a penis. The editor warns her male interviewer that "I could make you feel very low if I wanted to *very* easily," and goes on to a mystifying discourse on his&her penises. "Here's a little exercise," she explains. "There are positions where the penis goes in, but you can't really tell whose penis it is. The woman can straddle the man so their groins go together, and I can reach down and masturbate the penis between us, but you can't tell whose penis it is."

Listen carefully, in fact, and the language of gender shift—of women becoming men—is audible everywhere, from bars to bestsellers. Demi Moore speaks it when she shouts, "Suck my dick!" in *GI Jane*. Whoopi Goldberg speaks it when she orders a male coach, in *Coach*, to "Blow me!" Elizabeth Randall, capital projects manager for Harvard's Faculty of Arts and Sciences, speaks it when she says, "I have the balls to go one on one with contractors." Judith Regan, book editor, speaks it when she shouts down a critical underling by announcing, "You can't tell me what to do; I've got the biggest cock in this whole building!" "She's got big balls, that woman," says Geraldo Rivera, discussing Christiane Amanpour in *Esquire*. "She's got the biggest balls at Dow Jones," says *Vanity Fair*, quoting an unnamed informant discussing a *Wall Street Journal* executive. "She's ballsy," says the actress Catherine Zeta-Jones about the character she plays in the film *The Mask of Zorro*. "She knows cojones from cowardice," says a photo caption for a *New Yorker* profile of Secretary of State Madeleine Albright. "Janet Reno's going down to Miami [about Elián González] tomorrow," says Bill Maher on *Politically Incorrect*. "Of course. She's the only one in this administration with any testicles." I find it funny, says Sharon Stone in *GQ*, "that certain Hollywood suits now refer to [me] as Sharon Stones."

Impatient horniness—the stereotypically male variety—shapes the credo of the on-line girlzine *Minx*. "Girls demand satisfaction. . . . Don't waste our time. . . . Make us come." Eagerness for solid knowledge of the particulars of uniquely male pain thrums on the Internet. Stefanie among others seeks info about what happens when guys are kicked "down there":

> I'm kinda curious about it. You see all the time in the movies and stuff, and so many different things happen I don't know which is real. Sometimes it shows a guy bend over for two seconds, then he gets up and keeps attacking, other times the guy's on the ground, out. What does it feel like when you're kicked/kneed/punched in the balls? Can anyone provide details of what happened and how it felt, what you did then, etc.?

Daily a crop of high-fashion interviewers and columnists—Diane Sawyer, Maureen Dowd—speaks the new language, as when Dowd mocks, in a tough-guy tone, "the little dears" (men) for "openly discussing their messy love lives at the office." In her own tough-guy tone Sawyer taunts Al Gore as a liar for claiming he once "mucked pigpens." Gender shift idioms grow in favor among "serious" discussants of public issues—women under mounting pressure to prove their machismo. And, predictably, men imitate the voguish talk of wised-up women, adopting old-style "femme" postures, sometimes with operatic extravagance, as a way of dramatizing their relaxed, buoyantly good-humored masculinity. Thus Governor George W. Bush disarms an independently powerful lieutenant governor, Bob Bullock, who ventures to cross him on a piece of legislation, by speaking—all ironical playfulness—in the voice of an aggrieved woman:

> At a breakfast meeting during the 1997 legislative session, Bullock told Bush he planned to back a bill Bush opposed. "I'm sorry, Governor," Bullock said, "but I'm going to have to fuck you on this one." In front of staff, Bush stood up, grabbed Bullock by the shoulders, pulled him forward, and kissed him. "If you're going to fuck me," Bush said, "you'll have to kiss me first."

This book offers no brief for humorlessness or vapid romanticisms, no salutes (hypocritical or other) to the "weaker sex" or to emotion for emotion's sake. But it is critical throughout of the notion that imitating stereotypes of the other sex significantly enriches the self. It argues that today's "killer woman" should be seen as a victim as well as an agent, wounded not only by perverted individual will but by savage new cultural precepts and mandates. (In an important dimension *Killer Woman Blues* is a lament for killer women themselves as well as for the rest of us.)

Part I of the book surveys the ascendant images, arguments, and narratives in popular culture and working lives, and also looks into the pertinent historical and political backgrounds. Part II compares gender shift attitudes with some habits of thought and feeling that liberationism at its best aims to nurture. Part III studies examples of conflict, confusion, and loss in life and contemporary writing traceable to the spread of the new culture, and Part IV assesses some recent, highly publicized, nostalgia-prone stirrings of resistance to the culture. The concluding chapter returns to the theme of engagement developed in Part II, celebrating moments of achieved variousness, models of character and vision superior to those that currently command veneration.

The beliefs controlling all four sections are the same. I believe that today's infatuation with hardness is tightly connected with the advent of enthusiasm for women-becoming-men, and that the gestating culture is subtly weakening the foundations of this country's sense of social justice. I believe that, by drawing attention to the obstacles that gender shift culture sets in the path of straight thinking, a book can contribute to the work of rebuilding those foundations. And I believe that wasting the intellectual and social promise of feminism—losing touch with the liberationist ideal of gender flexibility—could have costs far exceeding those that political accountants on either the right or the left know how to measure: could, in truth, disastrously blight our country's psycho-moral future.

1

Women-Becoming-Men

VOICES OF KICKBUTT CULTURE

AKE A RANDOM WALK through the culture, eyes on the trivial as well as the weighty, and new male and female images fill your gaze. Men and women looking and sounding roughly the same. Women mimicking male stereotypes, trying on "basically masculine" attitudes and feelings. Women represented as eager to appropriate the other sex's traditional roles, traits, styles of talk, body parts, illicit desires.

Item: A cover story in *Cosmopolitan* titled "Infidelity—It's Not Just for Men Any More." Rejecting cliché-idealizations of women as morality bearers, this snippet of gender shift in course affirms women's rights to parity in perfidy. Let all have equal opportunity access henceforth, says *Cosmo,* to the fun or whatever of straying.

Item: The National Fluid Milk Processor Promotion Board decides mustaches aren't just for men anymore and paints white ones on exercycling women. A jokey gender shift. The promoters of a food product assert, with a wink, that fitness and a healthy diet erase differences between "the weaker sex" and the stronger.

Item: Santa Claus drops down a chimney—in a Marshall's commercial—and emerges female. Another jokey gender shift. An equal opportunity employer curries seasonal favor with its predomi-

nantly female clientele by grinning at the silly patriarchal past. *I can be anything I want, including the voice of HoHoHo.*
Item: Joy Behar greets an all-female audience gathered for a Ms. Foundation fundraiser with these words: "Good evening, girls . . . No, it's 1998. Good evening, men."

The tone of such material is often sly, enigmatic, ironically self-protective, eager to undercut its own claims to seriousness. And none of the material is more amusing than *The New Yorker's* continuing series of cartoons about the masculinization and feminization of the middle classes. William Hamilton draws four young women who, in the manner of yesteryear's frat boys anatomizing prom dates, sit at a table smoking cigars and exchanging crude notes on a list of eligible men. ("Great legs, good cook, not half bad in the sack," runs the caption, "but hopelessly tied to his mother's apron strings.") Richard Cline draws junior law associates mockingly admiring each other's high-gloss unisex toughness. ("Thank you, Nathaniel," says a female suit&briefcase to a male suit&briefcase. "I think you, too, are a very scary young lawyer.") Peter Steiner draws a briefcase-bearing lobbyist-mother explaining herself—the U.S. Capitol in the background—as she walks hand in hand with her kindergartner: "Mommy can be tough like Janet Reno. But she can also be vulnerable like Al Gore." Ed Koren tweaks New Man inhibition. Five middle-aged urban cowboys—refugees, maybe, from the movie *City Slickers*—male-bond around a campfire, all but one drinking soda pop and making un-macho nice. The rascally fifth has a beer bottle and a beer glow, plus a question: "Would any of you guys be offended if I told a joke that is a touch prurient?" Stuart Leeds kids macho militiapersons. Five middle-aged women armed with knives, automatic pistols, and rifles, and dressed in ammo bandoliers and berets, sit around a table planning mayhem. Says the leader, "We've gathered enough. Let's hunt."

But it's not the wit or banality that warrants notice. It's the pervasiveness, the omnipresence of similar figures, concepts, and themes in every contemporary genre—sitcoms, road movies, first-person confessionals, wedding pages, consumer columns, tall stories, fables, porn flicks, lyric poetry, ballets, beer ads . . .

A pretty young woman on a bar stool gossips (for Miller Lite) about a mutual acquaintance to an aggressively inattentive friend; suddenly the pretty young woman begins speaking in an All-Pro lineman's voice, deep and gruff, whereupon the friend listens. (*I can be anything I want, including bass-voiced.*) A woman driver in a Chevy Camaro commercial passes a leering truck driver and—almost off camera—gives him the finger. A woman driver in a Dodge Avenger ad lets her mate, Tim, have the keys to the fun car "because he knows who really sits in the driver's seat." "Why Women Love Trucks," a column in *New Woman,* spends pages comparing compacts with half-tons, advancing at the end to a rhapsody on the power boost conferred by a pickup perch. "The appeal is one of control—even of intimidation. . . . When you're up higher . . . you're in charge. . . . There's a feeling of power you get from riding high in the cabin of a four-wheel drive truck that makes you think you could, if you really had to, drive up and over the problems around you."

A "little old lady" golfer with a swing arc resembling Tiger Woods's strokes a 300-yard drive to the green (for O'Doul's pseudo-beer), cowing the wiseass males who are tailgating her and her partner, expecting an invitation to play through. Two ferocious deep-voiced old ladies, furious because the Stovetop Stuffing they've just tasted is so much better than their own homemade dressing, lash out viciously at the camera lens, trying to smash it. Trencherwomen party on at a single-sex barbecue for Baked Lay's; as the camera lingers over the gluttonizing—tight shots of women's hands wrist-deep in chow, women's faces sauce-smeared and sweaty—a relishing male voiceover intones, "Now girls can eat like guys."

And stand and sit like them as well, in a thousand Sunday supplement fashion layouts. A model with the familiar menacing look brushes back her scarlet Jones New York jacket, hands on her hips

Texas Ranger style (thumbs behind, fingers forward); on the facing page a model in an Albert Nippon pegged pantsuit sits mannishly forward on her chair, hands and arms action-ready, no jewelry, legs way akimbo, feet planted so firmly they communicate booted ruggedness although she's wearing slingbacks. Fashion magazines push "bruiser chic"—brown eyeshadow for the black-eyed look, "biker gear for glamazons," "beefy leathers, brassy cuffs, big boots," kickboxer postures for models. At Helmut Lang's New York show "the models march about in combat trousers, khaki anoraks [and] flight suits." The magazine *Teen* promotes boys' clothes for girls in a cover story ("Steal His Look/Boy-Meets-Girl Style").

Bruiser chic guy-talk resounds in ad copy. "When Was the Last Time You Got Screwed?" asks the top line of an ad for EOT, "the new long distance company" (in the artwork three young women frown at a phone bill). "Testosterone Isn't Just a Guy Thing Anymore" announces a seven-page spread, in *Prevention*, on the "hormone of desire." "Don't Ask Me to Be Faithful," warns a defiant sports heroine in Reebok's Monogamy/This is my Planet campaign. Sandra Bernhard tells *Vanity Fair* her motto is "Kiss 'em, slap 'em, send 'em home." Hydro Clara, journeyman technician for a big city daily, tells *Moxie* magazine she handles male co-workers with a series of fixed commands: "Don't call me dear, dear. Don't wait for me to leave to get out of the elevator so you can look at my ass. Quit staring at my tits while I try to explain something to you. No, I don't need your opinions on my hair."

Celebrity magazines admiringly profile rich widows who terrorize male staffs. Courtney Ross, hard-driving widow of the late Warner chairman, has the professionals in her employ bowing and scraping, according to *Vanity Fair;* she's turned museum curators into "dusters and polishers" who tremble at her approach, and her young chef is "a nervous wreck." *Marie Claire* features "Women Who Sell Men's Bodies," model agency bigwigs who intimidate males aspiring to modeling careers. (The piece opens with a get-cracking order—"Take off your shirt. . . . Now your pants"—addressed to "a beautiful young man, 6' 2", blue eyes, short blond hair," by a bored young woman executive.)

Talk profiles a professional wrestler (six-three, two hundred pounds) who performs under the name Chyna and describes herself as "an empowered woman who kicks guys in the nuts for a living." *People* reports that Christy Martin, lightweight boxing champ, woman's division, 35–2–2 with twenty-five KOs, could easily trash half the men who fight at her weight. (So says Martin's chief sparring partner, well ranked in his pro class.) Martin's trainer, who's also her husband, acknowledges that he never thought he'd be kissing one of his fighters, "but after one fight I was so proud of her I just gave her a hug and a kiss." ("If he didn't kiss me that night," she tells a girlfriend, "I was going to lay one on him.") The award for best direction at the Sundance 2000 Film Festival goes to *Girlfight*, a movie about a high school senior who "lives to fight," hangs out in boxing gyms, and has a "snapping hook [that makes] her look like a natural." Muhammad Ali's daughter—Joe Frazier's as well—are embarked on ring careers.

Fights grow more common at women's pro basketball games: "Suddenly, eight more players arrived, and the Liberty's backup center, Venus Lacy (six-four, two hundred and thirty-four pounds), leaned over to help. [Debbie] Black let go of [Teresa] Weatherspoon's neck to take a swing at Lacy, who retaliated by slapping Black," etc. The cover story of the premier issue of *Jump*, a "magazine for girls who dare to be real," is called "Girls Who Kick Guys' Butts," and profiles girls who are teenage wrestlers, football and hockey players, and water poloists. Brandi Chastain kicks the winning goal in World Cup soccer, tears off her shirt guy-fashion, and is saluted for having "met the androgynous ideal of women as men who can have babies: muscular, irreverent, aggressive."

The *New York Times* reports that female "Killer Instinct" players—they beat half the top-seeded males in a recent national electronic games tournament—are needling the industry about wimpy products. " 'Barbie Super Model' is stupid," declares Kate Crook, teenaged semifinalist in the Blockbuster World Game Championship. "Games should be made for both sexes [because girls] like fighting games and role-playing adventures."

The industry's response was to create a new game called Sissyfight 2000 in which the players are girls on a playground. ("It's not just that Sissyfight is fun," writes one young female player. "This game has stirred something inside of me I thought was dead: the urge to bludgeon someone. . . . It's a vicious pleasure that I never got to indulge as a child. . . . The object is to fight your opponents until [only] two of you remain.") Levi's Jeans for Women derisively lists bygone noncombatant fantasies in its ads—"the princess dream . . . the pony dream . . . the pretty bride dream"—and then asks, "Ready for the kick-butt dream?" (The art focuses on the jeans-clad behind of a woman in karate first posture.) Finlandia vodka ads pose young women on high diving boards and detail their inner thoughts: "In a past life I was an Amazon Queen. As for men . . . Well, as long as they had dinner on the table, we kept them around." Alone and underarmed, beach book heroines conquer teams of killer bad guys. In Joseph Finder's *Zero Hour* (1996), FBI agent Sarah Cahill not only whips mercenary terrorists and paranoid billionaires but also saves the nation's banking system.

TV for its part has warrior princesses (*Xena*), mobster matriarchs (*The Sopranos*), female Harley-riding cop killers (*Renegade*), and a heroine who takes a wrench to the private parts of a bearish male auto mechanic (*3rd Rock from the Sun*). "Babes with Blades," an "all-woman's showcase of stage combat," runs at Chicago's Footsteps Theater ("these fightin' females kick ass," says the *Chicago Reader*'s reviewer). At moviehouses adolescent heroines play outlaws, kidnappers, and thieves (*Foxfire, Manny and Lo, Girls Town*). ("As an actress," says Heather Graham—Rollergirl in *Boogie Nights*—"it's fun to do rageful things.") The heroine of Disney's animated epic *Mulan* dons "male military drag" and "bur[ies] a horde of enemy Huns under tons of snow." In other highly promoted movies women are killers—trigger-happy cops, trigger-ready moms, kickboxer-avengers, hit "men," soldiers of fortune, and the like. Sony ads depict a downed woman flyer crawling intrepidly through deep brush, computer mouse grenade in hand. "I've Committed Murder," sings Macy Gray in the "gutsiest track" of her debut album. (Gray imagines herself killing her lover's oppressive female boss in an instance of "class revolt for which she refuses to apologize.") "Goodbye Earl," a hit from the Dixie Chicks, tells how Maryanne and Wanda murder Wanda's abusive husband ("We'll pack a lunch, stuff you in a trunk, Earl/Is that alright?").

"I have a confession to make," says the producer Elizabeth Hurley to an interviewer. "I grew up dreaming of being a gangster." "I pattern myself after Frank [Sinatra]," said Roseanne shortly before the singer died. "He beats people up, I beat people up." "Quite often," says Lynne Russell of CNN's *Headline News*, "even the suggestion of a woman's ability to hit a guy so hard that when he stops rolling his clothes will be out of style is all you need to improve your day." Geena Davis, a pirate in *Cutthroat Island* and a paid assassin in *The Long Kiss Goodnight*, taunts her enemies remorselessly: "You're gonna die screaming and I'm gonna watch."

"Go Ahead, Be a Bitch," says a cover story plugging aggression in *Woman's Own*. The piece notes that "bitches don't settle," that "bitches have that my-girlfriend-can-beat-up-your-girlfriend sex appeal," and that bitches "will stiletto-kick [anybody] who gets in their way." Bitchery is obligatory, the magazine explains, because men nowadays "stay nice by having their worse halves do their dirty work." Gina, young wife of John, observes that "I'm always the one to do battle. John is not good at confrontation. While I'm fighting the landlord, John's off getting a Coke." Or else having himself a spa day. The actor Richard T. Jones recommends, in *Jane*, five-hour spa stints — a loofah glove scrub and deep massage plus a eucalyptus leaf beating. ("I think more men should do the spa thing. Men *need* this kind of thing.")

Eyewitnesses tell the *New York Post* about a battle between O. J. Simpson and a woman named Christine Prody that took place recently in a Miami airport hotel. (A hotel security guard said Prody, twenty-five, "was slapping and kicking the shit" out of Simpson.) Men's magazines fill up with first-person narratives by males physically abused by females. "It happened several years ago," writes Daniel Frankel in a representative *Men's Fitness* piece, "in an office where I used to work."

> A female colleague said something during a meeting that pushed my button. "You know, if this was grade school, I'd sock you for that," I replied, mostly in jest. "Well, we're not in grade school, and it's me who could kick your ass," she shot back, not in jest. (A martial artist, she regularly kept us apprised of her belt status.) . . . I found myself replaying the conversation over and over again in my head. You see, I've had my ass kicked by chicks before. . . . My career as a cross-gender punching bag goes back to when I was eight, hanging out with Jan, my next door neighbor.

Frankel's memoir climaxes with a bout in which a girlfriend kicks him three times in the face. ("It could have been worse; she held back a bit.")

Males beaten by their mates are favorite talk show guests. Rick tells Oprah that his wife "liked to slap my face a lot, she enjoyed kicking me—going for the ribs—punching me in the face. A lot of kicking. A *lot* of kicking." Now dependent on Mace for protection, Rick feels "betrayed by the system." Patty, a Catholic schoolgirl, beats up a new boyfriend in *Downtown*, the MTV cartoon series. ("She's mean," says the narrator. "She put her last boy in the hospital.") A freshly shaven man in a Norelco shaver ad eyes a passing woman and she pats his face approvingly; the woman seated beside the freshly shaven man hits him hard with a rubber bat. In the porn flick *Hardwood* (1999) Bobbi finds Dave, her man, packing a suitcase to leave her because she's too male in her behavior. ("You work like a guy. Hell, you even drink beer like a guy.") Bobbi socks Dave hard in the jaw, whereupon he moans, "You even hit like a guy."

Male novelists introduce male protagonists who idolize female achievers in their chosen profession, women who command heights men see as unscalable (the reporter-protagonist of Christopher John Farley's *My Favorite War* [1996], a well-received debut work, is infatuated—from afar—with a hard-hitting woman columnist for the *Washington Post*). Male dancers no longer "lead" in the work of Mark Morris and other top-ranking choreographers, nor do they carry; women dancers carry them. Reversing traditional placements, life insurance and car ads aimed at heads of families elevate women, pictorially and textually, and demote men. Mom faces the reader directly, Dad looks off at the kids; Mom sits higher than Dad, on a chair, while Dad crouches on his knees; Mom cups Dad's chin in her hand; Mom, not Dad, gets quoted. ("If something happened to me," says Mom in a Savings Bank Life promo, "I'd be looking down and seeing that they're making it." "I feel safe in this [Ford Taurus]," says Anne Kimble, chin-cupper.) Wrangler tells women its jeans are "perfect for your ten-year-old son, perfect for your ten-year-old husband."

Sitcoms about single fathers multiply—men struggling to bring up a younger sibling or their own child alone (*Boy Meets World, In the House, Brotherly Love, The Gregory Hines Show, Meego, You Wish, The Tom Show, The Tony Danza Show*, and *Sister, Sister*). In Dave Eggers's *A Heartbreaking Work of Staggering Genius* (2000)— a best-selling memoir about an older brother serving as parent to a younger brother—the older brother, in his early twenties, fumes at a friend who deprecates his work as a parent: "I am a forty-year-old mother. As far as you and everyone else is concerned, I am a forty-year-old mother. Don't ever forget that."

Self-pity becomes standard in male comics' voices. A teary cheerleader laments his powerlessness in a Reebok commercial ("Pom-poms, my only means of expression"). "Soon women will be conceiving children without us," says Conan O'Brien, all rue. "What few men are left on earth will be slave laborers at a desalination plant in the Philippines." A guest comic on O'Brien's show,

Robert Schimmel, recalls the time he logged on to the lesbian chat room on America Online, under a woman's name, and found excitement denied to men. ("In about a minute," Schimmel says, "a woman named Monica beeps me and says, 'I'm really hot.' ") "The most uproarious comic set piece" in the Broadway hit *Closer,* says James Wolcott in *Vanity Fair,* has the two male leads "engaging in anonymous cyberchat," one of them "pretending to be female."

Vicki Shick and Tere O'Connor collaborate on a word and dance performance wherein female dancers ridicule a male dancer who "mouths his desire to give birth." Visa runs a commercial showing a male leaving a hospital in a wheelchair, a newborn babe in his arms. Arnold Schwarzenegger plays a pregnant man in the movie *Junior* (1994). In a commercial for the "Jamie Foxx Music and Sports Festival," Foxx falls while skateboarding and tells an upright passerby, "My water just broke." *TV Guide*'s cover hails Tom Hanks for "tak[ing] time for kids" in a new special in which famous dads explain how to care for children. Gail Sheehy, pitching her book *Understanding Men's Passages* on *Today,* describes the male mid-life crisis as "man-o-pause."

The *National Enquirer* chronicles a tough male cop's fulfillment-through-sex-change. ("I love being a lady about town," says Bob Reeve, father of two, still living with his wife and family.) *Salon* runs a piece in which a woman contributor reports having had "my revelation about the patriarchy when—I challenge the gentle reader to put this more delicately—I strapped on a dildo and fucked my boyfriend in the ass." *The New Yorker* prints a poem in which a female speaker remembers riding "our shared penis" with a lover:

> a glistening pillar
> sliding between us . . .

Fairy tales, novels, ballets, and children's stories are redone in transposed versions. Madeline in the movie version of the Bemelmans books kicks a man in the groin. Cinderella dons combat boots in *Cinderella Wore Combat Boots* (a play for "family audiences"). There's *Olivia Twist* (a Children's Theater/Chicago show), Matthew Bourne's *Swan Lake* (bare-chested men as swans, praised by Anna Kisselgoff of the *New York Times* as "polished entertainment"), "Martha @ Mother" (a New York dance showcase with Richard Move as Martha Graham and Robert La Fosse as Isadora Duncan), *R & J* (a four-man version of Shakespeare's *Romeo and Juliet*), *Ms. Scrooge* (a TV movie with Cicely Tyson as Ebenezer), and much more.

The cover of *Spy* pictures Hillary Clinton in the White House backyard about to take off for Camp David. A copter's whirring lifts her skirt; the First Lady wears jockey shorts and has a penis and scrotum. The sexual needs column in *Woman's Own* recommends man-style groping. ("I began to act differently, I smiled at strangers," says a woman successful at "igniting [her] own sexual glow." "I fondled Kent in elevators. I became really bold and totally energized.") In the film *Fever* the hero and an old girlfriend listen to an Otis Redding hit in a bar. The hero says that whenever he hears the tune he gets a hard-on. "So do I," says the old girlfriend. A volume of new essays by famous women—Germaine Greer, Terry McMillan, and others—tells what they would do "if endowed with male genitals for 24 hours." The book's title: *Dick for a Day: What Would You Do If You Had One?*

Similar raids on gender identity occur in many more settings and mediums—unimaginably many more—than any quick survey can suggest; they are identifying marks of the culture of gender shift.

Old patterns of thought don't disappear, to be sure—old having-it-both-ways patterns of thought. The insurance company promo that gives Mom pride of place as family earner and planner refers to her as a "homemaker," not a "breadwinner." *People's* Christy Martin profile reveals that the fighter who talks of laying one on her trainer-husband is a clotheshorse (Martin is shown selecting from hundreds of outfits in her walk-in Imelda Marcos–style closet). Some cartoons find humor in residual timidities and stubbornly durable domestic patterns. One trousered young woman to another in a *New Yorker* drawing by Richard Cline: "He's great, and not too much of a threat to me." "Despite my best efforts," says a harried, Koren-invented wife to her husband—she has a babe in arms and is serving dinner to two seated kids and the husband, who's reading the paper—"Despite my best efforts, you're still the man and I'm still the woman." Cartoon humor provides a constant reminder of the slipperiness of the material, its shrewd, audience-teasing interest in embracing gender shift and spoofing it simultaneously.

Some ad campaigns shuttle between poles, presenting women famous in youth for their take-no-prisoners ferocity as, in middle life, quiet souls, wives settling into "personalized" versions of domesticity. Panel one of a two-panel ad for Spice Island's Good Harvest rice consists of a distraught female face, deranged eyes evoking rape terror, mouth filled with a yellow tennis ball. Caption: "Eating What Chris Evert Served, 1972–1989." Panel two shows Evert (the retired champ is demurely dressed, gently smiling) and her husband—Andy Mill, ski champ—seated at a kitchen–dining area table, happy homemakers holding aloft a platter of rice. Caption: "Andy Mill Eating What Chris Evert Serves Today." Other ad campaigns promote serial expression of women's violent and tender impulses. "Ever want to tear your man limb from limb?" asks a Drexler ad. With the "Love-Hate Playmate," the company's $19.95 blow-up toy, the satisfactions of both the male batterer and the female cuddler are brought close to hand: *The doll has every part a man has and is held together with Velcro. Vent your anger by ripping off his arm, his leg or . . . When all is forgiven, put the little softie back together again and cozy up to him.*

Occasional news stories and interviews labor to comprehend the tone and mindset of interviewees who seem to combine fury with forbearance. "Sometimes I think about dismembering him," says

Eileen McGann, talking to *Newsweek*'s Eleanor Clift about her prostitute-patronizing husband, Dick Morris. "And good friends have offered to help me dig up the backyard and bury him." But she adds, to the reporter's evident puzzlement, "I am taking it day by day. . . . [Dick] is suffering terribly."

The new inventory of tones includes a sermon-like strain. ("There are no genders, there are no infirmities," a solemn voice announces in an MCI Internet Access commercial.) A large body of academic writing—remote from pop and assiduously read in women's studies departments—examines gender exchange, polyvalence, and allied topics. Research from social science organizations and government agencies provides timely statistical backup for women-becoming-men fantasy. "Average American civilian women" load trucks, fix heavy equipment, and jog for miles wearing seventy-five-pound backpacks as well as most men, at least in training labs, say the latest numbers from the U.S. Army Research Institute of Environmental Medicine. A current Highway Safety Institute report notes that, whereas a generation ago five times as many male drivers as female were killed in crashes, today the ratio has dropped to three to one. (Invited to comment, a captain in the Rhode Island state troopers observes that "women used to get in the right-hand lane and stay there. Now . . . it's not unusual to see them bombing up behind you at 80 miles an hour.") A new attitudinal survey of ten thousand undergraduates, underwritten by the American Psychological Association, affirms—with numbers—that "college women are getting more masculine—assertive, goal-driven, action-oriented."

There is, in addition, a whole new gender shift rhetoric of celebration, an idiom heard at Rose Garden ceremonies introducing woman appointees to high office, at university commencements, and other public occasions. Addressing Smith College seniors in 1995, Gloria Steinem saluted contemporary advance from benightedness and contrasted her frustration at her own graduation day (Class of '56) with the sense of promise and possibility alive in her

listeners. Her words echoing over a sunny, densely packed quad-
rangle, Steinem rose to a near-panegyric on gender transformation: "At my graduation I thought we had to marry what we wanted
to become. Now, you are becoming the men you once would have
wanted to marry."

I thought we had to marry what we wanted to become: as the pre-
liberation forties and fifties disappear from the memory of all but
one living generation, the feelings Steinem evokes lose definition
even for women now in their middle years, and conceivably are
downright puzzling to twenty- and thirty-year-olds. Could there
have been a time—a recent time—when young women were practically forbidden to be "goal-driven, action-oriented"? When helpless dependency on men's lives was the norm? When consent was
nearly universal to the degrading proposition that one could attain
ambition and achievement only by marrying them?

The realities of that time filtered through succeeding decades are
important factors in the rise of kickbutt sensibility. They partly explain the reluctance of elders to criticize that sensibility and the decline of the ideals of flexibility and variousness. When details of the
past grow indistinct, smudged by generalities about "oppression"
and "male domination," memoirists and others call them back,
reanimating an age when serious talk for women was limited,
as Betty Fussell remembers in *My Kitchen Wars,* "to children and
schools and houses," when the only work for women was "to please
the men in my life . . . with the small gifts that the men might or
might not notice when they chose to stop work," when wariness of
victories for "rights" had to be the rule ("I had invested too much
in my decades of caretaking. . . . I couldn't simply exchange one
role for another, so like countless other women I took on both
[writing-teaching/caretaking], doing double the work in the same
amount of time").

Not for Fussell and Steinem alone but for millions of survivors,
pre-liberation life stirs, in the memory, a sense of gender shame:
anger at insults and impotence unprotestingly accepted, a will to

deny and erase gender, to stomp and kick it into nothingness if that alone will prevent the return of humiliation. Revisited fury is, as I say, an important factor in the background of gender shift. Of equal rank is the ineradicable national proclivity for "individualistic" solutions — politics that asserts the superiority of the single self to the group. (Women-become-men are driven upward one soul at a time; classic feminism envisaged broad-scale one-for-all solidarity.) A third factor, probably, is the mortification of some males at the record of other males' absurdly self-glorifying domination. (Absent mortification, male voices would surely be speaking out — they have not been — against the idiocy that equates paradise with "becoming men.") Many other factors in the phenomenon of gender shift deserve notice and will receive it in their place.

But what counts more than the question of origins is simply the astonishing ubiquity of images of women-becoming-men: the ceaseless weaving of the key themes of gender shift into the texture of dailiness, the saturation of the public air with sounds, gestures, and behavior that dumb down women's struggle into a campaign for universal masculinization — and declare its total victory. The ascendant discourse — attacks, salutes, "neutral" reports — dissolves the feminist analysis of forces underpinning sexism. It overwhelms the feminist challenge to market value dominance, silences the feminist call for models of humane interaction between the sexes and for institutions capable of nourishing its growth. The understandings and values that lent saliency to the ideal of gender flexibility itself begin to disappear: reverence for human potentiality and for openness and social and imaginative access; the sense of the irreducibility of the human creature however sexed; the belief that settling for thinned-out, role-constrained, culturally implanted versions of male or female "personality" or "character" amounts, for the individual, to an act of self-mutilation.

The collapse of such beliefs testifies compellingly to gender shift's political clout — and to the power still exerted, despite women's advance, by stereotypical masculinity. But in this context standard mutterings against the masculine regime aren't helpful. How are we to explain the spell the culture casts on widely different audiences? Exactly which traits and attributes stamp the culture's archetypal heroines and heroes? These are the first questions needing answers.

2

Anatomy of Gender Shift (1)

POLITICS AND PERSONAE

RIME FACTORS in the rise of gender shift—aside from memory of the oppressive past—are its big-tent politics and its self-heroicizing personae.

Virtually all the defining gestures of this culture, commercial and noncommercial, reflect preoccupation with problems of self-development and self-realization. And almost without exception those defining gestures also manifest fascination with what is perceived as the supremely estimable masculine attribute, namely, toughness.

But as there are many kinds of toughness, so there are many ways of constructing the theme of toughness. Toughness in one version equals aggressive egalitarianism. (I base my claim to superiority on my membership in the producer or working classes, and on my separateness from elites who know nothing about what Theodore Roosevelt called "the rough hurly-burly of the actual work of the world.") In another version toughness equals the spirit of rebellion against regulatory authority, official or unofficial. (I base my claim to superiority on my refusal to be coerced by any entity purporting to act, without my consent, for my own good.) In still another version toughness equals willingness to face the rupture of ties to loved ones rather than risk loss of self-respect. (I base my claim to superiority on my refusal to be coerced by so-called moral obligations, including duty to family, as convention-ally defined.)

Partly because promoters have stayed on message—masculinity equals toughness—while developing subthemes on separate styles of toughness, gender shift's appeal isn't narrow. The resentments and fantasies it articulates are, by turns, populist, generational, elit-ist. It aims barbs at "softness" wherever detected—in privileged women, privileged men, whining bottom dogs, elders, bosses. Now egalitarian in idiom, now liberationist, now individualist, it stands for nothing except the proposition that toughness is redemptive and individualism the only truly worthy creed. The differences of idiom ensure not only that the cause of women-becoming-men at-tracts multiple sectors of the mass audience, but also that spokes-persons for the cause will never function as representatives of groups, only as advocates for the sacred entity of The Self.

For an illustration of how this blurry big-tent *a*politics works, consider the contrasting examples of Camille Paglia and Katie Roiphe, gender shifters who approach the pertinent cultural issues from widely different viewpoints. Paglia first came to notice as the author of *Sexual Personae: Art and Decadence from Nefertiti to Emily Dickinson* (1990), a meditation on Dionysian impulses and Rousseau's doctrine of natural goodness which fired barrages, in-termittently, at elitist feminists. Although *Sexual Personae* owes some large, unacknowledged debts, it's learned and lively, alert to the significance of popular culture (Rolling Stones, Rita Hayworth, Elvis Presley), unstuffy in manner and choice of detail. It's also a work in which the author couples devout masculinism with ad-mirable if inconsistent hostility to assumptions of moral superior-ity based on class or gender.

Paglia's initial contrasts between masculinity and femininity celebrate hardhat manhood's vigorous wrestling with the world and deride "feminine" withdrawal. ("If civilization had been left in female hands, we would still be living in grass huts.") And there-after, in this and other works, her deprecation of women centers simultaneously on feminism—viewed as "infested with white, middle-class, literary twits"— and privilege: "airy, rich-bitch, affected dilettant[es]" and the like. (There are complementary assaults on non-macho men that revile them as suckups and bookworms: "lily-livered, dead-ass trash-talkers," "brown-nosers," and "timorous nerds.")

Paglia's affirmations of the superiority of red-blooded male experience—like her denunciations of wimpy womankind—regularly erupt in class-based indictments of "expensive Northeastern colleges and universities," "the protected, white middle-class world," "pampered homes," the "stale WASP world of prep schools, English departments, fast-track careers, [and] good manners." And she bans upscale euphemisms from her blunt, pugnacious guy talk. "If a guy tells a girl she's got great tits," Paglia observes, "she can charge him with sexual harassment. [But that's] chickenshit stuff. . . . Don't slink off to whimper and simper. . . . Say, 'Shut up, you jerk! . . . Crawl back to the barnyard where you belong!' "

Paglia tells her lecture audiences that she loves the "simple, swaggering masculinity of the jock," and that when she was young, she was an Amazon. "People *remember* this," she cries. "I mean before feminism was, Paglia was! Out there punching and kicking and fighting with people." She denounces Ivy League condescension to state universities like her own alma mater (SUNY-Binghamton). She denounces WASP putdowns of Italian Americans and others of immigrant background. Most vehemently she denounces top-class ignorance of the world of real work. ("I've been on the unemployment line," Paglia writes. "I have taught in factories.") Always she links her basic theme—let women be tough hombres—with anger at inequality and snobbery. Gender shift in this version becomes associated with the murky resentments of a society presumably pissed off across the board, as Paglia would put it, at hierarchies that are not merely anti-democratic but self-righteous and corrupt; it takes on an of-the-people dimension.

Not so Katie Roiphe's version. Her masculinism is only a shade less ardent than Paglia's, but it is developed in contexts different from people's politics. And it opens up significant alternative entrances to the big tent—entrances through which libertarians, free marketeers, elitists of many kinds can comfortably pass.

Holder of a Ph.D. in literature, author of *The Morning After* (1993) and *Last Night in Paradise* (1997), Roiphe attended private schools for thirteen years before graduating from Harvard. The social detail in her writing—allusions to chic Manhattan bars and restaurants, hundred-dollar haircuts and Chanel suits and Prada bags—situates her in the urban upper-middle classes. Conceivably she's never seen a factory floor. Nevertheless she talks authentic gender shift talk. She savors masculinist bluntness—recalls admiringly a Harvard classmate who "intimidated obscene phone callers with the line 'Listen, honey, I was blow job queen of my high school. . . .'" She presents herself as fearless: "When I used to walk the golf course to the [Princeton] graduate college, I was more afraid of wild geese than rapists." And she's as contemptuous as Paglia both of weak women and of male wimps who preen themselves on their sensitivity. "[Peter] goes on to tell me that in the jungle of insensitive men, the male feminist is a rare and welcome flower."

But while Paglia associates the enemy, whining woman-kind, with privileged classes hiding out in velvet-armpit enclaves, Roiphe associates the same enemy with Big-Brother brainwashing. Her masculinism isn't that of workingmen but of entrepreneurial rugged individualists who revile governmental and quasi-governmental regulators—pothole-tenders of the road to serfdom. Roiphe's spin is, in a word, Reaganesque.

Managers of "sexual harassment and assault-education and counseling program[s]" are the specific bureaucrats who most infuriate her. These characters constantly invade others' mental space, she argues. They tell others how to think. They intimidate others with rituals ("candles . . . silence . . . promise[s] of transformation . . . substitute[s] for religion"). They turn nebulous experience into criminal offenses. They advertise their anti-rape marches as a means of " 'finding your own healing practices' and 'taking back who you are and what you need and want. This is your journey,' " they whisper, " 'your reclaiming of a strong sense of self.' "

Against the gullibility that the harassment bureaucracies manipulate, Roiphe sets the tough independence of her models of women-becoming-men—self-reliant Emersonians all. She hails the spikiness that rejects "regulation from the right or the left." She upholds in absolute terms the freedom to leer: "People have the right to leer at whomever they want to leer at. By offering protection to the woman against the leer, the movement against sexual harassment is curtailing her personal power." A ground theme everywhere in Roiphe's writing is that the whole of contemporary feminism is, quite simply, an oppressive "regulatory force."

> From Catharine MacKinnon to the protesters against the *Sports Illustrated* swimsuit issue to more mainstream theorists of sexual harassment, feminists are the front lines of sexual regulation. Much of today's feminism in its most popular forms provides yet another source of repression. . . . Feminism has come more and more to represent sexual thoughts and images censored, behavior checked, fantasies regulated.

Neither Roiphe nor Paglia imagines herself in political competition with the other. The left flank of Paglia's offensive against middle-class insulation and obliviousness moves in rough synchrony with the right flank of Roiphe's offensive against bureaucracy and government control. Shared enthusiasms and hostilities—esteem for masculinist independence and ruggedness, distaste for "feminine" weakness and whining—bridge the gap between left-leaning and corporate perspectives. The capacity of the toughness message to sound, by turns, pro-entrepreneur, pro–wage slave, pro–open shop, pro–closed shop—pro–male, pro-female—guarantees expanding audiences and minimal danger of factionalism.

But only, of course, if those who deliver the message are themselves *interesting.* Gender shift's rise owes much to the protean politics just described. But take away its persona and it's nothing. Prototypical gender shifters are arresting presences with unimpeachable bona fides as contemporary. They entertain and instruct. They take up wholly unexpected stances toward experience. Their expressive gestures and manners—their attitudes toward others, their psychosocial postures—conjoin in a distinct persona or self. And it's this persona that is most directly responsible for gender shift's ascent to influence.

A prime element of the persona is the air of having escaped into freedom and self-sovereignty. Yesterday I was the prisoner of so-called normal responses, socially approved emotions (pity, compassion), conventional timidities and anxieties. I worried about offending others. I was frightened of conflict, of anger, even of criminality. I actually consumed—gratefully—the pabulum that the master class feeds its servants. Now I emerge from the void. I learn derision and disdain for certified right thinking, "political correctness," et al. I rid myself of naïveté, dependency, groupthink illusion. In midflight from credulousness, scornful of consensus thought, women-becoming-men rejoice in their free spirit—and the jubilation is *exciting.*

Both Paglia and Roiphe dramatize themselves as happy loners and express full-throated scorn of groupthink. Comparably free-spirited isolates are everywhere in mass entertainments, and, especially striking, they fill the burgeoning literature of women-becoming-men self-help, a body of work that repeatedly portrays indifference to common opinion and to human attachment as essential to personal growth.

Consider, for example, a recent volume adapting Machiavelli's *The Prince* to the needs of ambitious career women—*The Princessa: Machiavelli for Women* (1997), by Harriet Rubin. The author, a publishing executive, reports that, as a business book editor, she became the confidante of many "business leaders and . . . strategists." By studying them carefully, she learned "how to take command of underlings and lieges. . . . How to take what I wanted from the world."

The first and most important lesson Rubin learned from male movers and shakers is that women warriors on their way to becoming men need to shed their attachments. They must understand, that is, that commitments to others inevitably mean subservience to others—a condition seriously disadvantaging to would-be princessas. "The person who wields unfair advantage over you," says Rubin, "may be your mother, your boss, your spouse or lover, your child. . . . Anyone or anything with a hold on your emotions has got you by the short hairs."

Therefore disengage. Study indifference. Rubin cites a soldier who survived a jungle prison camp by refusing to set his heart on anything—even a teaspoon of water—that others controlled. "What is as vital as this water to the princessa? Her child's smile, her mother's approval, her boss's praise?" You "may be parched for these things," but, Rubin says, you mustn't let on. You must "treat the things you value most—your health, your love, your prestigious job—indifferently." Further, the princessa-to-be must be ceaselessly mindful that her way of inhabiting her circumstances differs from that of ordinary folk. "The princessa has a different relationship to the world than most women. She thinks of herself as a hunter. She feels the world is there to feed her."

But she also knows—because Rubin stresses this unrelentingly—that she can't grow big except by refusing commitments, whether to people or manners or codes. "In the princessa's situation, normal rules do not apply. Obeying the law becomes a dangerous addiction. Flaunting [sic] it is the way to succeed."

Ordinary, dutiful women fret about manners. They tremble before their own rage. They "regret the[ir] outburst[s]. They might apologize or compromise. Ordinary women make an effort to get over their anger, as if it were the flu. They cuddle anger out of a child." Not the successful man-aping princessa: she "*acts in order to build tension.*" Again: ordinary, dutiful, subservient women turn away from those they abhor—but not the princessa-to-be. "Behave like the people you hate," Rubin commands, "be even more like the hated than they are themselves." Choose models, male or female, who abide by the principle of absolute iron separateness from others.

Rubin's models of choice, Rocky Marciano and Lady Macbeth, disciplined themselves into sovereign levels of indifference to all common concerns. Marciano's gift was for total absorption in combat:

> *He concentrated on his strength—he became a bullet of a man.... In front of a mirror in her mind's eye, [the princessa] is Rocky.*

Lady Macbeth's gift was for total concentration on the throne:

> Everyone in Shakespeare's play follows her agenda before their own. She pulls the future to her—she creates the future—because she, alone in the play, demonstrates the greatest desire.

Rubin has an obvious taste for pugnacity. The solemn promise of her introduction is that "I will teach you war," and she offers chapters on such subjects as "The Use of Men as Weapons" and "How the Right Weapons Turn the War in Your Favor." In some passages her pugnacity matches that of Camille Paglia, socker-scholar.

But important as pugnacity is in the persona, it's less crucial—as I've said—than the sense of escape into freedom. When Rubin orders the princessa-to-be who's also a parent to shut down the flow of lovingkindness to her child, it's not pugnacity that connects the advice with Paglia and a thousand other gender shifters; it's the release from mother love as mandated feeling. The same holds for Paglia's insistence that emoting about wife beating is soppy and that rape isn't "that big a deal." The link to others in the tribe is the longing for breakout from containment in stock response. Paglia ridicules off-the-rack outrage at wife beating:

> Many of these working-class relationships where women get beat up have hot sex. . . . If gay men go down to bars and like to get tied up,

beaten up, and have their asses whipped, how come we can't allow that a lot of wives like that kind of sex they are getting in these battered wife relationships?

And, says Paglia, although pampered cowards fear rape, it's really a challenge and a learning experience:

My sixties attitude is, yes, go for it, take the risk, take the challenge — if you get raped, if you get beat up in a dark alley in a street, it's okay. That was part of the risk of freedom, that's part of what we've demanded as women. Go with it. Pick yourself up, dust yourself off, and go on.

Disdain for groupthink sanctimony is still more vivid in Katie Roiphe. The latter's mocking account of a Princeton anti-rape rally ranks, in fact, among the most sharply definitive representations of gender shift "attitude" in print. Roiphe moves through the crowd feeling repugnance for every cliché-ridden voice, every banal emotion, laughing within at every groupthink claim that "sex should be gentle, it should not be aggressive; [that] it should be absolutely equal, [and] should not involve domination and submission," chortling at rape victims who, "oversaturated with self-esteem," praise themselves "for getting out of bed every morning and eating breakfast," and who "give intensely personal accounts" of their misery that all "begin to sound the same."

Certainty that anti-rape rallies are congresses of shammers and cheats is one mark of the unreservedly committed partisan of toughness. Another mark is the belief that it's better to turn oneself into a pity-proof bullet of an observer than to be gulled into wasting pity on any gatherings of the wounded not blood-tested for malingering and cowardice. Not once during the anti-rape rally does Roiphe hear a word—a bid for fellow feeling by someone brutalized—sufficiently heart-shattering to moderate her stony scorn.

Derision, impatience, self-importance—these draw us close to the insides of the fully realized masculinist mentality, and to the toughness on others that is its signature characteristic. Typically

the gender-shifting princessa forms no human attachments, refuses to hug her child, and wears the zealot's fiercely ardent face. It
is the face of Lady Macbeth telling her lord that, when he swore to
her he would murder the king, "then you were a man" — and telling
him, further, that if she herself had sworn such an oath and broken
it, shame would have made her smash her baby's brains out:

> I have given suck, and know
> How tender 'tis to love the babe that milks me:
> I would, while it was smiling in my face,
> Have plucked my nipple from his boneless gums
> And dashed the brains out, had I so sworn as you
> Have done to this.

The advent of princessa-style ferocity in biographical business literature has given currency to a language differing from that of old-
style appreciations of distinguished commercial predators. Traces
of disfavor that once lingered in those appreciations — hints of reluctance to accord full reverence to ruthless sharks — have all but
disappeared; the will to emulate knows no inhibition, and flat-out
homage to homicide is a convention. "She's a killer," the co-founder
of Schwab says excitedly, to *Brill's Content*, about Kelly Ann Sole,
general manager of the *Los Angeles Times*. "She's a cutthroat killer
underneath," Martha Stewart gushes to *Fortune* about Darla
Moore, head of a giant investment partnership. She knows "who
you have to kill, and when and how," Richard Avedon tells *The New
Yorker* about Sharon Stone, actress-producer. Nor is the unmoder-
ated enthusiasm reflected only in verbal usage.

Consider, for instance, the behavior of Bijou Phillips, young
celebrity-habitué of Manhattan clubs. In her eighteenth year, in the
summer of 1997, at a club called Spy, Phillips "got hold of a nine-
inch sex toy . . . threw a girlfriend on the floor, and performed a
mock sex attack on her." Thereafter, reported the *New York Post:*

> A screaming fight broke out among Bijou, her pal and onlookers.
> Asked by another friend what was going on, Bijou replied, "Just
> spending time with some friends." When she was asked to leave, the

argument moved onto the sidewalk, where she was overheard telling her enraged galpal, "So I raped you—deal with it."

Or there's Tonya Harding, charged with domestic violence for belting her live-in mate "with a hubcap, after punching and hitting him." Or there's Mia Farrow reporting a bout between herself and her daughter Soon-Yi. "She kicked me," says Farrow, "and I hit her on the side of the face and shoulder."

Or there's Sarah Jacobson, film critic for *Wire on the Scene*, enthusiast of a movie called *Grace Has Mace*, in which the heroine is transformed "from a victim businesswoman" to a "Don't-mess-with-me-shitkicker." Jacobson's review of *Grace Has Mace* cited as "one of the film's highlights" a "head-spinning sequence of guy after guy getting maced in a row, only to be the heroine's masturbation fantasy as she satisfies herself with her phallic-shaped Mace can." The reviewer added: "It's nice to see girls [who are independent filmmakers] being gross and strange and making amazing movies." Or there's Jessica Hundley, in *Salon,* hailing non-indie movie directors who are learning "to manipulate male sexuality according to our own observations and whims." "After too many years," says Hundley, "it's finally our turn to objectify, sexualize, fear, worship, battle, adore, and best of all, lust after."

Or there's Foxy Brown—or Kathleen Hanna of the riot grrrl group Bikini Kill, or Lynn Breedlove of the San Francisco group Tribe 8. Foxy Brown is a seventeen-year-old rap star hauled into court in Raleigh, North Carolina, for spitting at Holiday Inn desk clerks and repeatedly "threatening to hit them with a glass bowl." (The problem arose from Foxy's "anger at Holiday Inn appointments. . . . The motel did not have an iron she could use.") Kathleen Hanna screams "Suck my left one!" and bares her breasts in defiant fury during her group's show. During her performance, Lynn Breedlove wears a dildo as an accessory and hacks it off with a knife in rage.

Or there's Roni Lowe, the sixteen-year-old Lubbock, Texas, beauty queen who, allegedly furious at a group of cheerleaders, "told them they would all 'disappear from the face of the earth and everyone will know who did it.' " (Beauty pageant officials stripped Lowe of her crown, sash, and title as Miss Lubbock, Texas, USA.) Or there are the seven teenaged Vancouver girls who, in the company of one teenaged boy, "swarmed" an unpopular fourteen-year-old named Reena Virk, beating, torturing, and killing her. ("Kelly Ellard boasted to another teenager," according to one newspaper account, "that she placed her foot on Reena Virk's head and smoked a cigarette, as the 14-year-old drowned.")

Extremists in the gender shift party, members of the Bijou–Foxy–Jacobson–Kelly Ellard cohort, exhibit exceptional levels of egocentricity. Like Paglia "out there punching and kicking" or Roiphe shrugging off the brutalized or Rubin teaching war, they're unimpressed by the claims of others ("So I raped you—deal with it"). And the toploftiness of the stance—its confidence in its own peerlessness—speaks strongly to frustrated pride, depressed by obscurity.

It's partly for that reason that white racist groups have been increasingly successful in their efforts to "move beyond their traditional 'angry white male' constituency [and] recruit as many new female members as they can find." Anti-Semitic and anti-black postures of superiority boost the status of the statusless. Even when the tone and diction are leveling, like Paglia's, the promise to bottom dogs is that, by seeing through everything, mercilessly dismissing every kind of value, compassion not excluded, they can become top dogs. Gender shift is tuned, in sum, to high individualism's fantasy life. Listening to its promoters, the merely average citizen—our cousin, one of us, the parent who knows no better than to cuddle an unhappy child and to become "entangled" with a beloved—hears a seductive summons to the tough uncaringness that is presumed to give the masculinist regime its edge. *Harden yourselves, citizens, and ascend thereby to exceptionality.*

3

Anatomy of Gender Shift (2)

HARDENING PROCESSES

A T ITS EXTREMES the new culture explodes, as we've just
seen, in spectacles of egotistical frenzy—kicking, spitting,
far-out furious contempt, torture, murder. Elsewhere the
culture is less showy; it imposes regimens of self-simplification and
internal hardening, adjusts them to personal temperament and
economic resource, and usually keeps them out of the public gaze.
The hardening processes—signs of burgeoning influence—weed
out this or that element of character, select this or that aspect of
"femininity" and "masculinity" for abuse or emulation. One mark
of the culture's influence is the shedding of familial and domestic
attachments on the ground that they distract from career interests.
Another mark is the adoption of a standard of judgment that assesses actions solely according to whether they enhance or diminish personal reputation for toughness.

Still another mark is attraction to the stance of the aggressively
gung-ho company "man"—she or he who represents as a weakling
or sentimentalist anyone who appears to mistrust corporate America's word.

Obviously no single framework of articulated assumptions binds
the gender shift middle with the freakish cutouts and killer women
who dominate talk shows, self-help shelves, and rock clubs. But a

unifying horror of softness is everywhere, spinning webs of connection among behaviors ranging from grotesque to civilized, mindless to thoughtful. And evidence of general impact is mounting. Now change registers as serial shocks (rendered less stunning by repetition). Now change registers as small, barely noticeable movements of mind and feeling—a hum and buzz of implication, toughness measuring its own meanings, anger effortfully reenergizing itself, work obsession mocking aspirations to wholeness. Again it's the tones of voice that draw us close to centers of being.

i. "I'd rather be alone than bored." Esther Dyson

The *New York Times* describes her as "the most powerful woman in the Net-erati." Six hundred computer honchos (Bill Gates and Michael Crichton among them) pay $3,000 each to attend her annual high-tech computer conference. She manages her own venture-capital fund. She advises Al Gore about the "national information infrastructure." She presides over Icann, an international group professedly bent on creating the Internet's first democracy. At public meetings on Internet governance she tells backers of democratic elective procedures that those procedures lead to the nomination of "people who are stupid." She writes books. (Broadway Books buys her treatise on Internet issues for a million dollars.) The deputy CEO of Lazard Frères says that "if the Pope could be a woman, she would be it."

Pushing fifty, Esther Dyson works ceaselessly (nights, holidays, Christmas, round the clock), walks to appointments reading, never (says a foundation executive who knows her) "wastes time on bullshit." Her brother claims to be close to her but adds, "I talk to her five minutes a year. I read about her in the *Wall Street Journal*." Her mother says, "She's never been to my place. She is too busy, and she's just not interested. She is very hard-nosed and determined. . . . When I travel, I always let her know where I am, and chances are that once in a while we can spend fifteen minutes at some airport lounge. She fits me in." Her father asks, "Who is my daughter? . . . What is it that drives her?"

Not, certainly, personal or familial involvements. (Dyson has no husband, lover, children, intimate friends, pets.) "The notion of having children was never appealing to me," she says. "I wanted to have my own identity. . . . I've never felt lonely on a Saturday night; I'd rather be alone than bored. There seem to be a lot of people who are just desperate for companionship. I'm not."

Vanity Fair's portrait of this extraordinary achiever doubts that "if she were a man," her brand of workaholism would seem noteworthy. The magazine quotes a "longtime observer" who argues that the right approach to Esther Dyson is, in fact, to see her *as* a man: "The easiest way to understand Esther is to think of her as Ed Dyson and not make the assumptions we all make, in our deeply ingrained sexist way, about what are a woman's needs and what are a man's needs."

Asked about her larger life goals, Dyson responds briskly, "The goal is to help the industry grow and to define itself, and to help the world be more efficient." Efficiency: key objective of self-simplifying women-becoming-men.

ii. "I would have told him to go fuck himself." Marcia Clark

For a long while they *could not get* Marcia Clark, lead prosecutor in the criminal trial of O. J. Simpson, to focus on the domestic violence aspects of the case. Clark recalls that "when Scott Gordon [a prosecution team member] would collar me in the hall, as he did at least seven times a day, with 'Marcia, we've got to get to work on DV,' I'd say 'Yeah, yeah, Scott. Why don't you write me up a memo on that?' "

One reason for Clark's lack of interest was that—as she puts it in her autobiography—"from a strictly legal standpoint, we would never have needed to address [the Simpsons'] history of marital violence. . . . The [DNA] evidence was so amazingly strong. I felt that we could probably put him away relying on that alone." But concern about her own self-image and reputation appears to have been the determining factor. Clark presented herself to the world as a commanding person made of absolute steel. She stormed into and out of meetings, slamming doors Bette Davis–style. "Marcia had the reputation," said Christopher Darden, her co-counsel, "as the toughest woman in the [court building]. . . . She could use her 100 pounds to unleash a string of profanities that would quiet a dock full of longshoremen . . . She barked orders with no misgivings about how men might feel about being ordered around by a woman." Darden's own nickname for Clark was "G," meaning gangster.

About a colleague who disapproved of her manners Clark herself said, "If he'd offered his etiquette tips directly to me, I would have told him go fuck himself." About Judge Lance Ito she said time and again—not without provocation—that she'd "never seen a man with so little spine." Her bosses were constantly at her because people "perceived [her] as 'hard.'" They wanted her to "speak more softly. I should get a softer hairdo. I should lose the business suits in favor of—get this—dresses."

And this talk of her need to soften herself seemed of a piece with the idea of elevating the domestic violence aspects of the case above the DNA and other scientific evidence. That strategy asked the lead prosecutor to identify with vulnerability—to put herself in the place of a woman who had actually *allowed* herself to be beaten. Which simply wasn't Marcia Clark.

> I've never gotten up on a pulpit to spout a feminist line. I never rushed in and charged spousal battery. . . . I have always hated the culture of victimization. . . . It's something I can't tolerate. I believe people have to take responsibility for themselves and their actions.

True, the tabloids at one point tried to turn her into a battered wife. They found "some dingbat" who lived next door when she was married to her first husband, Gaby. The dingbat "was claiming that I walked around in long-sleeved dresses all the time so that no one would see the bruises from Gaby's beatings." But no way, said Clark emphatically: "He never beat me. Never. He pushed. I shoved, we wrestled. That's as far as it went. . . . The pushing and the shoving were bad enough. But I always gave as good as I got. . . . I was not a battered woman! I was not a victim!"

A dozen explanations of the jury verdict in the Simpson criminal case are still in circulation. Marcia Clark's own explanation blames the defense's unscrupulous introduction of the race card; other versions, predictably, blame an incompetent prosecution for turning a winning case into a loser. What the court record shows, unambiguously, is that the prosecution did finally lead with the domestic violence evidence, and that—in the unanimous opinion of the best-regarded courtroom observers—the presentation of that evidence was terribly botched.

The problem was partly that, although her colleagues pressed her, week after week, month after month, to work on this evidence, Clark "kept putting [them] off." Not until nearly half a year after team members assembled the domestic violence material for analysis did the lead prosecutors get to it, and by then, Clark acknowledged, "we'd run out of time." There were sixty to seventy different episodes to scrutinize, stretching over a dozen years, and by the time that job was done, "the defense . . . complained that we'd given them the domestic violence stuff so late that they could not respond to it," and the "spineless" Judge Ito took the defense's side. "To sanction us for this supposed tardiness, Ito split the testimony in half, forcing us to hold off revealing the older episodes of abuse . . . until later in the trial. Unfortunately," Clark went on, "the power of these episodes was cumulative. You had to start from the beginning in order to see the pattern of pathological sadism. [Ito] crippled our domestic violence case from its infancy."

Doubtless the judge's decision preventing the prosecution from dramatizing the pattern of violence building over the years was crippling. But the "supposed tardiness" in forwarding the materials to the defense was, in fact, real tardiness—and real evasion. Furthermore, Clark's "deeply conflicted" feelings about domestic violence had had a direct impact on the prosecutor assigned to present the material. Christopher Darden by his own account lost interest in the subject. His presentation was poorly prepared and hapless—"amateurish," "inept," and "a fiasco" were among the labels courtroom observers applied—and hurt rather than helped the prosecution.

Whether a first-rate presentation would have made a difference is questionable: faithful observers of the proceedings scoffed at the notion that a guilty verdict was ever within these jurors' range. But the issue of final judgment isn't to the point. What is pertinent is the emergence of a *cherished* toughness, an abhorrence of weakness so deep it simultaneously chokes a flow of feeling that should have run strong and beclouds professional judgment. Nicole Simpson was a beaten, defenseless woman who failed to fight back, failed to give as good as she got. Marcia Clark, her courtroom surrogate, self-defined as a hard rock, gave that failure less than the compassionate response it deserved. One reason for this lay in Clark's ill-judged determination to play a "man's game"—law—like a man.

iii. "What is it about women's anger that scares us?"
Judy Oppenheimer

In the mid-nineties a magazine editor and freelance writer for the *Baltimore Sun*, Judy Oppenheimer, interviews a millionaire land developer who is launching a campaign for the Republican nomination to the U.S. Senate. The developer, Ruthann Aron, impresses Oppenheimer, although the two differ politically (Oppenheimer is a liberal, Aron a conservative). The interviewer has no notion that the woman she is interviewing will shortly induce in her remarkable intensities of self-examination—will prompt her to view the history of the women's movement as a chronicle of sellout, to see herself, Judy Oppenheimer, writer and feminist, as complicit in the sellout, and to imagine violent acts by women as inevitable responses to the collapse of the original feminist dream. All this in fact happens, however, and in a manner illuminating quiet alterations in course in the structure of contemporary feeling.

Ruthann Aron, millionaire developer and candidate for the Republican Senate nomination, is "one tough cookie," Oppenheimer writes, noting that "we [in Maryland] have a real fondness for tough, straight-talking women." Oppenheimer thinks it possible that her interviewee "could ride her tough cookie persona straight to [the Senate]." (Events prove her wrong; Aron fails even to win the nomination.) The candidate has energy and anger—and she doesn't shilly-shally. She attacks federal bureaucrats who won't listen when she and other land development types tell them "how to handle the banking crisis." She attacks an interloper—a former U.S. senator from Tennessee—who has suddenly decided to try to beat her out for the nomination she believes she deserves. She's furious at "political insiders who accuse her of being an outsider."

Oppenheimer reacts positively to these displays of anger. She has "no idea where [they will] lead," but nevertheless finds them "bracing, even energizing." Aron has overcome the handicaps imposed by her working-class background and by her sex. Measured by the masculinist standard, she's already a person of substantial achievement. She's aiming higher, at a place of power in the male-dominated public world, and—most bracing and energizing—she's assuming the right to full expression of masculinist emotional prerogatives, not excluding the right to anger.

Comes a reversal, not long after Oppenheimer publishes her interview with the woman: Aron is arrested, charged, and soon after convicted of attempting to hire a hit man to kill her husband and two lawyers. News reports disclose that Aron's house is heavily armed, that the owner is in the habit of "stroll[ing] around her homestead packing a piece," and that her anger has "fueled her complete estrangement from her father and brother."

At a different cultural moment, with a different structure of feeling in place, this news and the pending court trial might have restrained a journalist's impulse to continue celebrating her interviewee's rage. But not now. After the arrest, Oppenheimer returns to the subject of Ruthann Aron in the opinion pages of the *Sun*, noting that some of her acquaintances are mocking Aron, treating her as comparable to Lorena Bobbitt. A male lawyer she knows—someone who had worked for Aron—congratulates himself publicly "for managing to stay off her hit list." Others Oppenheimer knows simultaneously laugh and distance themselves. Oppenheimer acknowledges that she herself briefly shared their response:

> Every new tidbit, every new detail of the story, we seize on eagerly, because with each Ruthann Aron recedes, further and further, into some far-off, distant realm, the realm of the different, the bizarre, the not like us. Her anger was not like our anger (if in fact we are honest enough to admit we have any in the first place). Her anger led, after all, to this.

But her newspaper piece makes plain that Oppenheimer now regards this response as treachery—and despises it. She's angry at those who make merciless fun of Aron's anger, angry at herself for having joined in the laughter, angry at the manifold failures of feminism. Explaining herself, she voices loud protest against those who dare to condescend to the would-be murderer:

> Again and again, you hear it in the voices of former co-workers, former colleagues, when they talk of her—a certain smugness. Aron was tough, opinionated and liked to get her way. She also lacked flexibility and could hold a grudge forever. It's almost as if these are the real flaws, to hear them speak—the attempted hit-man hiring being only the natural fallout of a basic character deficiency. One man had even predicted, he said, that one day Aron would grab an automatic weapon, march into a building and start firing—she was that mad. He for one was not surprised at any of it.
>
> And you wonder. What is it about female anger that scares them all so much, scares all of us, actually? Scares us so that we need to cor-

don it off, make fun of it, leer at it—and if we find it in ourselves, press it down hard because there doesn't seem to be any socially approved, socially accepted place to put it?

The writer's protest on behalf of a "tough cookie's" right to anger signals no personal taste for violence; it's miles removed from riot grrrl shrillness. Cutting-edge, riot grrrl gender shift proclaims that toughness and anger in themselves can satisfy the needs of the good society for better values. Middle-class gender shift proposes, as with Judy Oppenheimer, only that respectable folk should reconsider their muscle-twitch negativism about toughness and anger, and allow for the possibility that fear of rage may equal cowardice ("What is it about female anger that scares all of us?"). The writer expresses *limited* hostility to softness—no fireworks. She ventures no further than the suggestion that shutting down criticism of toughness and anger could open up new paths to insight.

The suggestion—gender shift in its mild middle mode—represents molecular change under way.

iv. "Don't listen to her bitch." Girlbaum

A shade less mild is the style favored by *Bust,* a self-published 'zine catering to "garter-belt feminists in the Madonna mold," and to fans of Courtney Love and other "glamour-girl sexual aggressors." This journal's advice column, "Girlfriend to Girlfriend," written by the pseudonymous Girlbaum, harps on the theme that young women need to concentrate on Number One: stop fretting about the plight of your hapless friends, forget sympathy and "concern for others," grasp that the only happiness lies in unflagging self-involvement. Most advice columnists thrive on repetition: after two generations the *Playboy* Advisor continues to flog the themes of women's basic animality and hypocritical worry about appearances—themes that won the column its original audience.

Still: Girlbaum's repeated explosions of anger at souls entrapped in "caring" sisterhood—the taunting fury she directs time and again at "their" (probably written in-house) letters—are striking. Not only does this writer treat stoniness as high moral principle; she insists too, in a sort of low-rent aping of the Machiavellian princessa, that not until her correspondents learn how to cut themselves loose from others will they be able to conquer depression, anxiety, "transference," and related ills.

An example: Girlbaum quotes a letter in a recent *Bust*—it's signed "The Girl Next Desk"—from someone upset about the behavior of a friend at work. The friend has taken up with a male fellow worker given to "playing all these manipulative, freaky games where she can't call him because that's too much pressure, but he can come over to her place drunk at midnight, fuck her and pass out, and that's just fine." Girl Next Desk pronounces herself "horrified and disgusted" by this conduct and campaigns against it. She tells her friend "maybe she might want to move on and find someone more worthy of her"; gradually the friend seems to see the light and talks of getting rid of the man, whereupon Girl Next Desk cheers: "I'm all hooray! finally! and I tell her how much everyone else in the office hates him and pities her, and how glad I am that she woke up. . . . I give her the whole 'You are good, he is bad! You are good! He is bad!' feminist empathy cheer." Days later she sees Mr. Vile and her friend smoking intimately in the corridor together and the friend gives a mealy smile, "like, 'I knooooow, but what can I dooooo? I looooove him!' " And now, Girl Next Desk tells her adviser, "I feel so infuriated and betrayed; why am I taking this so hard? I mean, it's not my problem, is it?"

Girlbaum's answer weighs in, first, with mockery of this correspondent's protestation that she knows her friend's problem isn't her problem. "Oh yeah," says Girlbaum, "obviously it's not your problem. You're fine. You already had a jerk in your life, and you dumped him. And it was hard. And you wanted to take him back, but he was dating somebody else. And you were so mad you could hardly cry." The trouble is, Girlbaum continues, even though you think you know better, you've lost control of yourself. You're getting scared. You're holding out for a decent man, but "you're afraid you'll never find him, and that in three years . . . the pick of the slobs will all be taken, so, maybe you're feeling a little insecure and even jealous—yes, jealous—not because you wish you could be in a lousy relationship, but because you wish you wanted to be."

So what's to be done? Find your way back to total self-involvement, says the counselor. Stop caring about your office pal. Focus solely on Numero Uno. Don't even think about what Mr. Vile is doing to your friend:

> Nobody can learn from your mistakes but you. So learn from your mistakes, and decide that you will never engage in transference again, because that is what you're doing now, and stop, just stop. Don't bother telling your work pal that she's an idiot, don't listen to her bitch, and in a few weeks when she's miserable, don't let her turn to you. You can't empathize with her, and you shouldn't want to. You're over it. Voila. Now don't you feel better?

Violence and rage as traditionally understood play only marginal roles in this exchange; like its counterparts in other tough girl 'zines, "Girlfriend to Girlfriend" addresses symptoms of "feminine" softness as they come, working cell by cell at correcting the presumed underlying pathology. In the new culture happiness means cutting the connections between self and ordinary human response. *Harden yourselves, citizens; shed fellow feeling and ascend.*

v. "Would I? Sure I would." Maureen Dowd

Week in and week out in her *New York Times* column, "Liberties," Maureen Dowd dramatizes herself as a woman freed from the postures of deference, mannerliness, and softness in which stereotypical femininity is entrapped. She mocks the First Couple as starstruck children caught in a "kooky connubial deal." ("Husband strays. Wife gets mad. Husband brings flowers, and if he's been really bad, earrings, and if he's been really, really bad, the health-care portfolio.") She puts down George W. Bush for "curl[ing] up with his feather pillow" and "softly moan[ing]," and for "coyness." (He wants "to have it both ways.") She slams John McCain for campaigning as "a martyr in the flames." ("He thought he was showing [people] his strength but he was showing them his weakness. And nobody finds weakness exciting for very long.") She laughs at Warren Beatty for vanity and manipulativeness:

> Once, while I was interviewing the star at his candle-lit dinner table in Hollywood, he wanted to read me something about Tennessee Williams. Instead of turning on a lamp, he fetched a tiny flashlight. . . . He kindles to the game of cat-and-mouse with reporters, manipulating the way he's portrayed. He scrupulously weighs every word for every possible effect. He dissects every question, flashing an ankle only when the angle is propitious.

Everywhere in her writing she takes up the position of satirical top dog, superior, proof against inanity, eager to laugh at the "kerfuffles" of the mighty, spelling out the defects and weaknesses of males and females whom others accord some measure of respect. And everywhere her writing is marked by the assumption that power relationships between men and women have been completely transformed, with women now on top. ("Now that we have feminized society and domesticated our men . . . now that we have forced them to help pick Martha Stewart stencils and watch Olympic ice-dancing" . . .)

Increasingly, as her routines, tones, and bits grow into a second nature, this columnist's top dog assertiveness functions as an unforeseen having-it-both-ways trap. The imperatives of clever hardness drive Dowd to commit herself unwittingly to stances that exactly mirror the behavior she believes herself to be chiding. Her critiques become self-canceling.

An example: In a column titled "Sure I Would," Dowd slates an *Esquire* writer for an article evoking Hillary Clinton as a sex object. The writer of the piece, Tom Junod, praised the First Lady for her "pretty, almond-shaped, slightly catty eyes" and "mighty cheekbones," speculated about her intimate language ("One could imagine her talking dirty"), and announced he'd consider making love to her ("Would I? Sure I would"). Dowd objects: "The problem with this is that it yanks us back to judging women on their looks and desirability. That is where women have been through history, relying on their appearance to get approval and get ahead, and that can be debilitating."

Then, for the purpose of showing "how trivializing it is to sexualize Hillary Clinton in this way," she proceeds to "apply the Junod approach (and much of his own panting vocabulary) to male candidates." Al Gore "looks like the smartest guy at the dance. . . . Would I? Sure I would." Sometimes Rudy Giuliani "seem[s] open to the intrigue of dishevelment. . . . Would I? I sure would." Alan Keyes is "irresistibly saucy. . . . Would I? Sure I would." George W. Bush is a cowboy and "cowboys make me weak. Would I? Sure I would." Bill Bradley's "chin packs a lewd wallop. . . . Would I? Sure I would."

Arriving at Gary Bauer, the columnist slips and falls on her own conceit: "One could imagine Gary Bauer talking dirty. His lips form a curving line as though nothing could please him more than his own hunger. Would I? Let me get back to you on that."

I'm Dowd, not dowdy, is the message. I criticize the masculinist standard that rates "looks and desirability" as crucial—but, do understand: when push comes to Bauer, I embrace the standard. The writer's grin assures readers that none of this is serious, and she thereby lays claim to a hard-nosed, mannish solidarity with trivializing males—characters addicted to having things both ways. Week by week, for an audience of millions, the solidarity deepens; week by week, Maureen Dowd's critiques confuse high-fashion hardness with pointed seriousness, lose their momentum, dwindle into inconsequence.

vi. "I'm willing to take quite a lot of risks." Marsha Angell, M.D.

An accomplished woman professional in the sciences chastises public hostility to corporate America—particularly hostility to drug companies—at a gathering of journalists, lobbyists, and legislators. Her manner is cool, businesslike, unflappable; her sentences are clipped. ("No evidence, no conclusion. That in a nutshell is the scientific method.") She's angriest at damage awards by juries that, she says, have "brought Dow Chemical to its knees." And she holds up for special scorn the notion spread by lawyers and media folk about who gets hurt when drug companies have to pay billions in questionable claims. Lawyers aver it's the corporations that are hurt, but in fact, says the speaker, corporations are you and me and the others who buy manufactured products; we are the ones punished by the damage awards.

The speaker is Marsha Angell, M.D., editor of the *New England Journal of Medicine,* and the occasion is a National Press Club luncheon. Her focus is the controversy over "silicone gel–filled breast implants, a controversy that's raged in this country for nearly a decade, and still isn't resolved." She fixes blame for the controversy on "liberals and feminists," and her talk begins by excoriating Connie Chung, guilty of a "breathless treatment" of breast implants on TV in late 1990.

Chung "interviewed several women who claimed to have autoimmune disease caused by their breast implants," and "she conveyed the clear message that implants were dangerous devices foisted off on unsuspecting women." Nobody questioned the "presumed link between the implants and the illness"—whereupon chaos. "Many women rushed back to their plastic surgeons to have the implants removed and, not surprisingly, the trickle of lawsuits became a flood." Juries commenced awarding huge sums to women for alleged damages. The Federal Drug Administration banned the sale of implants. Dow Corning nearly collapsed. An "astonishing saga," says Marsha Angell, pulling her listeners up short with an angry question:

> What did we actually know about the medical risks from breast implants? Well, we knew implants could rupture. And we knew they could cause excessive scarring of the tissue around them. But as for serious disease in the rest of the body, we knew next to nothing. To be sure, the local complications could be painful and disfiguring but it was the specter of systemic disease, generalized disease, that had led to the FDA ban and was the cause of all the legal activity.

And about that, she reiterates, "we knew next to nothing." Worse, once something *was* known — once respectable epidemiological studies proved that "breast implants [are] probably reasonably safe" — juries "seemed uninterested in the science." Women kept on suing and juries kept on finding Dow Chemical guilty of negligence.

Dr. Angell berates "liberals and feminists" for their hostility to the drug companies — their predisposition to believe that breast implants cause disease. Liberals, she argues, "feel certain that corporations would as soon make harmful products as not and that the government would as soon cover for them as not." Feminists "dislike the idea of breast implants in the first place and are ready to believe the worst of them." Both are immeasurably guiltier than the manufacturers involved. Both fail to grasp that corporate America's sole concern is to provide consumers with the best possible products at the lowest possible price:

> Make no mistake about it, there is big money in breast implants, as there is in other health scares and nostrums. Billions of dollars are now being transferred from the implant manufacturers — which means the consumers who buy their products — to plaintiffs' attorneys and women who claim their implants made them ill.

Breast implants were produced for the purpose of profiting from women's compliance with male standards of female sexual attractiveness; pain and disfigurement resulted in thousands of instances from the implants; the manufacturers evinced little concern, before marketing the products, about possible harmful effects. In reserving pity for a corporate giant "brought to its knees," the editor of the *New England Journal of Medicine* proves her commitment to bottom-line rationality—but also to a troublingly lordly attitude toward ordinary human credulousness.

To women whom a marketing program cons into buying a product that harms them, her counsel is: You have only yourselves to blame for your gullibility. To members of her audience fretting in the question period about an array of environmental-ecological problems, her counsel is to relax: "*I'm* willing to take quite a lot of risks." She denies legitimacy to any objection to Research and its products not specifically tied to methodological or evidentiary issues, dismisses moral concerns as superstitious and fuzzyheaded, presents bottom-line concerns as superior to all others.

The impression overall is that Dr. Marsha Angell thinks in a groove, treating all nonprofessional considerations as frivolous; one of her major goals appears to be that of establishing her level of toughness as equal or superior to that of any man who might serve in her place. In a word: a model citizen of the gender-purged republic to come.

vii. "Doing just as [we] like with the car keys." Rebecca Mead

Rebecca Mead, a reporter for *The New Yorker*, travels to New Canaan, Connecticut, to do a humorous then-and-now story about life thereabouts for the "Talk of the Town." The occasion is the release of *The Ice Storm*, a movie chronicling exurban wars between the sexes a quarter century ago. Set in New Canaan in the seventies, the movie centers on wife-swapping and couples therapy, and its climactic scenes detail a so-called key party, at which husbands "drop their keys in a bowl, not knowing which women they are going to take home until the evening's end, when the wives pluck out a set of keys, grab-bag style."

Mead shapes her piece, called "The Good Old Days," as a story of tables turned—contemporary women trading places with men, not just going to work and taking charge of their lives but reducing their mates to the condition of wretched helplessness women endured in yesteryear. Ida Davidoff, a ninety-four-year-old marital and family therapist who's practiced in the town since the mid-fifties, serves the reporter as alter ego. Yes, there were key parties in those days, Davidoff says; yes, college-educated women back then were "spinning their wheels." Disillusioned by marriage and too passive to think of doing anything else, "they used to say, 'I'm so lonely; what's wrong with me? I'm angry at my husband; he takes me for granted.' " Furthermore, "when couples came seeking therapy, it was always the woman pleading with the man, and he telling her that she was no good."

But not now. Together, Davidoff and Mead hail a new day worth celebrating because—as indicated—miserable women have been replaced by miserable men and "triumphant" rule-defining men have been replaced by triumphant rule-defining women. Today's women say, "This is what I want, this is what I am going to do, and there are no longer rules that I am breaking." Today's men are in socio-sexual disarray, passive, humiliated, at odds with themselves. In today's couples "the man comes in pathetic and apologetic . . . [is] absolutely to be pitied, because the women are in the driver's seat." And today's women, says Mead in a sly closing sentence, are "doing just as they like with the car keys."

Measure for measure. "The Good Old Days" is a mini–revenger's fantasy in which seventies women, pitiably childish and victimized, get their own back by becoming (vicariously, through the successor generation) punishers and victimizers—people who relish dominance precisely as did their mates in earlier times. The pretended truculence is amusing, as are the faces slightly flushed with success; the hint of controlled heartlessness inside the joke is a telling mark of the evolving ethos.

A woman entrepreneur who dismisses human attachment as boring . . . A woman editor who denies that a will to violence is per se either reprehensible or comic and affirms that murderous rage has a dignity that mockery of rage lacks . . . A woman prosecutor so obsessed with her reputation for toughness that she can't bear to rehearse a narrative of female vulnerability because it requires her to speak in defense of weakness . . . A pop psychological counselor who promotes total cutoffs of fellow feeling . . . A woman columnist seemingly fixated on the task of proving that males—especially elected officials—are frailer than females . . . A woman scientist who transforms a complex issue involving competing concepts of justice and injustice into a bare-knuckles scrap between commerce and sentimentality . . . A woman reporter saluting, in print, the contemporary state of relations between the sexes because now the oppressed are oppressors and vice versa . . .

Unlike riot grrrls, working professionals of this sort don't bid for sensational notice. But the pressure of gender shift is nevertheless evident in their behavior—in the masculinist postures of superiority, in displays of detachment from ordinary feeling, in teeth-gritted toughness and knowing scorn of values not keyed to the bottom line. Feminism had argued that women want structural and attitudinal change supporting the ideal of gender flexibility—change aimed at transforming women's experience, knowledge, and abilities into significant influences on the whole life of society. The pressure of the new culture wears away that ideal, replacing broad-scale feminist visions of a more humane future with hardening processes: internal makeovers presumably preparing for the full conversion of women into men.

As the displacement of the earlier idealism proceeds, mass entertainment comes to function in new ways, as an unofficial public explicator of the hardening processes at which we've just been glancing. Yesteryear's bitchery lacked standing as an ideal; it had little authority as the possessor of rare and marketable skills, little capacity to terrorize. But contemporary bitchery is formidable not negligible, powerful not impotent; explanation (non-pedantic, unpretentious, even tongue in cheek) is welcome.

The explanation arrived at in Sitcom and Movie America is at once simple in outline and devastating in impact. It presents the hardening processes we've been surveying—the yielding to egomaniacal ambition and utter feelinglessness for the claims of others—as *natural:* the hidden core of the female, hence the very soul of feminism itself. Female characters contemptuous of attachment, scornful of male weakness, eager to become oppressors are not seen as exhibiting psychosocial patterns with a strange inner dynamic, an initially narrow audience, and an unarticulated agenda. They are seen as women allowed—thanks to feminism's success—to be and to reveal themselves.

It follows, obviously, that womankind as promulgator of ideal visions of change vanishes almost entirely from the world of mass communication, and that feminism is reduced simply to a force generating hard women—creatures increasingly powerful, increasingly villainous. Keying itself directly to representations of feminine/feminist sensibility as mean, cold, and destructive of humane values, pop explodes in an extraordinary gender shift campaign of its own. And, in a turn completely and unsurprisingly supportive of things as they are, the campaign in question emerges as a crucial front in the contemporary war on possibility. How the campaign is waged is the subject to which we now turn.

4

The Media's Love-Hate Relationship
with Women-Becoming-Men

Women's demands for change are rooted in women's hunger to become men.

Egocentricity, a taste for sexual bullying, and obliviousness of social ills and injustice are marks of the character of contemporary women; warmth, kindness, and alertness to social ills and injustice are marks of the character of contemporary men.

At the tasks of nurturance that truly matter — e.g., instilling a sense of security through lovingkind constancy of concern — men qualify as superior.

Women's moral authority is declining, men's is on the rise.

W ILD AND SOBERING by turns, the extended narratives that transform women-becoming-men into mass entertainment include cineplex movies, TV movies, sitcoms, hits, bombs, much else besides. But patterns exist, together with endlessly recurring themes. Whether the stories deal with figures from yesteryear's myths (wicked witches and spider women metamorphosed into gun-crazed killer bitches), or with "sexually liberated" women who pattern their behavior on that of male sexual marauders, or simply with mediocre nurturers in need of male tutoring, they dramatize women as fanciers of their new mastery of stereotypically male patterns of sexual aggression and as despisers of stereotypical feminine passivity. They delete women as care-givers and truth-tellers from history and contemporary life. They show women forth as bitter, mean, or worse in daily dealings with others in both private and public worlds. And quite often they argue that the true gifts of nurturance belong to men.

The overall effect is, unsurprisingly, subversive of women's claim to moral authority—and totally destructive of the moral politics of liberation and equality. The female braggarts and miscreants who populate the tales, cold-cocking the good, teaching deviousness and cynicism to one another and to the young, don't invariably escape punishment. Nor do the tender-minded males in their shadows invariably come in for salutes. But cheers and boos, if they materialize, are incidental—mere nods at rating systems. The serious, for-profit projects lie elsewhere, in the demonstration that no alternatives exist to the bottom-line monomania ruling the country's still largely male corporate hierarchies.

The shows over the past ten years dramatize the intensity of women's longing to become men—the longing that launched and still powers, so audiences are meant to conclude, the "women's movement." On occasion a movie or sitcom alludes to the trade union issues, such as pay disparities, that figured in the original launch, and that gave rise to the despairing, furious conviction that women could overcome the stacking of the deck against them only by matching the ruthlessness of the most ruthless men. But the allusions amount for the most part merely to period detail, and trigger minimum scrutiny of the morality of ruthlessness. The shows reestablish men's moral preeminence by depicting them both as instinctively truthful and as naturally apt at (and selflessly devoted to) the arts of caring. And the shows remove from consciousness any lingering hope or delusion that women's ascent to power will effect fundamental change in social, political, or moral-intellectual attitudes and values.

An example: *Disclosure,* a top-grossing film about upper-echelon corporate life in the presumed age of equality. The movie's heroine, handsome Meredith Johnson (Demi Moore), is a knowing, hard-driving executive who's also a sexual harasser. Throughout most of the film, whether seen pumping her exercycle or mounting a podium to con shareholders, she stands forth as a glisteningly imposing figure. Characters attack her behind her back, lamenting that she doesn't "fight fair." She's cited as proof that "a woman in power can be every bit as abusive as a man." She's charged with incompetence. (On field assignment in South Asia she contracts for bottom-wage labor, ruining quality standards on a Malaysian production line.) She's locked in an extended black-hat/white-hat moral contrast with the man she beats out for promotion and harasses. When a fortuitously discovered tape attests, at a mediation hearing, that she's guilty of harassment, she's publicly punished — reviled, fired from her job.

But these various chastisements, severe as they are, nevertheless belong to the margins; they concern what *Disclosure* moralizes about, not what it animates. What *Disclosure* animates is a woman aping stereotypically male patterns of sexual aggression, suffering forced retreat from "masculinity" to stereotypical femininity, scorning femininity as humiliation, battling thereafter to recover the heights of maleness from which she has been banished. The cycle begins with a sexual harassment scene, progresses to an interval of cowering "feminine" self-defense, and completes itself in the woman's near-exultant recovery of an unintimidated "masculine" voice.

Meredith Johnson invites Tom Sanders (Michael Douglas), the executive she's beaten out for promotion, to her office after hours (the two had an affair some years before). Fully relaxed as she welcomes him (he's ill at ease), she gives orders quietly (tells a secretary to leave, turns off a phone), opens wine, asks him to show her his family snapshots, insists when he hesitates, sets the pace and direction of their talk. She's unhurried, evidently the stronger of the two (her corporate rank and her well-conditioned physicality are factors, as is the man's nervousness). Her casual confidence and no-problem manner hold firm as she proposes that he see his prospective infidelity as both private and unmomentous; her voice hardens a little with impatience, but there's never a trace of wheedling. *I'm showing restraint and forbearance,* is the unspoken message. *My indulgence has limits.*

Nor is there, at the physical crisis, any shrinking from challenge. Johnson orders the man to rub her shoulders. She taunts him sharply for inhibition—reminds him of his vulnerability. ("Do you have a problem working for me?") Reasoning with his inner child, far quicker than he, she suddenly lays strong hands on him. "No!" he cries out. "No, Meredith!" They wrestle evenly for a breathless moment. Only by summoning all his strength can he hold her off! Her mouth is on his penis before he manages to break free. She threatens him, warns him he's in deep trouble if he leaves without "finish[ing] what you started—"

The test of combat is, in other words, almost passed. By way of proving to herself that she can confirm each new increment of power through action, the heroine imagines a quasi-rape and commits to it daringly, pursuing her concept of masculinist freedom—the freedom of brutality and cynicism. And as the movie dramatizes her confident, nearly successful approach to her goal, it affirms that these heady masculinisms are indeed prizes worth coveting.

Minutes later, moreover, the movie combines with that affirmation the necessary corollary: female self-hatred. When she is brought up on charges of harassment, Johnson's only possible defense is to claim that she was the victim, not the victimizer—which means she has to drop the heady masculinisms. The self that moments before comfortably manipulated and condescended—the self that plainly hates prissiness, meekness, frilly idioms and tears, that relishes four-letter-word liberty, that knows with rich satisfaction *what a man feels*—has to be shed, and Meredith Johnson sheds it. In front of the assembled authorities she breaks character—

breaks down. She sniffles. She feigns bewilderment that a Good Husband and Responsible Executive could contemplate infidelity to his wife, makes ritual obeisance to "beautiful children" and sadly deceived mothers, speaks (an ultimate indignity) of her underwear as "my panties" (when not play-acting, Johnson calls her underwear underwear).

And she makes the audience taste the repugnance seething within her at these "ladylike" acts. The character of Meredith Johnson has cartoon aspects, but in several scenes Demi Moore overcomes the role's limits. The striking element of her performance is her success in communicating that, for her character, descent into weak whimpering "womanliness" is hell. Drawing us close to the mixed despair and hatred presumed to torment a would-be woman-become-man, Moore demonstrates that, for such a person, it's a positive debasement to be obliged to register shock as some harmless obscenity passes your lips.

"I told him the children were beautiful," Meredith Johnson forces herself to say, in plaintive voice, to the lawyers. "He said looking at them made him feel old. . . . He said seeing me again after these years made him feel young and marriage was a tough tradeoff." The camera finds the victim's wife at a little distance from the conference table, alone, and waits for her tears. "He began to rub my shoulder," Meredith Johnson continues, pretending she's near the edge. "I struggled with him and told him to stop. He grabbed my hair and forced me to his knees. He put his penis in my mouth. He said, 'You want to get fucked? Is that what you want?' He pulled off my panties."

She's quickly found out, as I said, but being found out—found guilty—is, for this woman, a relief: she can at least recover quasi-manliness. Before the movie is over the recovery is well launched. We see Johnson in effect rebuking herself for the shame of her collapse, in front of the lawyers, into "feminine" moral elevation. Regaining her lost voice (the voice of impatient masculine command), she talks down-and-dirty to a fussy woman lawyer. ("I *like* it [sex]. You wouldn't understand that.") She speaks up boldly for equal opportunity harassment—the right of the strong, that is, to enforce their will on the weak. "I'm an aggressive woman," she says. "We expect a woman to do a man's job for a man's money and then walk around and wait like a pillow for a man to fuck her." At the end she's assuring her enemies that headhunters in number are after her and that in ten years she'll own the firm that's firing her. Her voice as she speaks calls up the whole history of male revenge fantasy, from braggart soldiers to comeback kids.

A straightforward story, then, about a bad apple luckily found and discarded before it rots the basket? Hardly. *Disclosure* is a message movie, crammed from beginning to end with direct instruction about how to respond to any utopian sounds still issuing from women agitators for change. Don't be suckered, is the lesson. Ignore the preaching and the pretensions, the tired pieties about "openness," "social justice," and the rest. Feminists have had but one serious objective from the start, namely, raiding and pillaging men's nature and men's worlds. Their only hunger is for the freedom of cynicism and the joys of sexual bullying. This is why they wander the earth embarrassing themselves and others with visions of themselves as men.

On the prime time cartoon sitcom King of the Hill, *Debbie — a Demi Moore/Meredith Johnson knockoff — repeatedly attempts sexual assaults on Hank Hill, a nerdy married fellow employee at Strickland Propane. He flees from her, locks himself in his car, cries out in fear: "No, sir, at this point in time, I'm going to have to reject your advances." (Debbie rages in closeup: "Nobody rejects Debbie Grunge.") On* Frasier, *the hero's assistant, Roz, sexually bullies a tight-jeaned stranger in a café by staring at his private parts. (Frasier hopes the man's tailor can "fix the two holes you just burned into his jacket." Roz corrects him: "They're not in his jacket.") On* Stark Raving Mad, *Audrey, the hard-driving publisher, bids farewell to a writer she's just signed with these words: "I'd kiss you good-bye but as you know my lips have been on your ass for the last half hour." On* Townies, *Denise lets fall that her husband, Ryan, was one of several possible progenitors of her baby boy; she made him marry her "after seeing how good he was with the baby." On* Caroline in the City, *Caroline deals with Joe—a youngster casually met and fucked who persists in telling her that he loves her. "I could never have pictured a one-night stand ending up like this," says Caroline. Her associates are equally puzzled. One of them remarks, "Nothing says love like dirt." Caroline's inventive insults finally persuade Joe the jerk to knock it off with the I-love-you's. On* Sex and the City, *Miranda sets Charlotte and Carrie straight about their wimpy practice of faking orgasms:*

> Miranda: Orgasm? Major thing in a relationship.
> Charlotte: Yeah, but not the only thing. Orgasms don't send you
>   Valentine's Day cards and they don't hold your hand in a sad movie.
> Carrie: Mine do.
> Miranda (disbelieving): You're seriously advocating faking?
> Charlotte: No, but if you really like the guy, what's one little moment
>   of oooh-oooh versus spending the whole night in bed alone?
> Miranda (horrified): These are my options?
> Charlotte: And who's to say that one moment is any more important
>   than when he gets up and pours you a cup of coffee in the morning?
> Miranda: I'll take an orgasm over a cup of French drip Colombian any
>   day.

Sara on Men Behaving Badly *has to straighten out Kevin, her doltish boyfriend, because he's given to talking soppy when they're together. ("When you think of romance, I want you to think of me," etc.) Sara tells the dumbbell that romance is out, but notes that "in case you haven't noticed, I'm [in bed] with you."*

> Kevin: Yeah, I know. But why?
> Sara (trolling): Well, let's not pick it apart, OK?
> Kevin: I mean it.
> Sara (leading him deeper): You don't want to hear this.
> Kevin: Oh yes I do.
> Sara: OK, I'll tell you. (Feigning a difficult confession) I guess it started

*with my childhood. You know, my—My brothers teased me and
made me feel inferior—and I think I sought out that pattern in the
men I dated. Then I met you. And I loved you because—because—*
Kevin *(taking the hook): Because I didn't treat you that way.*
Sara: *Because I felt superior to you.*
Kevin *(choking): Sara!*
Sara *(more confession): No, no, and I—No, I still do. I really do. And
I gotta tell you, it's a great feeling!*

On Boy Meets World, *male teenies are uniformly dorky, stupid,
and weak. (Eric calls his rear a "tushie" and treats himself to a bikini
wax over the summer.)* On Friends, *Chandler and Joey, former regular guy roomies, lose their identities when they move in with bossy
young women. Chandler to Joey: "You're turning into a woman." Joey
(in hurt tone): "No, I'm not. That's just mean. Not what you said but
the way you said it." Hearing his prissy tone, Joey puts hand to fore-
head at the revelation: "Oh my god! I'm a woman!"* On Odd Man
Out, *Andrew ("lone man of the family") and friend briefly demur
when Aunt Jordan and the other women of the house tell them to
switch channels from baseball to women's ice skating; the women
scam them by talking up the sexiness of women skaters and then, having gotten their way, exchange a wink at the boys' dimwittedness:
"They're such simple creatures."* On The Single Guy, *Johnny wakes
up to the fact he's a kept man. Valerie, a rich executive, has been using him as combined lover and personal servant—having him pick up
her cleaning, exchange her pantyhose, carry her briefcase, and so on—
and he's been in denial. But now he tells Valerie she'll have to choose
between Johnny the lover and Johnny the personal aide:*

Valerie: *Oh my god. You're absolutely right. . . . How does $15 an hour
sound?*
Johnny: *Please tell me you're offering to pay me to be your boyfriend.*
Valerie: *Plus lunch and dinner. You're not gonna do better than
that anywhere in town. Deal?*
Johnny *(sighing): So that's it. You'd rather I work for you than
date you.*

Valerie: Oh, Johnny. I mean, there's a lot of handsome, eligible guys in this town but . . . Try finding an assistant with your attention to detail.

The varieties are endless. Women staring at men's genitals—like men staring at women's breasts. Women mocking the language of romantic attachment—like men joking about women's reluctance to Come Across until babied with "I love you." Women laughing in masculinist disdain, following sexual encounters, at men's fantasies of equality. Lying, condescension, trickery . . . In a beer commercial a woman stands at the door of her apartment with a man. He's carrying a six-pack. She wants the six-pack, not him, so she asks him for a commitment. He flees, naturally, and she sails in to her roommates, gleeful sexual despot, Bud in hand. Deal?

Cousin to the female sexual bully is the figure of total self-absorption, incapable of imaginative engagement with others, career- and profit-driven, unrelentingly self-involved. *The Paper*, a movie recounting the crimes and punishment of the managing editor of an underfinanced tabloid, studies this kind of egomania.

Alicia (Glenn Close), the managing editor, is gripped by the deranging passion of the would-be man—and by frustrations arising from dimness about the reality of minds other than her own. She can't comprehend that her publisher is himself too hard-pressed financially to pay her enough to support her Manhattan East Side lifestyle (designer clothes, luxe apartments, fashionable decorators). She doesn't understand that her co-workers' hostility stems from her failure to engage with them, one at a time, as individual human beings. She doesn't understand that the fast-track celebrities whose company she seeks are as blind to her as she is to her co-workers. Fury goads her into a series of confrontations that comment on her "feminist" eagerness to be male. Desperate for money, she chases the paper's publisher into a hotel men's room and hears herself denounced—in front of a row of occupied urinals—as "cheap." Excluded from male after-hours camaraderie, she swears and blusters to prove she belongs. ("You think my job is easy? You assholes couldn't put up with the shit I put up with!") She tries—in a weird pressroom slugging match—to punch out a male assistant city editor who countermands her orders. At nearly every moment Alicia is defined as morally wanting (she offers to sleep with her publisher if he'll give her a raise); at every moment her words and deeds make plain that her longing to bond with guys lacks substantive human content.

The obliviousness that's central in Alicia's character soon becomes pivotal to the story. *The Paper* is structured as a whodunit: the plot concerns an urgent effort by Henry Hackett (Michael Keaton), assistant city editor, to save two young blacks from conviction for a murder they didn't commit. Mobilizing resources ranging from his eight-and-a-half-months-pregnant wife (a former reporter) to a golden-hearted cop, risking everything—job, reputation, marriage—in his effort to save the black kids, Hackett at length uncovers evidence sufficient to justify a last-minute stop-press order for a front-page screamer (THEY DIDN'T DO IT!).

Alicia, managing editor, won't run the screamer. Stone cold, she couldn't care less that Hackett's innocents have no shot at a fair trial unless the facts about the frame-up get out fast. The budget numbers tell her this edition's front page is locked for good; her head tells her only numbers count. Dollar-maddened, vigilant on behalf of no human interest save her own, the managing editor can't see beyond the bottom line.

The Paper isn't a humorless film; it grins at the melodramatic conventions (Stop the presses!) that it observes. Neither is it unforgiving. Alicia grasps in the end that her bottom-line monomania threatens her interests (including her desire to win over the guys in the after-hours corner bar); she relents and runs the screamer for the sake of journalistic honor (and for a happy ending). Never a sign in her, though, of fellow feeling for the kids whose just cause her male co-worker has made his own. For most of its length, *The*

Paper leaves the impression that, for its masculinist heroine, as for Meredith Johnson in *Disclosure,* toughness, harsh cynicism, and insensitivity to others are life-structuring values; lose hold of them and there's no escaping descent into self-hating chaos.

On Action, *Wendy, a prostitute, takes command: she seizes her pimp's gun, accepts appointment as "a motion picture producer," gives orders to the president of production for Dragonfire Productions, and lays it down, stompingly, that henceforth anyone calling her a bitch risks being shot. On* The Hughleys, *the genteel senior citizen lady who babysits for the family is impatient with Hughley for promoting nonviolent video games for the kids. She's a happy gun owner herself and loves a game called "Gut Splash." On* Ink, *Kate, managing editor, fires an underling and finds it pure delight. "In fact," she says, her voice filling with adrenalin, "I felt a rush of power. I could, I could do it again. I could fire more than one person. (Mounting excitement) I could fire groups of persons!" On* Drew Carey, *Drew tells Mrs. Lowder, a gung ho corporate executive, that he's witnessed an episode of sexual harassment and intends to testify for the victim in her lawsuit: "I'm gonna . . . make sure it never happens again." Worried that the suit could cost the corporation millions, Mrs. Lowder tells Drew, "I like your spirit. Now let's see what we can do to break it"—and comes up with bribes. On* Murphy Brown, *the female station boss swings into the office with, as usual, an insulting greeting to her employees: "Ah, good morning, my little worker ants. That's just a figure of speech. I would never compare you to insects . . . Not after that sensitivity seminar those maggots at the network forced me to attend." Later the same boss asks for opinions, gets them, and announces, "That's four opinions I don't care about." On* Cybill, *the heroine tells her buddy Maryann that "home security is like sex: if we want it done right, we have to do it ourselves." On* Almost Perfect, *Kim persuades her associates to join her in a scheme to put a business competitor out of action by framing him for a murder. Her male associates wryly observe that her unfeelingness marks her as no different from the rest of her kind:*

Kim (great relish): He'll be humiliated, his career will be ruined, his nerves will fray. . . . He'll lose his grip and end up a broken shell of a man.
Rob: You're a scary lady, Kim.
Gary: Scratch the surface, they're all like that.

Meaning, they're like men—enclosed in egotism, shut off from the life of other minds. Women preening themselves for toughness—like men establishing their bona fides as downsizers. Women adopting the tones and manners of "superiority"—like men assured that rank in a socioeconomic hierarchy defines human worth. Women erasing the impulse to feel with the losses of others—like men taught as boys that sympathy is weak and unmanly. Scratch the surface: they're all like that.

Increasingly gender shift narratives represent kindness, thoughtfulness, concern for others as indigenous to males. Stories that follow women-becoming-men also often follow, in a subsidiary line, one or more men-becoming-women—like, for example, Joey and Chandler on *Friends.* The shift is sometimes dramatized in scenes of domestic life (fathers performing stereotypically maternal roles in caring for the young), sometimes in workplace scenes (a male executive argues against a hard-nosed corporate policy). Invariably the moral contrasts drawn in such scenes between male and female characters favor males.

Well before we meet *Disclosure's* predatory sexual harasser, Meredith Johnson, we observe her victim, Tom Sanders, casually setting self aside on the very morning of a long-awaited promotion, feeding and dressing his kids for school, brushing their teeth, reminding them to pee. Finding a happy-face, hurry-home message from his kids on his office computer screen, he's moved almost to tears. He lingers so lovingly over snapshots of his son and daughter, in Meredith Johnson's office, that he seems for a minute almost to forget his harasser's very presence. He has strong feeling for the sanctity of other males' obligations as providers, and for the seriousness of other males' promises to their young—puts himself out to help a jobless father who's a total stranger, frets about a subordinate (a foreman in a Malaysian factory) who's headed for a California holiday with wife and kids minus tickets to Disneyland. (Sanders's wife, a lawyer with a demanding job, is mystified at her husband's concern with the weak or poorly placed. "You're the only person I know," she says sourly, "who sucks up to his underlings.")

Lightly sketched in *Disclosure,* female bewilderment at the phenomenon of self-forgetfulness is foregrounded elsewhere. Alicia, for instance, in *The Paper,* isn't the only ego-imprisoned soul in that movie. The wife of the crusading city editor can't fathom her husband's exertions on behalf of the framed black kids; from the start she hounds Hackett to take a job he's been offered by the competition—an Establishment paper that pays well but cares little about the wronged or the helpless. The wife's close friend, moreover, an embittered female ex-reporter, delivers a monologue warning with boozed-up candor that having a baby means the end of life. "Loss of adult contact, less money coming in, feeling worthless around people who are working . . ." The movie repeatedly avers, through miscellaneous minor characters, that failed fathers and unfaithful husbands are far more grievously burdened by the memory of their failures than their female counterparts. At the birth of the Hacketts' child it is the father, not the mother, whom the miracle of birth overwhelms.

And *The Paper* is, by emerging standards, relatively nuanced regarding the pertinent issues—capable of acknowledging that male talents for child rearing tend to be late-blooming and that male child rearers may have shortcomings. As the film industry grasps more clearly the nature of the opportunities presented by the new ethos, it worries less about nuance and dramatizes male kindness and sensitivity both as the rock on which justice in the public world depends and as foundational for the civilized home and hearth.

As in *Jerry Maguire*. The eponymous hero of this box office hit—played by Tom Cruise—stands forth as lone spokesperson for lovingkindness in a violent, profit-crazed world. The film owes debts to earlier Hollywood renderings of male *sensitifs*, including *Mrs. Doubtfire* and *Rain Man* (the latter also starring Tom Cruise). And it faithfully follows basic conventions of the media campaign against women-becoming-men (i.e., against feminism as Hollywood understands feminism). It specifies that female power executives are ferociously hardhearted, enraged by any whisper of utopian "reform," and prepared to duke it out with any male who crosses them.

But in its portrait of Maguire the nurturer, the movie reaches well beyond the conventions. This hero, who works for a mega–sports agency, is awakened by a child, at the start of the film, to the corruption of the business. (The child is the son of one of Maguire's clients—a terribly injured hockey player whom Maguire, unawakened company man, exhorts to return to the game; the kid, worried sick about his dad, sees the exhortation as villainous and calls the exhorter a son of a bitch.) Conscience-stricken, Maguire produces a "mission statement" for his employer—a document whose policy recommendations (downsizing the client list, caring more about individuals and less about the bottom line, and the like) are aimed at introducing soul into a viciously greedy commercial enterprise. His co-workers jeer at his naïveté; his fiancé, an executive in the agency he's set out to reform, decks him contemptuously with a fiendish roundhouse right to the jaw and a knee to the groin; he quits and, with but one client left, sets out to humanize the world of pro sports.

Maguire's humanitarianism reaches well beyond mere anger at a brutal, selfish world. In the course of the movie, the man becomes the infinitely tender guardian angel of a five-year-old named Roy. The lad has a gifted, caring mother; she was, in fact, Maguire's secretary and stood with him when he fought for his mission statement. But, on spying Jerry Maguire, Roy conceives an irresistible need for him as a significant elder. In scene after scene Maguire embraces the bespectacled needy lad, feels the lad's rapture in his presence — obeys fate's instruction to become Roy's dad.

Nor is this all: Maguire the humanitarian and surrogate father also becomes parent figure to a black man, an undisciplined wide receiver, teaching him trust and loyalty. At one point in the film, Jerry Maguire is sufficiently confident of his place among the morally elect to harangue a divorced women's support group on the meaning of woman's love. An apogee of the new ethos, *Jerry Maguire* reinvents the ordinary male — elevates him to the highest mythological status: truth-teller sublime, social reformer, originator of mother love.

On Coach, *Hayden again shames his wife, Christine; she's just not as good as Coach himself at feeding and diapering the couple's newly adopted son. On* 3rd Rock from the Sun, *Commander Dick, emotionally vulnerable alien, weeps because "the woman I love won't let me be a woman." On* Mad About You, *Paul, zealous protector of infant innocence, teaches pregnant Jamie about the dangers of playing Sinatra records to a fetus:*

> *Paul: "Live at the Sands"?*
> *Jamie: Yah.*
> *Paul (anxious): You played this for the baby?*
> *Jamie: Yeah, so?*
> *Paul: You don't play Sinatra at the Sands for a fetus. Everybody knows that.*
> *Jamie: Why?*
> *Paul: Because it's "Live at the Sands." It's loud and brassy. Plus, Las Vegas. You know . . . It's smoky. It's gambling. The baby doesn't need that.*

On Grace Under Fire, *when Grace's daughter asks her mom if she can have a dog, Grace answers curtly, "Look, I got you a baby brother. You can teach him to fetch." On* Late Night with Conan O'Brien, *Laura Kightlinger, a comic, does an extended turn about remote, heartless mothers, including her own:*

Actually I was watching this guy in a park. And, ah, just a young cute dad tossing a ball to his two, ah, little kids. And I thought: "Oh, that's nice. I wonder what it'd be like to have a family."' Then, all of a sudden, the mom comes over. She starts swearing at her husband. She hits the two kids, takes their ball and throws it in a garbage can. And that just shook me up. Because my mom never did anything with us.

On Malcolm in the Middle, *sensitive Malcolm's tough-guy mom is bandaging some cuts and bruises on Malcolm's knee when she suddenly becomes impatient with her boy. (Malcolm has been running on, in monologue, about how sorry he is for having hurt a younger kid in an argument.) Malcolm's mom pinches his knee hard where he's been cut, he screams in pain, and she tells him he's a nice boy: "I'll kick the conniption out of anybody who says you aren't."* On 3rd Rock from the Sun, *young Tommy and two other hooligans pass through the living room and Sally asks, in a cheerful maternal tone, where they're going and what they're going to do.*

Tommy: You know. Burn stuff. Throw junk at cars.
Sally: All right. Have a good time.

On Life's Work, *when Lisa's daughter asks why she and her little friend don't have play dates anymore, Lisa cites a Mafia movie: "You know how, in* The Godfather, *when Tessio sets up Michael to be assassinated?" Tess nods. "After that," Lisa explains, "Michael and Tessio don't play together anymore."* On Boston Common, *Tasha insists to Wiley that if he comes on to Meredith, who's barely into her teens, Joy, the woman Wiley really wants, will be jealous and become more interested in him. But Wiley's natural truthfulness swiftly breaks out and he tells all to Meredith: "I was using you to make someone else jealous. That's the honest truth. It was wrong and I'm sorry."* On Friends, *Monica and Rachel advise Chandler that Janice won't commit herself to him unless he lies and pretends to be aloof and grumpy; Chandler's natural truthfulness swiftly breaks out. He tells Janice how he feels, honestly, and wins her heart.* On Men Behaving Badly, *Sara is again talking about babies and motherhood, and, knowing no better, Kevin thinks she wants them to start a family. He burns their condoms and announces he's ready for fatherhood. Sara is horrified. Babies! God, no. Sure, she wanted to talk, but no, no action, positively. That evening, caught up still in loony mixed imaginings of a Mom&Dad self, Kevin, sweet innocent, plays a tape of a fetus in the womb, and, to the transporting sound of the heartbeat, Kevin's sleaze-ball buddy Jamie dozes on the couch. Observing him, Kevin lifts the bag of chips from Jamie's tummy and covers him gently with a throw, in the manner of a loving parent charmed by the sight of his sleeping babe.*

Others besides Kevin and Commander Dick are teased on the tube for their longings to become women. On its season premiere Everybody Loves Raymond *focused on Raymond's fixation first on busty women, then on his personal defects of figure. In the closing scene Raymond, on a stool in the bathroom (the better to study himself in the mirror), presses his arms into his sides to create a cleavage—and is surprised by his wife. "I thought," Raymond yelps defensively, "I thought I saw a mouse." The comedy program* Girls Night Out *features a rising woman comic imitating a man breastfeeding "his" baby. But Team Jerry Maguire and real-life followers aren't fazed by teasing. A Manhattan journalist, James Atlas, describes at length in self-congratulating wonder, in* The New Yorker, *the richly fulfilling parenting demands he meets as a street cop/dad of a St. Bernard's schoolboy. Clint Eastwood tells an interviewer of the satisfaction he finds in changing diapers. The actor Pierce Brosnan advises* Entertainment Tonight *at the Academy Awards show that he and his mate, parents of a new baby, won't be partying afterward because "we have to go nurse"* . . .

In the film *To Die For,* Suzanne Stone Maretto (Nicole Kidman) arranges the murder of her husband, Larry (Matt Dillon). She commits this crime because, after three years or so of marriage, she's tired of Larry. (She began to tire of him early, a few hours after their wedding, and slept with another man during their honeymoon.) Larry keeps pestering her about having children, and, worse, wants her to work with him in his new restaurant. Suzanne's primary interest lies in television (she does weather and news documentaries for a local cable station, and anticipates a call shortly from the networks or PBS). Larry is becoming a distraction, and the problem is how to get rid of him.

The solution comes in the form of a trio of high school students whom Suzanne meets while doing interviews. The kids, two boys and a girl, are working-class teens with zero prospects. Suzanne offers them various bribes to perform the actual killing. She has torrid sex with one, convinces another that she truly cares about her as a friend, promises all three careers in show biz when her own big California break comes. (The movie is set in small-town-headed-nowhere New Hampshire.) The kids murder the husband, and then, when suspicion turns in Suzanne's direction, she betrays them. She also betrays the good name of her dead mate by claiming that Larry Maretto was a cocaine addict, that the kids were his suppliers, and that his murder was the result of a botched drug deal.

Suzanne's cruelty to the youngsters—especially to the girl she persuades to believe in her affection—is unsettling. As it grows clearer that she may well get off, we wait for some faint sign of remorse. Nothing. To the very end (a contract killer determines the end; he's hired by Suzanne's father-in-law to take her life), this character combines deceit and murderous selfishness with seemingly total obliviousness of everything but the trajectory of her fantasy career. Minutes before the hit man gets her, she's taping her life story as a promo for book and film deals, positively chirping into a video camera; at the fadeout, we watch Suzanne's sister-in-law, a professional ice skater, celebrating the act of revenge by dancing on ice, jocund and blithe, to a song called "Season of the Witch."*

---

*A monograph on the background of female-killer films such as *To Die For* would glance at a few breakthrough works from earlier years, including *Alien* (1979),

KILLER WOMAN BLUES // 68

On tonight's Ally McBeal, *Ally's beautiful black roommate punches out a guy who comes on too confidently after the two hook up at a dance club. Seeing the dude on the floor when she arrives home—he has a broken neck bone—Ally asks her roomie, deadpan, "So. How was your date?" The star of* Roseanne *tells an enemy on her show, "I'll snap your spine like a potato chip, bitch." On* Cold Feet, *a mother making baby food in a blender hears her suited husband say, heading out, that he may be late returning; the camera tracks her thumb pressing the* PULVERIZE *button. On one* Seinfeld *episode, Elaine squares off against George's elderly father in a sock 'em, rock 'em police station*

Fatal Attraction (1985), and *The Silence of the Lambs* (1991). Approaching the present, scholarship would lose focus owing to a near blizzard of films about women killers (on both sides of the law). Some notion of the quantity of relevant recent "product" can be gained from a partial list of nineties films—TV, junk action movies, and remakes mingling with more pretentious work—in which women kill or are about to kill or plot to kill other human beings: *Eye for an Eye* (1995), *Final Analysis* (1992), *Body Language* (1995), *Thelma and Louise* (1991), *Malice* (1993), *Overkill: The Aileen Wuornos Story* (1992), *Boys on the Side* (1995), *Natural Born Killers* (1994), *Mi Vida Loca* (1993), *Poison Ivy* (1992), *The Hand That Rocks the Cradle* (1992), *Serial Mom* (1994), *The Positively True Adventures of the Alleged Texas Cheerleader-Murdering Mom* (1993), *China Moon* (1994), *Blonde Heaven* (1995), *Sibling Rivalry* (1990), *Double Tap* (1997), *Single White Female* (1992), *Diabolique* (1996), *Shattered* (1991), *Widow's Kiss* (1994), *Mortal Thoughts* (1991), *A Passion to Kill* (1994), *Playmaker* (1994), *Blue Steel* (1990), *Hourglass* (1995), *Nightmare* (1991), *Copycat* (1996), *Illegal in Blue* (1995), *Body Count* (1996), *The Juror* (1996), *Payback* (1994), *Payback* (1999), *Till Murder Do Us Part* (1992), *The Apocalypse Watch* (1996), *Profile for Murder* (1997), *The Quick and the Dead* (1995), *Assassins* (1995), *Strange Days* (1995), *The Bodyguard* (1992), *The Silencer* (1992), *The Dangerous* (1994), *Doppelganger: The Evil Within* (1992), *Double Jeopardy* (1992), *Double Jeopardy* (1999), *Spitfire* (1994), *Two Days in the Valley* (1996), *Nick of Time* (1995), *The Disappearance of Christina* (1993), *The Alibi* (1997), *No Contest* (1994), *Childhood Sweetheart* (1997), *Die Hard with a Vengeance* (1995), *Selena* (1997), *Cyborg Soldier* (1997), *Stalked* (1994), *The Spy Within* (1994), *The Sister-in-Law* (1995), *Skeletons* (1996), *The Getaway* (1994), *Last Man Standing* (1996), *Bound* (1996), *Stay the Night* (1992), *Scream* (1996), *Bad to the Bone* (1996), *Scream 2* (1997), *Desperate Trail* (1995), *Courage Under Fire* (1996), *The Girl Gets Moe* (1997), *Austin Powers: International Man of Mystery* (1997), *Austin Powers: The Spy Who Shagged Me* (1999), *River of Grass* (1995), *In My Daughter's Name* (1998), *Office Killer* (1997), *Dead Cold* (1995), *Bodily Harm* (1995), *Tomorrow Never Dies* (1997), *The Replacement Killers* (1998), *Murder at 1600* (1998), *Misbegotten* (1997), *Heaven's Prisoners* (1996), *Rebecca's Secret* (1997), *Wild Things* (1998), *battle. (Elaine later explains to Seinfeld, "Well, he wrote the check and I cashed it.") On another Seinfeld episode, Jerry is mocked by his blind date Holly and by Elaine for picky, effete eating habits: "You don't eat meat? What are you, one of those—" Proving himself, Jerry fakes a macho-masticating style at a mutton chop dinner while stuffing his pockets full of chops. On* Futurama, *two women in exercise tops berate two male slobs of the future—beer-swigging Bender and*

Executive Power (1997), *Presumed Innocent* (1990), *Bella Mafia* (1997), *Wounded* (1997), *Supreme Sanction* (1998), *Montana* (1998), *Wife, Mother, Murderer: The Marie Hilley Story* (1991), *Turbulence* (1997), *Conspiracy Theory* (1998), *Poodle Springs* (1998), *U.S. Marshalls* (1998), *36 Hours to Die* (1999), *Hit and Run* (1996), *Jawbreaker* (1999), *Executioners* (1993), *Chosen One: Legend of the Raven* (1998), *A Child Lost Forever* (1992), *Pressure Point* (1997), *Murder in Mind* (1997), *The Bone Collector* (1999), *Dead by Dawn* (1998), *Crazy in Alabama* (1999), *Undercover* (1995), *The Gingerbread Man* (1998), *Iria: Zeiram the Animation, Part 2* (1994), *Fist of Justice* (1994), *If Someone Had Known* (1995), *The Price She Paid* (1992), *Cries Unheard: The Donna Yaklich Story* (1994), *Palmetto* (1998), *Daddy's Girl* (1996), *Prison Heat* (1993), *Cellblock Sisters* (1995), *A Killer Among Friends* (1992), *Naked Lies* (1998), *Dead End* (1997), *The Landlady* (1998), *Route 9* (1998), *Ratchet* (1996), *Point of No Return* (1993), *Hidden Assassin* (1995), *Another Day in Paradise* (1999), *Hollow Point* (1995), *Scarred City* (1998), *The Beneficiary* (1997), *Scorned* (1994), *Seduced by Madness* (1996), *Hush* (1998), *Eye of the Beholder* (2000), *The Huntress* (2000), *The Whole Nine Yards* (2000), etc. Worth noting, in addition, is that television talk shows and "magazines" often feature at least one segment—sometimes more—on women accused or convicted of murdering their children. During the week of November 17, 1997, for example: *Leeza* studied "The Conviction of a Death Row Mom" (Darlie Routier, killer of her two small sons); HBO's *Autopsy* reported on Paula Sims, who killed two baby daughters several years apart; *Prime Time* analyzed parents, mainly mothers, who murder their babies for "self-aggrandizement"; and *Geraldo Rivera* ran a mock trial of the (unnamed) murderer of JonBenet Ramsey.

A number of court cases are pending on issues relating to the real-life impact of killer movies. One case involves the acts committed, in 1995, by Sarah Edmondson and Ben Darrus in Mississippi and Louisiana. After tripping on acid and watching *Natural Born Killers*, Edmondson and Darrus killed a cotton gin manager and turned a convenience store clerk into a quadriplegic. A civil suit on behalf of the now deceased clerk and against Edmondson, Darrus, Oliver Stone, and Time Warner was brought in Louisiana. An irony of the case is that, as Susan J. Douglas points out, *Natural Born Killers* was intended as a "satiric look at American media's cynical exploitation of violence to maximize profits." Edmondson and Darrus "weren't seeing biting social commentary; they saw a how-to manual." See Susan J. Douglas, "The Devil Made Me Do It: Is *Natural Born Killers* the Ford Pinto of Movies?" *Nation*, April 5–12, 1999, pp. 50ff.

Bavarian-cream–loving Fry. "Fry," says one woman, "you've become a fat sack of crap." "Bender," says the other, "your beer belly's so big your door won't close. C'mon. We're taking you to the gym." Sally in 3rd Rock from the Sun smashes a suitor down time after time on a couch to yucks plus cheers. On Life's Work, Lisa, prosecuting attorney, celebrates victory over a defense attorney by shouting to a colleague, "C'mon, Deeda, he's down, kick him!"

On Cybill, Maryann makes a tape about her ex-, Dr. Dick, that includes the sound of "Dr. Dick's head exploding." Cybill's friend, a karate specialist, commences teaching the two women "the fine art of kicking someone's ass," quoting Elizabeth Cady Stanton: " 'Women will continue to be the victims of men until they learn to use the weapons of men.' " Demonstrating prowess with a pistol at a firing range, Cybill reveals she was given a shotgun and a Barbie doll for her twelfth birthday, and that she blew "Barbie's head off at fifty yards." "Wow! Cool!" Maryann exclaims, blasting away at a target with her own monster handgun, shouting "Dick! Dick!" after each salvo (the target is in tatters below the belt). Home from target practice, Cybill forgets about the male dummy she's bought to scare off intruders. She rushes the dummy and decapitates him, and she and Maryann toss the head back and forth disgustedly in the living room. Maryann hikes it between her legs, and, with the two buddies racing downfield for the long bomb, we go to commercial . . .

Implicit in the original vision of gender flexibility were the lineaments of a transformed world. Achievements of mental, moral, and physical self-reliance resonated, in this world, for women as for men. The sexes combined candor about their sexuality with awareness of each other's complex humanity—awareness that ruled out men and women treating each other as sexual objects. The sexes united in rejecting servitude and subjection as the defining lot of either; they regarded shared scutwork as the norm (not as anybody's act of noblesse oblige), and they recognized that, for both nurturers and nurtured, the meaning of nurturance lies in the gradual realization that *sustained* selflessness in the service of others is within—although narrowly so—the range of ordinary human beings. And the sexes grasped, finally, that, demands of nurturance aside, contending against excessively rigid genderization is arduous labor: it involves pushing hard, hour by hour, against habit, culture, and the internalized intimidators who forever recommend the conciliatory shrug when only a firmly expressed No! can be life-giving.

The lineaments of a transformed, more sanely genderized world.

No memory of this vision survives at the multiplex or on the tube: gender shift, feminism, and the death of altruism become, in these settings, interchangeable. Cybill's shotgun blasting Barbie's head away and the bullet in Larry Moretto's brain equate independence and autonomy with rage and violence. Women who rape or who ogle male genitals reduce equal sexual candor to equal rights to objectify and humiliate. Sitcom Sallies and Maguire-like males who instantly shape-shift from girlie to hardrock or from business tiger to teary softie reduce the discipline of continual self-interrogation to careless indulgence of whim. The recurring characters—woman as merciless revenger, man as helpless penitent—proclaim as fact a coup that's only a fantasy. But it's a fantasy that's influential among the credulous, lending further moral authority to males.

The pop attack on women-becoming-men functions, then—to repeat—as a handmaid to the assault on feminism and feminism's vision of gender flexibility. Presenting banal switches and trades—this for that, toughness for tenderness and vice versa—as momentous changes, it buries the understandings and aspirations inherent in the ideal of flexibility under layers of poisonous distortion. Unsurprisingly, this assault is wedded to paeans on capitalism and censure of capitalism's disparagers. Although pop flirts with anti-materialism (*Jerry Maguire*), smirks at careerists (*Disclosure*), and genuflects at birthing and babies (*The Paper* and assorted sitcoms), it rarely forgets its mission of serving things-as-they-are. Tirelessly, endlessly tangled in unacknowledged, unresolved paradoxes and contradictions, the familiar ground theme nevertheless resounds: there's no hope for an ideal human future anywhere on earth except in market-dominated values.

Still, there is a certain novelty here, something relatively fresh in pop's socioeconomic lessons about women-becoming-men, namely, the refashioning of Woman herself into an incarnation of—a stand-in for—the corporate ethos. In one of its dimensions the pop attack on masculinized women adds up simply to a standard endorsement of the status quo. But in another dimension the attack recycles old sex war cliché in ways that invaluably soften the harsh exterior of corporate bullying.

Praised as a cutthroat with balls and the biggest cock in the building, the figure of the killer woman emerges, through the recycling, as an instrument of corporate extenuation, an embodiment of a venerable corporate aspiration: to be ruthless in action yet gentle by reputation. How can a firm that commits mass firings solely to gain a narrow profit edge be other than ruthless? In the culture of women-becoming-men this question subtly modulates into a different query: How can the dragon lady at the top who orders such firings be a dragon lady? She is, after all, "just a woman," hence herself a victim of oppression. So how can corporate America be blamed for her excesses? Who else but corporate America accepted the burden of lifting her up from underdog nothingness? Seen clearly, the killer woman functions as a whole new line of defense—a new savior—for the country's profit-maddened.

5

Killer Women and Corporate Kindness

THE POINT BEARS stronger formulation: no institution in America has gained more than the U.S. corporation from the proliferation of images of the killer woman—the socker, the husband-beater and murderer, the child-hater, the fiercely driven manager on the way up. Choking on these images, the society is hard put to register the impact of institutional profit obsession— increasingly incapable of drawing connections between that obses- sion and the collapse of families, the wrecking of homes and neigh- borhoods, the advent of millions of subteens and teens minus a moral center. The features of the killer woman loom overbearingly; let her accept the blame.

And let there be less carping about corporate America—more sympathy, less criticism. One sign of the current mindset is the blandness of criticism of policies reflecting the bottom-line fixa- tion: wage and benefit cuts, downsizing, environmental code viola- tions, voiding of community commitments and loyalties, dumbing down of communication in virtually every public sector, buying of legislators, and the rest.

Another sign is the overpreoccupation of critics and whistle blowers, season after season, with the same targets—tobacco com- panies that lie about the addictive properties of nicotine, chemical companies that solve disposal problems by dumping toxic waste in minority neighborhoods. *Sixty Minutes* runs no exposé of, say, Lehman Brothers and other "fine old firms" that bankrolled the First Alliance Corporation, the home equity lender under investigation by the U.S. Justice Department for allegedly earning huge sums by cheating uninformed loan applicants. (Skilled in the art of scamming uneducated loan seekers into paying massive "origination fees" and unusually high interest rates, First Alliance's loan officers followed verbatim, during interviews, a twenty-seven-page sales pitch called "The Loan Officer's Track to Run On," a document advising salespersons that when customers question rates and fees, they should say, "May I ignore your concern about the rates and costs if I can show you these are minor issues in a loan?") The deal between this company and the fine old Wall Street firms involved billions and is the kind that, taken together with numberless others similar in nature, has massive social consequences. It helps to explain both the preposterous expectations of rich private individuals and institutions regarding rightful rates of return on risk-free investments and the collapse of funding for public sector needs.

But with the ascent of women-becoming-men, corporate America's transgressions become less visible and its harshness to the helpless becomes easier to mask. Whether the figure of the killer woman belongs to real life or to fiction, whether she's Harriet Rubin instructing would-be princessas in the fine points of brutality or Judith Regan boasting about her male genitals or Meredith Johnson in *Disclosure* ruining a colleague's career and family life, the killer woman's behavior functions to channel antipathy to ruthlessness away from the profit-mad. Clarity about greed is displaced by a muddle of mindless options:

1. The culture of dog-eat-dog reflects the ascendancy of women.

2. The culture of dog-eat-dog reflects the battle between habitually oppressive men and women who are merely struggling to breathe.

3. The culture of dog-eat-dog reflects the triumph of equality, fairness, and evenhandedness—values to which corporate America

and market democracy have proudly demonstrated their allegiance by elevating the status of women.

Befuddled heads can't easily see the bottom-line fixation steadily and whole—and killer women narratives intensify the befuddlement. Time and again the narratives dramatize conflicts between underlings who disobey corporate authority (for good reason or bad) and woman executives deputed to curb rebellion. Time and again threats are exchanged, combat ensues, and in the sequel blame for corporate policy is redirected either toward the killer woman herself or toward what is termed "sexism"—but in any event away from the corporate ethos in which the policy has roots. And time and again audiences learn that the changes in train do not matter because, come on, they're *funny.*

Pause once more to sample pertinent material—for example, a yuck-filled episode of the comedy series *The Larry Sanders Show.* Sanders is a talk show host harassed by the network executive who runs late-night programming. Melanie Parrish, the executive, is a broad-shouldered black suit of a lady with a razor voice and a mixed-race entourage, and at her first meeting with Sanders and staff she takes command within seconds.

> *Melanie: Gentlemen, I'll be brief. We all know what the economic climate of network television is like out there right now. We're getting kicked in the balls. There's video markets. There's cable. It's trench warfare. So our number one problem, mathwise: Lost viewers. Equals lost advertisers. Equals lost revenues. What do we do to keep our advertisers happy? other than giving them free handjobs? Now, Larry, we've talked to some of your sponsors. We've asked them what we can do for them. It's come back to us this way: They want you to do live commercials as part of the show. They want it. That means we want it.*

The star, an egotistical coward, doesn't want it. He waffles, calls on his producer to run interference for him, plays show biz wit games for a bit, aiming to distract the corporate hard-nose. Melanie Parrish doesn't distract.

Melanie (interrupting male blather): Mr. Sanders, look. I'm going to have to be blunt here.
Larry: Is that right?
Melanie: In a fiscal sense, your show just isn't cutting it. Now, I think you should take a serious interest in that fact, and do whatever you can to reverse it, because— Well, I'm warning you. Our parent company cannot and will not carry your show in deficit. And that comes directly from [she brings the firm's name forth reverently] Unidac Electronics.

Sanders is told that the commercial he's to read is for a tool called the Garden Weasel. He jokes that this is a nickname for Melanie Parrish. Nobody laughs. Sanders tells Parrish that "I just don't feel right about this. I mean, you know, there are no other talk show hosts who do their own commercials." "Exactly," says the woman executive: we'll beat the competition and get an edge. More rows. Sanders mocks the commercial on air with golf and sex innuendo and by pretending the Weasel has uncovered a buried corpse ("Oh, hello, Mr. Hoffa"). At the crisis Sanders proposes, on air, that the Weasel might better be called "the amazing Rat Stick," and the woman executive storms toward him, screaming.

Melanie: I'm talking to you.
Larry (avoiding confrontation):—
Melanie (commandingly): Mister Sanders—
Larry (turning toward her reluctantly): Ms. Parrish, please—

In his office, Sanders tells the woman she must never talk to him again in that way "on his set" in front of "his people."

Melanie: I pay your people, my friend, and I pay you. And I can talk to you any damn way I see fit. . . . It bugs you to have to take orders from a woman. I think that's it. Is that it?
Larry: You know what. If you were a guy I'd take you outside right now—
Melanie: If you were a guy, I'd go.

Larry: You know, as a rule, I don't hit women. But this rule doesn't apply.

Cut to Sanders sitting in the makeup room, black-eyed, half his face covered with a huge red-black bruise. "All right," Sanders suddenly acknowledges. "All right. A woman hit me." "Melanie," says the makeup man knowingly. The whole crew is aware that the star has had the shit beaten out of him by Corporate Woman. Nobody in the crew finds this distressing. The audience of millions chuckles.

Erase for a moment the yucks and this episode can be read for faint echoes of nearly forgotten labor-management conflicts. Demented though he be, the talk show host (played by Garry Shandling) speaks for workers' dignity and against universal shilling; he claims solidarity with craft and asserts that the craft has standards. He speaks also in the voice of the paternal caring employer: "My people." "My set." For her part, Parrish the network executive speaks for time-honored corporate assumptions: no mere employee owns anything, no craft rule trumps rules based on time study.

But obviously *The Larry Sanders Show* isn't about property relations or worker abuse or management arrogance or sellouts to "product placement." It's about men who think they can beat up women and learn that they can't. It's about women who, when faced with an obnoxious male challenge to their earned authority, cope with the challenge as the situation requires. It's about women whose taste for brutal violence matches or exceeds that of the men they're replacing in corporate hierarchies. It's about the absurd silliness of naifs who imagined that the sharing of power by the genders might change things as they are. And it's about, indirectly, the "truth" that women made common cause for no other purpose, no higher goal, than to secure power and smash the men who had hitherto been smashing them.

Gone from the public stage is any issue with a bearing on the sleazeball commercialization that sucks honor and principle from contemporary life. Gone, too, therefore, is all ground for critical scrutiny of corporate USA. The "issues" racking the nation don't concern institutional greed and amorality; the issues arise from the character of women.

It's fair to acknowledge that only the beamish ever believed that women's rise to corporate power would necessarily have humanizing, civilizing consequences. (The revolutionary iconography idealizing heroic woman as "Liberty on the Barricades" was practically stillborn at birth, circa 1830.) One needs also to guard against exaggerated assessments of the power of a few passages of comic bedlam to shape public opinion. (*Larry Sanders* matters not in itself but as part of a massive confluence of ads, sitcoms, news stories, movies: the nearly immeasurable tide that these chapters have been surveying.)

And it's worth recalling, finally, that the corporate mind has never lacked for means of diverting public attention from its profit obsession, and wouldn't be bereft if the figure of the killer woman disappeared tomorrow. She is, as I've been arguing, an uncommonly effective distraction; when attention focuses on her, structural issues and inequities retreat to the margins; heartless labor policies become infinitely less interesting than the question whether unscrupulous Ms. Executive Veepee will succeed in destroying hapless Mr. Nice Guy—the chap unlucky enough to have to compete with her.

But other kinds of distraction exist, other corporate-devised schemes for hiding the bottom-line banana. Since the time a half century ago when corporations were awarded the status of individual, rights-possessing human beings, these institutions have grown immensely shrewd at promoting themselves as the little people's friends, givers of small gifts to those with large needs (needs that would diminish if corporate America were induced to pay its fair share of taxes). Beginning with relatively routine alms—subsidies for indigent string quartets, dance companies, opera companies; support for high school science projects, neighborhood basketball courts; judiciously advertised college scholarships—corporations have advanced to truly inspired innovations, among them the award, to themselves, of monetary good conduct or conscience prizes for moderating the ferocity of their exploitation of agricultural and other workers abroad. Corporate kindness to the killer woman ranks, in short, well down the list of management self-burnishing ploys. The point of looking hard at her rise isn't that she provides corporate America with an indispensable stratagem for masking its transgressions. The point in looking hard at the functions of killer women in the corporate context is that, when women's highest ambitions are seen as identical with corporate ambitions, a human past beyond price or valuing is buried.

Thinking straight about gender and power demands the recovery of what is in process of being buried. Activists, scholars, thinkers in many fields have worked and continue to work at refining the understandings in question—defining feasible social changes, reimagining life between the sexes (including erotic life) in terms that look beyond stereotypical "masculinity" and "femininity," developing ways of thinking and feeling more congruent with the values of sound democratic culture. Their vision of variousness for both sexes—an embattled, energizing dream wherein fullness of being conjoins social equity—still breathes in sectors of American cultural life.

That vision wasn't hammered out on high, wasn't shaped at tidy foundation-sponsored conferences, and can't be potted in handy position paper–style summary. Knowledgeable observers disagree, furthermore, about which contributors are and are not seminal. My attempt over the next few chapters to represent the vision is based on personal conviction: I believe that the work of the writers I've chosen qualifies as paradigmatic. It offers, that is, a view of the chief themes that derive strength from the idea of variousness and the chief forms in which the idea currently finds expression.

Time now to remind ourselves of these forms and themes.

TWO

A Vision of Variousness

6

Gender Flexibility

THE FRONT LINE

THE CRUCIAL THEME is, of course, *engagement.*
The ideal of gender flexibility stands opposed to rigid separations of the sexes on the basis of genital fact. The ideal carries no suggestion that women can become men (or vice versa). Its partisans don't make light of the weighty historical and cultural conditioning that supports fixed ideas of "the masculine" and "the feminine." Nor do they badmouth these historically and culturally derived identities as superstitions, obstacles in the path of progress, nuisances. They take history seriously, and part of their purpose is to initiate a disciplined discourse about the costs and benefits—more costs than benefits—of the divisions between the sexes that have been sanctified over time.

The assumption is that when iron classifications are treated less solemnly, viewed analytically, it becomes possible for the sexes to engage each other's knowledge, experience, and power—to see anew and to imagine changing and enriching each other in ways that are beneficial to the larger society. No claim is made that any of this happens decorously or painlessly. The impulse to demonize others and romanticize the self—to figure the struggle as between unalloyed virtue and unalloyed vice—will live on, regrettably, after the command Engage! replaces the command Imitate!

But over time, engagement has consequences. It induces shrewder realism about self and other, and about the institutions in which self and other are embedded. Minds edge forward from anatomizing the other side's faults and conspiracies (ancient, modern, postmodern); skepticism mounts that deals aimed at enabling women to become men are good deals. Intelligence begins saying No! to the proposition that *Women instantly elevate themselves when they adopt formerly male-only codes of conduct, standards of excellence, styles of behavior,* and No! again to the proposition that *Asserting the sexes differ slows progress and asserting the sexes are the same speeds progress,* and No! yet again to the proposition that *Gaining admission to all-male educational, recreational, corporate, military, or professional enclaves automatically improves women's quality of life, and that of the society as a whole as well.* Engagement values difference, in other words; it grasps that difference can be used to larger human purpose than hitherto. On the basis of knowledge, not supposition or self-idealization, engaged partisans of gender flexibility begin to speak—in non-utopian, practical terms—about new institutional models, new models of mind, fresh understandings of the insides of intimacy itself.

It bears repeating that the processes of engagement are gritty: anger, resentment, condescension, contempt belong to the mix. The rote-learned, imitative, provoked toughness from which proponents of gender flexibility battle to extricate themselves can be incapacitating. But the effort continues—the search for a language commensurate with the complications and contradictions with which real engagement (as distinguished from slavish imitation) learns it must deal.

And successes are scored. Advocates of gender flexibility teach that men and women who narrow themselves, adapting to gender stereotypes, are enemies of any progress worth the title. They explore the full meaning of the paradox that although women's past powerlessness damaged the human essence, the accumulated experience of powerlessness constitutes precious capital: ways of thinking and standards for judgment and action deserving equal regard with standards rooted in masculinist power. They draw and explain the distinction between cosmetic change and ground-up rebuilding as that distinction applies to public institutions and to private selves. And at their best they drive their lessons home not as grist for end-of-term bluebooks but as a summons to the reanimation of a movement.

An example: Catharine MacKinnon, lawyer, teacher of law, sometime bourgeoisie-baiter. A striking platform presence and a forceful writer, MacKinnon has exceptional command of sex discrimination case law and related fields. She has wit, in addition, often expressed in fierce observations on "classless America." (To the bromide about women's place being in the home, MacKinnon appends that "black women's place is in other people's homes.") She's a fine humorous relisher of earthy talk. ("I would like you to address a question," she tells an audience of women wryly: "whether a good fuck is any compensation for getting fucked.") Her militant self-certainty provokes charges of arrogance that direct attention toward "character" and away from her determination to effect immediate, real-world social change. In law journal articles, popular magazine pieces, interviews, and public lectures, she has lent prestige to a version of political history in which males are seen as exercising total, conscious—and deforming—control of the world from millennium to millennium.

Yet the complicating fact is that from the start of her career to the present, Catharine MacKinnon has been invaluably clear about the difference between sham change and real. Sham change ignores the historical processes that created the genders—created capital out of horrors, qualities and aptitudes out of subjection, gifts of command out of fatuous, unearned dominance. Sham change presents the imitation of men as they are by women as they are as a necessarily positive event. Sham change associates the idea of the sameness of the sexes with progress, and associates "the non-

sameness of women and men" with regression. Sham change ignores the problem of hierarchy. Sham change strengthens the status quo. Substantive change profoundly alters the status quo.

True equality, MacKinnon writes, "means the aspiration to
eradicate not gender differentiation, but gender hierarchy." Far from
eradicating or even moderating hierarchy, sameness dogma—the
masculinizing craze, women-becoming-men—enforces gender hierarchy. Masculinizers claim that women should "measure ourselves
by male standards, on male terms," and they mistakenly trace
the flaws and failings of the general society to barriers between the
sexes rather than to basic structures of value.

Smart feminists don't make that mistake. Yes, says MacKinnon,
"we *do* criticize our exclusion from male pursuits." But "we also
criticize male pursuits from women's point of view, from the standpoint of our social experience as women." To define "equality as
sameness" and salute women-becoming-men means jettisoning
rights of criticism and all that goes with them. It means failing to
engage—assenting to a miniaturization of the feminist agenda, reducing the agenda to a plea for access to this or that job or this or
that tone of voice or level of rage, when what is actually demanded
is "access to the process of the definition of value itself. . . . Our demand for access [is] a demand for change."

Time and again, in essays, lectures, and conference papers on a
wide variety of topics, MacKinnon returns to this theme: "Feminists do not seek sameness with men"; "we more criticize what men
have made of themselves and the world that we, too, inhabit." Time
and again she emphasizes that mere role reversal—replacing the
long-powerful with the long-powerless—isn't the goal: "We do not
seek dominance over men. To us it is a male notion that power
means someone must dominate. We seek a transformation in the
terms and conditions of power itself."

Change that meets this standard ends the custom of ignoring
power relations between the sexes. Encouraged to become knowledgeable about how power affects those who do and do not possess

it, men and women both arrive at clearer-headed views of the making of "masculinity" and "femininity." They stop undervaluing either the power historically denied or the experience of powerlessness that became, during centuries of denial, formative for women's selves. They take a step away from mindless imitation toward responsiveness to male and female examples of richness of being—models of humanity unfettered by stereotypes.

MacKinnon doesn't offer up such examples, but their absence from her pages hardly weakens her broad historical and political argument. Naming personal models of achieved richness of being—my own list would include Abigail Adams, Jane Addams, Mary Cassatt, Chekhov, Lincoln, Walt Whitman, Eleanor Roosevelt, the filmmaker Mike Leigh, the writer John Berger, the civil rights activist Bob Moses—doesn't invariably advance argument on these matters. It shifts the focus to the idiosyncrasies of the list maker and to the barren issue of where exactly "the feminine" and "the masculine" conjoin to create compositive being. Immured in particulars and self-justification, list maker and list critic alike lose feeling for the subject of large consequence: the difference between narrowing stereotypes and a true vision of wholeness. MacKinnon does not lose her feeling for this difference.

Her vision is complex, to be sure. Hostile to the assumption that "those things that men have been, psychologically and physically, so also women should be allowed to become"—angry at the notion that women should "act as though they don't have any particular perspective"—MacKinnon proposes a double perspective, conscious of but not incapacitated by its inner paradox: a perspective that "criticizes all the ways women have been created by being excluded and kept down" but that goes beyond this to assert "the validity of our own experience." Put another way, her double perspective combines "an embrace of what [women] have become with a criticism of the process of having been forced to become it, together with a similar dual take on everything we've never been allowed to be." The passionate stringency of the criticism functions, together with a glimpse of compositiveness as a potential value, as a guarantee that the perspective will not leave the status quo unchanged.

And there are other guarantees, not the least of them a determined resistance to claims that advancement equals simple admission to existing slots. The "dual take on everything we've never been allowed to be" stands as a summons to inventiveness—a demand for reconceptions of human pursuits that connect personal causes with public causes, personal advancement with transformations of slots, roles, institutions, concepts of excellence.

Consider, for instance, the world of women's sports. Enthusiastic about "the new, improved image of the [woman] athlete"—the fact that "it has become more acceptable, hence less stigmatic, for women to be physical"—MacKinnon nevertheless raises a question: "What has athletics meant to men? and what can it mean to women?" Surveying masculinist understandings, she speculates on what being deprived of the sports experience would mean to men, developing a contrast between sports for men and sports for women.

For men, sports are "a form of combat . . . a sphere in which one asserts oneself against an object, a person, or a standard. It is a form of coming against and subduing someone who is on the other side, vanquishing enemies. It's competitive." Occasionally men experience "kinesthesis, pleasure in motion, cooperation (and by this I do not mean the male bond) . . . and fun," but these "are not allowed to be the central purpose of male athletics." The reason: "Physicality for men has meant male dominance; it has meant force, coercion, and the ability to subdue and subject the natural world, one central part of which has been us."

Not so women's physicality; therefore women find "ritualized violence alien and dangerous as well as faintly ridiculous" and find "sex-scripted cheering from the sidelines demeaning and vicarious and silly." But the question persists: Given that women aspire to self-realization that neither repudiates their historical experience of subjection nor duplicates existing patterns of self-absorbed ambition, what can sports mean to them? Answer: it can mean, ideally, "claiming and possessing a physicality that is our own."

Women have something to fight for in athletic arenas, MacKinnon contends: not mere personal victories or "personal bests" but an altered sense of their physicality capable of sharpening their alertness to mechanisms of oppression. Through sports women gain

> a relation to our bodies *as if they are our own* . . . our bodies as acting rather than as acted upon . . . our bodies that *we* do things with, that we in fact are and identify with as ourselves, rather than our bodies as things to be looked at or for us to look at in preparation for the crucialness of how we will appear . . . . The place of women's athletics is that women *as women* have a survival stake in reclaiming our bodies in our physical relations with other people.

MacKinnon's account of the world of men's athletics is an obvious oversimplification—too many thuggish jocks, too few men with multifaceted and broadly life-enhancing feelings for their sport. But the retrogressive male-bashing is marginal to the larger undertaking, which is to vitalize awareness of the difference between "access to the process of the definition of value itself" and access to means of imitating men.

Gender shift regimes preach that sports for women is about equal rights to equipment and coaching, about team W's and L's, about how closely this or that shooting guard on a woman's pro basketball team approaches a man's ability to stop and pop— about, in other words, *women-becoming-men*. For advocates of gender flexibility, like MacKinnon, sports for women is a microworld of change—a release, political in implication, from the alienating pressure of belief that one's physicality exists only "to be looked at."

Viewing sport in these terms is neither a "sentimentalization of our oppression as women nor an embrace of the model of the oppressor." It's a recognition that by reflecting on their unique historical experience, women attain a better grasp of the difference between phony change and real progress. You cannot reclaim your body without confronting the arbitrariness that deprived you of it in the first place, without taking a step toward understanding how power regimes tease men and women into regarding as natural and irrevocable self-conceptions and political arrangements that are in fact, at this moment and every moment, open to change. Take the step and you put distance between yourself and habitual yeasaying to the status quo. Take the step and you grasp your own athletic self-expression as politically consequential.

Nor is this step different from that which women have to take to ensure that their breakthroughs in the professions attain substantial meaning. The MacKinnon critique of law school and corporate legal apprenticeships begins with an analysis of the relation between the history of women's subjugation and a defect "women [lawyers] are regularly faulted for," namely, lack of "the ability not to care which side of the argument you are on." Since most women experience sexual harassment of one kind or another, and since they "make half a man's income," and since "the only occupations [for which] this society . . . pays women as a group more than men are prostitution and modeling," women lean toward "identifying with the interests of all women." By extension they have an instinct for solidarity with the licked and unlucky. This is the unique resource that they bring to the law. What exactly is its impact?

Not enough thus far, says MacKinnon. The law's traditional discipline labors to stamp out feeling for associated life, is impatient with habits of thought that assess individual achievement in light of community well-being. "What law school does for you is this: it tells you that to become a lawyer means to forget your feelings, forget your community, most of all, if you are a woman, forget your experience. Become a maze-bright rat." In the legal work world, "the role of a successful lawyer is a male role regardless of the biology of its occupant." It is consistent with what men are taught to be:

> ... ambitious, upwardly striving, capable of hostility, aggressive not just assertive, not particularly receptive or set off from the track of an argument by what someone else might be saying or, god forbid, feeling. It also requires one to be unserious. By this I mean what I think Virginia Woolf meant when she spoke of "unreal loyalties." Not being present in what you say in a way that might make you vulnerable, skilled at false and manipulative passion and manufactured intensity. The lawyer role has as its implicit norms the same qualities that are the explicit norms of masculinity as it is socially defined. It is a power role.

Women lawyers are supposed to play this role—required "to take on the male context and integrate—in [a] word, assimilate," and become men. The "cardinal quality" is that "you *not identify as a woman.*"

But women lawyers need not capitulate; they have within themselves the power of resistance, and if change is to mean more than dressing in a suit and tie, they must exercise the power. In a memorable speech celebrating the elevation of two women lawyers to the Minnesota Supreme Court, MacKinnon challenged sisters-become-judges to build a career on their awareness of what powerlessness means, on their knowledge of "what our identifications are[,] ... who our community is, to whom we are accountable," and to refuse to become comfortable—however exalted their place—in a profession pleased to brush the teeth of power. Here as everywhere she imagines the possibility of a humanizing transformation, in time, of institutional ways and values:

> I'm evoking for women a role that we have yet to make, in the name of a voice that, unsilenced, might say something that has never been heard. I will hazard a little bit about its content. In the legal world of win and lose, where success is measured by other people's failures, in this world of kicking or getting kicked, I want to say: there is another

way. Women who refuse to forget the way women everywhere are treated every day, who refuse to forget that *that* is the meaning of being a woman, no matter how secure we may feel in having temporarily escaped it, women as women will find that way.

Famously controversial, Catharine MacKinnon comes off as extravagant in many of her pronouncements on the universal daily abuse of women. But extreme immoderacy marks many responses to the perceived extravagance. Her support for a civil rights ordinance against pornography, coauthored with Andrea Dworkin, is labeled "fascistic." (The terms of the ordinance are seldom accurately reported; it permits rape victims to sue pornographers if they can show that pornography caused the assault, and also defines coercion into pornography and forcing pornography on a person as causes for action.) Her statistics on the incidence of rape and harassment are dismissed as inflated. (The attacks tend to be less convincing than MacKinnon's defenses of her figures and citations of sources.) Accusations that this writer is the founder of contemporary heterophobia, monomaniacally averse to males, are overblown. (Some passages in MacKinnon's work allow for the existence of principled men.)

But, as I said, her work overall does leave the impression that the present order of things results from consciously directed, male conspiracies stretching over centuries. ("Male power produces the world," she once wrote, "before it distorts it.") Stereotyped male oppressors surface regularly in *Only Words, Sexual Harassment,* and her other books, and her version of lawyering in general is itself an oversimplification (an excess of corporate lackeys, a dearth of serious professionals who value precedent-mindedness and the disciplines of impersonality as means of restraining wishfulness and sentiment). A large capacity for coping with double and triple truths is absolutely essential for any reader intent on arriving at a balanced assessment of this writer's work.

But recall the key point: Catharine MacKinnon is an embattled writer attempting to preserve a vision of serious engagement at a moment when the entire society is inundated with claims that imitation is a soul-transformingly momentous reform. Kickers, brutalizers, spokespersons for "Infidelity: It's Not Just for Women Any More," "tough babe" CEOs hailed for super-deviousness, female stomper-sneerers ("So I raped you—deal with it")—the whole of kickbutt gender shift culture, awash with cynicism, promotes the adoption by women of the crudest masculinist ways as the culmination of the feminist revolution. The culture thus spawned commands Marcia Clark–style attorneys at law to play the male role to the limit, battling one another for the title of "toughest woman in the court building"; it promotes unrelentingly the notion that women set their cause at risk when they associate themselves too unguardedly with the cause of the insulted and the injured, the vulnerable and the beaten. Talk back to the promoters in nuanced voice and you will not be heard.

MacKinnon is heard—and the complication as well as the challenge in her case for engagement comes across. Others join her in spelling out the difference between power that merely imitates and power that aims to shape new terms and conditions. "The corporate culture women are trying to get equal in doesn't have empathy for the people who are at the bottom," argues Arlie Hochschild; therefore "women need to fight to change that culture," even as they try to rise within it. Mariah Burton Nelson, former pro basketball player, links athletic training with fighting back—"Surely it must be appropriate, sometimes, to 'act like men' "—against aggressors. But she then goes on, echoing MacKinnon, to speak for larger than personal causes:

> The woman athlete dedicates herself to women's rights, beginning with her own. The team athlete cares for women, respects women, and becomes willing to take risks for and with women. Sport for women represents autonomy, strength, pleasure, community, control, justice, and power.

These and other writers sound the basic gender flexibility theme: progress is neither a successful takeover bid of one sex by the other nor an exchange of styles of corruption. Progress is a matter of the insertion of different values, motives, and hopes into existing patterns of lived life. It involves reconceiving institutions, selves, and bases of respect across the board. And it entails building communities, whether on the margins of mainstream society or at the center, where powerlessness and power are better able to learn from each other, freer to revise established orders of thought and structures of opportunity. This is the spearhead for effort at changing life between the sexes. The sanest American optimism works forward from here.

7

The Pursuit of Compositives

I T WORKS FORWARD — sane optimism does — on many fronts, including some that build foundations for engagement on social science survey research: inquiry into sex and gender difference in modes of thought and feeling.

The development of so-called difference studies over the past generation has wrung considerable tendentiousness and piety out of claims that the sexes have much to teach each other. It has lent discipline and particulars to the discourse of "women's point of view," a discourse formerly synonymous with self-flattery. It clarifies strengths, weaknesses, gaps, excesses in the ideas and values that it probes. And despite distractions and temptations, it is uncommonly free of academic sermonizing on tattered themes of inequality, power imbalance, and the like.

Gender shift fantasy holds, remember, that by "becoming men," in whatever metaphorical sense, women win big: they move from the category of powerless inferiors — social, political, economic, moral, and intellectual inferiors — to the category of powerful superiors. Particularizers of "women's point of view" avoid win-lose talk, as I say. They do so not because they are uninterested in power (they stand firmly behind women's struggle to wrest a fair share of it from the powerful). They do so because they remain convinced that power fixations imprison both sexes in versions of "masculine" and "feminine" built on unexamined assumption and cliché rather than real-life observation. No hope of liberation except through sharply intensified self-knowledge. No answer to abstraction and unreality—no verifiable vision of variousness—except by stepping back from obsession with hierarchy, clarifying male and female ways of seeing, and trusting the clarity to stimulate new agendas for engagement.

In the modern world as in the ancient, few men who set up as authorities on women's nature step back from the hierarchical obsession. Not, certainly, Old Testament prophets or New Testament saints. Not John Milton, the seventeenth-century poet who defined rank order in the Christian epic *Paradise Lost* ("He [Adam] for God only, shee [Eve] for God in him"). Not the nineteenth-century elders who patronizingly celebrated maternal angels in the house for their selfless service, their gold medal religious and aesthetic sensibilities and intuition. Not Freud opining that the "undoubted intellectual inferiority of so many women" results from "the inhibition of thought necessitated by sexual suppression." Not the array of social scientists who presented themselves, well into the second half of the twentieth century, as experts on "human" development, despite dealing with exclusively male population samples.

But difference scholars are aware that taking difference seriously *demands* stepping back. Taking difference seriously calls for comparative study of male and female patterns of thought with attention to distinguishing characteristics rather than to scoring points for or against or about existing rank orders. Because certain difference studies delve into the impact of protracted experience of rule and submission on moral and psychological outlooks, they are marked by a degree of venting at past neglect of women's experience, and sometimes figure in polemics. Extremists turn the research into ammunition for attacks on "patriarchy" (indicted as impersonal, objectifying, heartless, brutal)—attacks that match, in mindlessness, the effusions of extremist gender shifters.

But this use of the research is alien to its spirit, which is anti-judgmental. The whole weight of difference studies falls against the sexes constricting themselves; the primary contribution of this work is to the imagination of a *detailed* wholeness of feeling and perception.

An example: Carol Gilligan's *In a Different Voice* (1982, 1993). An educational psychologist, Gilligan studied in graduate school with Lawrence Kohlberg, known for a theory distinguishing stages in individual human (read male) progress toward moral maturity. The theory grew out of interviews with eighty-four boys whose development Kohlberg followed over a period of more than two decades. (As Gilligan acerbically notes, the study assumed that "females simply don't exist.") On the basis of the interviews, Kohlberg theorized that moral development has six stages: the first and second stages are egocentric and infantile (what's moral is what I want), the third stage conceives morality in interpersonal terms and equates goodness with helping and pleasing others, the fourth stage subordinates interpersonal relationships to rules, and stages five and six subordinate rules to universal principles of justice. Originally published in journal articles, Kohlberg's theory was packaged with tables, graphs, descriptions of the hypothetical cases the interviewees were questioned about, discussions of classical Western moral philosophers, and implicit claims for the theory's universal applicability.

A problem arose when, testing his theory on women, Kohlberg "discovered" that they don't mature, are "less developed in justice stage sequence than males." Their judgments appear fixed at the third stage, where morality is purely interpersonal and goodness equals serving others. Kohlberg tried to shrug off the problem with the observation that, while Stage 3 goodness was doubtless functional for grown-up women so long as they stayed home, it constituted a kind of impairment; only if women entered male worlds and accepted "complicated work responsibility" were they likely to

acquire those "societal role-taking abilities necessary for the development of Stage 4 and 5 reasoning."

No! in thunder, says Gilligan in *In a Different Voice:* it makes no
sense to say that "the very traits that traditionally have defined the
'goodness' of women, their care for and sensitivity to the needs of
others, are those that mark them as deficient in moral development." The deficiency isn't in women but in the theory. The deficiency is that the theory is based solely on men's lives.

Interviews with girls and women disclose, Gilligan reported,
that because they think of morality in terms of "the activity of
care," their moral development involves growth in "the understanding of responsibility and relationships" rather than growth in
"the understanding of rights and rules." Moral maturity for them
hasn't to do with arriving at an "objectively fair or just resolution to
moral dilemmas upon which all rational persons could agree"; it
has to do with achieving a realistic grasp both of "the limitations of
any particular resolution" and of the post-resolution conflicts that
are bound to remain. What's more, this difference between the
sexes—this "alternative conception of maturity"—is connected to
many other differences: "different priorities," the belief that moral
problems arise from "conflicting responsibilities rather than from
competing rights," "a mode of thinking that is contextual and narrative rather than formal and abstract."

In a Different Voice assigns itself the task of bringing these differences alive for a general audience. The author undertakes to in-
stall herself in other minds, heedful of inner currents that spoken
words shape and are shaped (or silenced) by. Whether the person
speaking is a confident preadolescent schoolboy (Gilligan ultimately included a large number of boys in her interview sample)
or—in a different study—a reticent guilt-ridden thirty-something
wife and mother facing a second abortion, her interpretive readings seek to combine humane concern with critical edge.

Consider her reading of Jake and Amy, smart sixth-graders invited to wrestle with the question whether a fictitious man named

Heinz should steal the expensive drug he needs—Heinz lacks the $2,000 it costs—to save his wife's life.

Eleven-year-old Jake is decisive from the start—he says Heinz should steal the drug—and never once deviates from certainty thereafter. In a conflict "between the values of property and life," life logically comes first; Jake draws on logic in justifying his choice ("if the druggist only makes $1,000 he is still going to live"). Interviewer: Why is life is worth more than money? "Because," says Jake, "the druggist can get a thousand dollars later from rich people with cancer, but Heinz can't get his wife again." Interviewer: Why not? "Because people are all different and so you couldn't get Heinz's wife again." Heinz has to win, in short, and the druggist has to lose, because Heinz as thief has logic on his side.

Young Jake doesn't take lawbreaking casually; crimes have to be punished (the judge "should give Heinz the lightest possible sentence"). But, as he tells his interviewer, if Heinz were caught, the judge would probably see the theft as right ("the laws have mistakes and you can't go writing up a law for everything that you can imagine"). Jake is fascinated by logic, as well as by math, which he thinks "is the only thing that is totally logical." Gilligan summarizes his thought process as follows:

Considering the moral dilemma to be "sort of like a math problem with humans," [Jake] sets it up as an equation and proceeds to work out the solution. Since his solution is rationally derived, he assumes that anyone following reason would arrive at the same conclusion and thus that a judge would also consider stealing the right thing for Heinz to do. Yet he is also aware of the limits of logic. Asked whether there is a right answer to moral problems, Jake replies that "there can only be right and wrong in judgment."

Throughout the interview the youngster comes across as sparky and likable. Asked to describe himself he says, "Perfect. That's my conceited side. What do you want—any way that I choose to describe myself?" Asked how a person should choose between responsibility to himself and responsibility to others he says, "You go about one-fourth to the others and three-fourths to yourself." Much taken with the lad, Gilligan places him at "what Piaget describes as the pinnacle of childhood intelligence, and beginning through thought to discover a wider universe of possibility." The boy "radiates the self-confidence of a child who has arrived," she says, "at a favorable balance of industry over inferiority—competent, sure of himself, and knowing well the rules of the game." And she adds—returning to the subject of developmental stages—that while according to Kohlberg's scale Jake is a mixture of Stages 3 and 4, "his ability to bring deductive logic to bear on the solution of moral dilemmas, to differentiate morality from law, and to see how laws can be considered to have mistakes points toward the principled conception of justice that Kohlberg equates with moral maturity."

All this places him, on the face of things, well above eleven-year-old Amy, the bright classmate who's separately interviewed and with whom Jake is compared. Her initial answer to whether Heinz should steal the drug lacks crisp decisiveness:

> Well, I don't think so. I think there might be other ways besides stealing it, like if he could borrow the money or make a loan or something, but he really shouldn't steal the drug—but his wife shouldn't die either.

When she's pushed a bit, Amy seems to wander and has nothing whatever to say about property and law:

> If he stole the drug, he might save his wife then, but if he did he might have to go to jail, and then his wife might get sicker again, and he couldn't get more of the drug, and it might not be good. So, they should really just talk it out and find some other way to make the money.

When she's pushed still harder, the logical problem that intrigued Jake recedes into total invisibility:

It's not right for someone to die when their life could be saved. . . .
He [the druggist] should just give it [the medicine] to the wife and
then have the husband pay back the money later. . . . The world
should just share things more and then people wouldn't have to
steal. . . . If somebody has something that would keep somebody
alive, then it's not right not to give it to them.

Using the Kohlberg meter for her measure, Gilligan assesses
these replies as "evasive and unsure." Amy hasn't a clue about how
to view "the dilemma as a self-contained problem in moral logic"
or as a "math problem with humans," can't begin to see the life-
property conflict as the kind that can be "resolved by logical de-
duction." Amy's interview is notable for "frustration" and "circular-
ity"; "the interviewer conveys through the repetition of questions
that the answers [Amy] gave were not heard or not right"; the child
herself presents "an image of development stunted by a failure of
logic," someone in whom we recognize

> a feeling of powerlessness in the world, an inability to think system-
> atically about the concepts of morality or law, a reluctance to chal-
> lenge authority or to examine the logic of received moral truths, a
> failure even to conceive of acting directly to save a life or to consider
> that such action, if taken, could possibly have an effect. As her re-
> liance on relationships seems to reveal a continuing dependence and
> vulnerability, so her belief in communication ["talk it out"] as the
> mode through which to resolve moral dilemmas appears naive and
> cognitively immature.

In sum: grade Amy's moral judgments (on the Kohlberg scale) "a
full stage lower in maturity than those of the boy."

But also pause for a moment to reconsider the adequacy of the
scale. Having shown where and why the Kohlberg measure grades
Amy as deficient, Gilligan induces readers to revisit the child's
replies and engage them from an alternative perspective.

Amy fails to simplify, objectify, and abstract, Gilligan acknowledges—fails to clean the world of irrelevancies that distract from

the job at hand. She doesn't understand—as Jake seems to understand—that it's best, for the purposes of solving the offered "problem," to get rid of clutter and imagine a world minus time, minus before and after, minus human attitudes, responses, relationships, and the rest.

But Gilligan's commentary advances the suggestion that this failure has an obverse side: at some level Amy sees a world without felt responses and relationships as the cause of Heinz's problem and, as well, of real problems facing tens of millions. The child utters goody commonplaces, to be sure ("the world should just share things more and then people wouldn't have to steal"); she's eleven years old. Yet the swiftness with which she animates Heinz and the druggist as persons—the instant recognition of human presence rather than x and y—is hardly maladroit; no protest against immoral indifference ever began anywhere else. Moreover, Gilligan's tracing out of the child's absorption with narrative reality and context reminds the reader of the benefits as opposed to the costs of failure to abstract. We're made conscious that there's a hospital room in Amy's mind, a man and a woman speaking together of terrible intentions and fears; that this mind moves from the concept of theft to the need for a weapon, and on to a drugstore aisle warily traversed, a threat delivered, resistance faced . . .

Subtly, patiently, Gilligan puts her reader in touch with the "subject's" sense of before and after, and with her nascent feeling for the almost inevitable eruption of unintended consequences. And the explication raises a new possibility: that the Kohlberg method and scale—the problems, questions to interviewees, evaluations of answers—elevate detachment and distance to the status of high values. As the commentary proceeds, analogies appear between this firmly stylized remoteness from fact—logical distance—and various aesthetic and legalistic counterparts. Reading Gilligan, the present writer found himself remembering W. H. Auden on Brueghel's *Icarus*. Suffering is nowhere *felt* in that painting, as Auden observes. A child falls from a terrible height, screams, chokes, drowns; the water closes over; nobody attends. A ploughman may have heard something, but for him it was not "an important failure"; he turns away. The same for a nearby craft on the water. The "expensive delicate ship," although perhaps it too saw

> Something amazing, a boy falling out of the sky,
> Had somewhere to get to and sailed calmly on.

An extraordinary painting—but the poet isn't praising it for "moral maturity." Is it wise to equate moral maturity with failure to attend?

Gilligan presses forward. The Kohlberg scale prizes logical detachment; Jake delivers it and thereby qualifies as advanced; Amy fails to deliver it and qualifies as retarded. Caught and held by the moment-to-moment stuff of "the interpersonal situation" and by dread of unresponsiveness as a seeming human norm, Amy can't find her way to moral right and wrong without living into the immediacy of the situation, into the before and after of selfishness and desperation, into the hopeless insolubility of the thing. How does Heinz's wife cope if Heinz is jailed? ("He might have to go to jail, and then his wife might get sicker again.") How does a merchant pay his bills and also respond to the needs of strangers? How do people like the druggist live with themselves if they shut down their response to others? ("He should just give it to the wife and then have the husband pay back the money later.")

Installing herself within this innocent mind as it approaches the borders of such questions, Gilligan calls up the urgencies: the child's sense of somehow coexisting imaginatively with the principals, the child's belief that something needs to be done, the child's "if only" longings—if only Heinz could make his "wife's condition more salient to the druggist or, that failing, [more] appealing to others who are in a position to help." Tracing Amy's replies back to the wordless originating currents, Gilligan shows forth her world as a place of

> relationships and psychological truths where an awareness of connection between people gives rise to a recognition of responsibility for one another, a perception of the need for response. Seen in this

light, her understanding of morality as arising from the recognition of relationship, her belief in communication as the mode of conflict resolution, and her conviction that the solution to the dilemma will follow from its compelling representation seem far from naive or cognitively immature. Instead, Amy's judgments contain the insights central to an ethic of care, just as Jake's judgments reflect the logic of the justice approach.

Jake's logic is entirely at home with hierarchy—with winning and losing, place above and place below. "Transposing a hierarchy of power into a hierarchy of values," Gilligan notes, Jake "defuses a potentially explosive conflict between people by casting it as an impersonal conflict of claims. . . . He abstracts the moral problem from the interpersonal situation, finding in the logic of fairness an objective way to decide who will win the dispute." But, she adds:

> This hierarchical ordering, with its imagery of winning and losing and the potential for violence which it contains, gives way in Amy's construction of the dilemma to a network of connection, a web of relationships that is sustained by a process of communication. With this shift, the moral problem changes from one of unfair domination, the imposition of property over life, to one of unnecessary exclusion, the failure of the druggist to respond to the wife.

In a Different Voice is filled with interpretive readings of interviews not alone with children but with grownups examining their own moral dilemmas (sometimes considering them in the light of the Heinz-druggist problem). Woman interviewees often choose responsiveness as a pivotal value—quickness to animate the reality of another's situation and "understand what someone else is experiencing." And repeatedly the growth and refinement of understanding of that value become crucial in women's personal histories centered on stages of moral development.

Not surprisingly, some of these interviewees, asked to comment on the Heinz-druggist problem, acknowledge a "sense of strain" with Kohlberg's apolitical construction of the problem (property rights versus life). They try to restate the problem in accord with the themes of socioeconomic exploitation which they see as pertinent. Ruth, an ambitious graduate student for whom it goes without question that Heinz must steal the drug, argues that the central issue arises from Heinz's "willingness to substitute himself for his wife and become, in her stead, the victim of exploitation by a society which breeds and legitimizes the druggist's irresponsibility and whose injustice is thus manifest in the very occurrence of the dilemma." Another woman expresses the same sense that the wrong questions are being asked, and adds: "I don't think that exploitation should really be a right."

But *In a Different Voice* is no conventional left-liberal tract, nor is it a work advocating the replacement of one sexist hierarchy with another. Male preoccupation with a morality of individual rights is considered evenhandedly. "A morality of rights and noninterference may appear frightening to women in its potential justification of indifference and unconcern," Gilligan observes, yet, "from a male perspective, a morality of responsibility appears inconclusive and diffuse, given its insistent contextual relativism." The contrast drawn between young Jake and Amy isn't between a chilly dehumanizer and a saint-to-be but between two attractive kids both of whom, Gilligan insists, are "highly intelligent and perceptive about life, although in different ways."

Furthermore, there's no romantic idolatry of "feminine goodness" and "self-sacrifice." Gilligan provides detailed accountings of negative aspects of women's affinity for "relationships of care." She shows how such relationships can function as barriers to moral development—studies the situations of women whose comments, in interviews, suggest how troubles burgeon when "only others [not the self] are legitimized as the recipients of [a] woman's care." Reflecting on these interviewees, she stresses that "concern [only] for the feelings of others imposes a deference" that can lead straight to vulnerability, duplicity, unreality. Everywhere she reminds her reader that affinity for caring—and deferential—relationships isn't biologically determined, but results from multiple forces, centuries of dark social history among them:

> When women feel excluded from direct participation in society, they see themselves as subject to a consensus or judgment made and enforced by the men on whose protection and support they depend and by whose names they are known. . . . Childlike in the vulnerability of their dependence and consequent fear of abandonment, they claim to wish only to please, but in return for their goodness they expect to be loved and cared for. This . . . "altruism" [is] always at risk, for it presupposes an innocence constantly in danger of being compromised by an awareness of the trade-off that has been made.

As these words attest, Gilligan is mindful that the qualities and aptitudes that figure in women's ways of constructing moral problems evolved from a history of suppression; in one of its dimensions engagement means for her, as for Catharine MacKinnon, embracing "what we have become with a criticism of the process of having been forced to become it." And there's anger in the criticism. Her hostility to Lawrence Kohlberg is linked, no question, with hostility to the assertion that women bring nothing to the intellectual table—are simply blank slates waiting through the millennia for inscription-by-masculinization.

But the central thrust of her work lies elsewhere, in the critique of standard-brand, off-the-rack, gender-frozen attitudes toward cognition—perspectives she views, correctly, as overattached to either-or simplifications, overcommitted to binary oppositions (subjective/objective, impressionistic/logical, hard/soft, intuitive/rational) that split the world of thought into pointlessly rank-ordered, noncommunicating sectors. *In a Different Voice* asks the reader to listen carefully to two voices, two languages; one is logical and detached, the other narrative, contextual, empathetic. Without obsessing about which language is "better," without denying in an extremist mode that both males and females are capable of speaking both tongues, Gilligan directs attention to the cultural machinery responsible for banning fluid movement between them, and she launches—through the discipline of educational psychology—on the project of dismantling it.

Others before her have regretted the walling off of different kinds of cognition from one another. (The historian R. H. Tawney, to cite just one distinguished mind, framed powerful arguments in support of the thesis that "sympathy is a form of knowledge.") Nobody hitherto, however, set the matter of cognitive styles in such clear relation to the problem of gender *in*flexibility. On nearly every page of In a Different Voice (and in much of the author's subsequent research), one implicit theme is that from the critical interaction of contrasting styles of thought, real cultural gains can be expected. The "different voice" of the title announces the possibility not that one sex will shortly become more like the other but, rather, the possibility of richer mentalities across the board—affectively penetrating, compositively disciplined, skilled in the uses of the constructive imagination. In the world of mind, the drama of engagement has many meanings; few hold more promise than this one.

8

Spies in the House of Love

I N THE WORLD of bodies, talk of productive male-female encounter—talk of engaging, not imitating—stirs snickers. Despite liberation, sexuality remains private terrain; it is not commonly viewed as open to reconstruction. *They made love, they did a* cattleya, *he took her (had her, laid her), she fucked him:* these and other received versions of the actualities of passion are not much altered by phrasing polite or crude; the pertinent meanings seem transparent. Claims like Catharine MacKinnon's that those meanings undergo transformation according to who has "access to the process of the definition of value" rouse skepticism.

But as it happens skepticism is, in this instance, off the mark. Positive concepts of gender flexibility point paths to change not just in the professions or in academically certified forms of moral reasoning but in intimate scenes as well. Versions of passion are sharply altered; models of masculine and feminine evoke new possibilities for the self and new patterns of social relations. And there's rather less vulnerability to trivializing and cheapening than might be supposed. Advocates of flexibility in sexual expression speak and act in ways that are hard to reduce to *Cosmo* cover teasers ("Infidelity: It's Not Just for Men Any More"). They expand and deepen the subject, connecting change in norms and conventions of sexual expression with steps toward change in the broader public life. What emerges is a conception of engagement that embraces ideas, policy, and dailiness simultaneously: a sexual politics with breadth.

An example: Joan Cocks's *The Oppositional Imagination: Feminism, Critique, and Political Theory* (1989). Cocks, a political theorist and professor of political science, takes as her starting point a familiar tenet of gender flexibility discourse, namely, that prevailing beliefs and attitudes about the masculine self and feminine self constitute a "regime" set in place by the power system. That system presents masculine and feminine as distinct, foundational truths—truths of nature—when in reality there's little that's natural about them. Masculine and feminine are in significant measure fictions imposed "on the sexed body." From which it follows that, like any political regime, the regime of "Masculine/feminine" can be engaged and resisted, conceivably even overthrown or otherwise transformed.

But resisted in the name of what and to what purpose? In the name of truths that the regime suppresses, Cocks answers—and for the purpose of "explod[ing] the identities of mastery and servitude that the system dictates"— and for the further purpose of fostering progress toward a good society wherein "all people think at the highest possible level." We're obviously not talking here about enabling women to exchange one freezing, constricting identity for another by "becoming men"; the subject is how to raise levels of realized freedom, intellectual and other, for both sexes everywhere in the polity.

For guidance on this subject, Cocks turns to lessons about resisting political regimes found in the major twentieth-century political theorists. She notes that the writers in question—Michel Foucault, Antonio Gramsci, Raymond Williams, Stuart Hampshire, and Edward Said among them—share hostility to ruler/ruling class notions of power, arguing that the "whole top-down, center-capillary conception of power has descended to us from the monarchical age and is altogether inappropriate to the conditions of modernity." The theorists also reject the notion that dominant classes stand apart from power systems as subordinate classes cannot. ("The dominant social class is not the given order's master but its creature as much as the subordinate class is [and] the subordinate class is no less likely than the dominant to be desirous, willful, and committed in bolstering the given order.") And they reject the notion that resistance can be well waged by insurgents convinced either that the power system in place is purely destructive (never productive) or that they, the virtuous insurgents, can build a counterforce sufficiently organized (i.e., bureaucratized and rank-ordered) to contest the vicious state while retaining their own immunity to corruption.

Implicit in these positions is a clear bias against grand "utopian fantasies" and for long-term molecular effort at "bending" particular local circumstances. There's a "vitality to power at the molecular level," says Michel Foucault, "and a fixity to it at the grand one," and for this reason approaching from the bottom is "the surer way not to miss [power's] variations, reversals and diversions." As Cocks summarizes the thinking:

> Whatever the great situation, this particular one, being particular, might bend in all sorts of ways — towards some new and intensified form of the power prevailing on the grand scale, or towards some humbled version of it, or towards its deterioration, or towards its inversion. Exactly how the local situation bends is the interesting question for what it illuminates not merely about life on the molecular level but about life on the grand scale. Molecular details that begin to diverge in increasing numbers from the massive fact eventually will add up to a different massive fact, after all.

The first lessons for activists aiming at changing the status quo anywhere are, in sum: avoid moral preening, shed conventional conceptions of differences between power and powerlessness, concentrate on bending local situations, think molecularly.

What has all this to do with resisting the regime of Masculine/feminine? Several things. First, resistance must avoid conceiving of the "enemy" as an all-powerful, monolithic "patriarchy" that exercises total top-down control, stomping ruthlessly on its enemies and erasing opposition before it dares to breathe. Second, resistance needs to purify its "oppositional imagination," insofar as possible, of self-flattering concepts and assumptions. (Examples of such assumptions: we the resisters are made of wholly different stuff from those we oppose, our way of thinking and feeling nowhere connects with theirs, an immense gap separates our satisfactions from theirs.) Third, resistance must learn to particularize—must push itself to come at situations freshly, thinking aside conventional readings of their content, reaching constantly behind the familiar facade to the interiors of actual feeling.

Cocks acknowledges that certain brands of extremist feminism ignore these rules. A throwback to the age preceding the cataclysmic totalitarianism that instructed the political theorists, extremist feminisms maintain the continuing existence of total top-down power, absolute and unchallengeable. They use the king term, patriarchy, to describe this power ("men's rule over women and the historical-cultural world [is] perfectly monolithic and self-identical across time and space"), and the king term "evokes exactly the wrong way in which power operates." They insist on men's seamless brutality and manipulativeness and on women's seamless innocence and goodness. ("Women do not act through imposing their own purposes and will on everything around them but respect the integrity and natural impulse of things in themselves. They look to care for, not master, the other, and so learn in all relations to move towards harmony, not conflict.")

And this withdrawal into self-romanticization is flat-out disabling—"infantilizing and embalming." It effectively denies that women are "complex enough in desire, sophisticated enough in imagination, and dynamic enough in will to act in vicious as well as virtuous ways, out of passions, predilections and motive forces that are not men's but their own." Together with several other "morally superior" postures, it blocks the achievement of understanding-through-engagement on which real change depends.

In the private arena of sexuality—in the *bedroom*—such achievements draw on individuals' experience as "spies in the house of love." The details of that experience, carefully read, quicken awareness that the Masculine/feminine script gets the experience wrong.

The Masculine/feminine script insists that both the masculine self and the feminine self emanate from, and have their essential natures dictated by, sexual facts of the flesh. "The penis means aggressive power and strength, the opening of a body to the penis means that body's submission to that strength, the embrace of a large body and a small one means the possession and protection of the second by the first, and so on." Follow the script and heterosexual eroticism becomes, necessarily—even in the postmodern, coming-unhinged age—a scene "infused with aggression and force." The masculine self finds the source of its dominance in its body, its center of arousal. Convinced that "power emanates out from [the] fleshly penis," the masculine self sees the body of the other as " 'lacking' a penis, and in addition as slighter in will because slighter in physique than himself. On it—the 'feminine'—he seeks to achieve his pleasure through exerting his power. He penetrates the body, he subjects it to his force; at the moment of his climax, he sees himself as having the body, taking it, conquering it, possessing it, and using it."

As for the feminine self, the quasi-official script sees her—again necessarily—as masochistic and self-abasing. How else explain that she desires someone "whose own desire is a cauldron of sex and violence, pleasure and domination, release and exploitation"? The conventional Masculine/feminine still affirms—despite occasional ritual bows to so-called New Women—that "to enjoy erotic entanglements with the masculine self is to enjoy bowing down before the supremacy of the phallic subject and finding excitement in being had, taken, conquered, possessed, and used as an object by him. For phallocentric and [extremist] feminism alike, this is the only possible drama of heterosexual eroticism."

Resisting such versions of eroticism means "mak[ing] room for the varieties of desire in actually felt life" that the quasi-official script renders inexpressible. It means putting in play evidence against "the brute body as a fundamentally determining force," against the overequation of the "thrusting of the penis . . . with the expression of power." It means challenging the Masculine/feminine principle that "the sexual will to power is intrinsically male . . . and that, being male, it is under all circumstances vicious and contemptible." Resistance means, for a writer, critically engaging the standard understandings: confronting their rigidities with liberating images, gestures, evocations of feelings—and also with probing questions.

Why should we suppose that when a man experiences himself as commanding, his lover does not experience him instead as entreating, or as meeting her power for power, or as merging with her beyond all notions of power, or as stupidly self-deluded in his arrogant view of himself? Why suppose that when a man experiences his lover as submitting, the woman does not have her own quite independent view? It is not that she *could* not see herself and him in the way that he did, but that she just as plausibly might have her own reading of their interactions.

Cocks imagines the feelings—delight, derision, laughter — of a woman who doesn't read her own moves of passion according to any given script of submission or self-annulment:

She does not see herself as the object of pleasure for him, nor does she take her own pleasures in abasing herself before him. To the contrary! She sees her physical agility as a trait quite as admirable as his physical strength. She delights in the powerful demands of her own bodily pleasure but is never the owner or final purpose of that pleasure. She would laugh at the crudeness of his perception, were she to discover that he could see action only where there was visible physical movement, and that he would see passivity where there in truth was a physical charge of shattering inwardness, magnitude, and depth. She would shout with derision were she able to hear him boast that only *he* acted on *her*, as if the host of interesting ways in which she also acted on him had simply vanished from his memory.

A proud woman contending against the Masculine/feminine script can expect some frustration; a masculine self entrapped in obedience to the regime can't easily cope with a lover who conceives of herself as free. Cocks calls up a free woman's bitterness affectingly:

> Although her desires spontaneously run the gamut from commanding to succumbing in love, and although she may be aroused by the refinements, not the extremities, that the gamut has to offer, she is stopped short in her pursuits before a masculine self who on the old grounds of bodily difference claims for himself the sole prerogatives of the active, the dominant, the masterful, and insists that she take up the position of the passive and the yielding. . . . Isn't this the truest erotic defeat: not to be rejected in love, not to be its pain-seeking victim, but rather to be forced to press the expansiveness of one's desires into stultifying limits, to consent to love within those limits for the sake of the partial pleasures they permit, to be defined as one who naturally indulges only in those pleasures, to be ridiculed for the indulgence, and, finally, to take one's pleasures precisely with the perpetrator of one's predicament?

But although *The Oppositional Imagination* doesn't evade darkness and nonfulfillment, it is in no sense a negative work. The author sketches scenarios of heterosexual eroticism in which *both* lovers win release from sex-specific, sex-prescribed dominance and subjection; during these scenarios readers breathe open egalitarian air. Joan Cocks warns against mistaking the territory for utopia; the acts and choices are molecular, not culturewide, and the lovers remain human beings, all contradictions intact. "Relations between the two lovers are not at all the intimate analogue of relations between citizens in a democratic state, who ideally at least treat one another in a perfectly reciprocal way." Where erotic freedom and equality thrive, flesh becomes "a field of adventure, unfenced by rules stipulating specific eroticisms for specific bodily types" — and therefore politesse and niceness can't be norms.

But vital, multidimensional engagement *is* a norm, and most strikingly at just those climaxes of genital intercourse when the heterosexual drama is supposed to stand revealed as a pure matter of power and subjugation. In the author's scenarios these moments stand revealed, instead, as extended experiences of shared various-ness:

> The masculine self is likely to exult in his physical power over the feminine, to exhibit that power in his thrusting movements, his pos sibly but not inevitably larger, stronger body descending like a wild bird on her own. But just as easily and quickly this same masculine self forsakes the use of his physical strength, offers himself up to the feminine self, abandons his body to her. By the merest relaxation of his grip, the turn of his head . . . the change in the look in his eye from imperiousness to pleading, he places himself under the mercy of her will, to be controlled in the ebb and flow of his passion by her move-ments, to be actively aroused, excited, placated, and stilled as she de-cides and commands. And yet there is one more attitude that, de-pending on the vagaries of mood at the particular moment, the masculine self is likely to assume. He may be swept up with the fem-inine in a mutual ecstasy of identity and fusion. Suddenly their physical merging will signify not the explosion of opposition and dif-ference between the most intensely inward and the most intensely outward domain of the body, but the utter dissolution of opposition and difference.
>
> The masculine self's contentment and excitement in moving from a posture of power and strength to one of abandonment and vulner-ability to one of reciprocity and fusion does not simply signal an ex-pansion of erotic repertoire. It also transforms each of its specific moments, so that his enjoyment of power and strength does not have the same meaning that it did before. How can he experience his movements over and on the female body as acts in an episode of con-quest and exploitation, orchestrated by him and for his own sake, when the moment after he exults in his force he succumbs to the

force of the feminine self, and the moment after that he joins with her as if they were a single self with a single erotic perspective?

As for the feminine self, the same trio of attitudes is open to her: She may become the commanding, the succumbing, or the fused self, although the different facts of her flesh will mean that she will embody these attitudes in her own distinctive way. But genital intercourse is hardly for her the only or key moment of "truth." That she derives pleasure from her lover's thrusting movements inside her, or from her taut and driving movements on him, or from the reciprocal rhythms of their physical union is only part of the story of her sexuality. The idea that it is the whole story is perhaps the supreme phallocentric delusion. With respect to her more intense and absorbing moments of physical passion, she can assume the attitude of one who forcefully takes her pleasure upon her lover, or who is served by him, or who gives herself up to his will and control. And how can her self-abandonment be called her subjugation, when she moves so freely from that stance to another during her most acute experiences of pleasure no less than during his?

As Cocks acknowledges, "sexuality is secretive and also idiosyncratic enough that the outward signs of an assuming or forsaking power are so graphic that it would take a poet or pornographer to describe them." But her own approach is fearless; she often risks— in the name of a molecular detail that will tell powerfully against stereotypical rigidities—offending the "taste" of the regime she's contesting. The lover, she writes, "knows immediately that his lover is assuming a stance of power the moment he catches an expression of slightly cruel concentration on her face, the moment he is beset by the searching movement of her hands, the moment he feels the hard pressure of her touch somewhere on or inside his body."

"How come we can't allow," Camille Paglia asks in a passage quoted earlier, "that a lot of wives like that kind of sex they are getting in these battered wife relationships?" And again: "If you get raped, if you get beat up in the street, it's okay. . . . Go with it." To their credit, Paglia and Katie Roiphe know better than to insist that "sex should be gentle, should not be aggressive." But they see the ferocity, dominance, and aggression that they savor as necessarily his (unique to his "nature"), and relatively untouched by contradiction.

Whereas the discussion of sexual encounter in *The Oppositional Imagination* isn't afflicted by cliché. It vivifies the contrast between women-becoming-men (becoming locked, that is, into styles of aggression owing everything to dogma about the hard-driving male member), and men and women answering a summons to gender flexibility that is characterized not by monolithic top-down toughness but rather by fluidity of movement between command and compliance, compliance and fusion, fusion and command.

Nor does *The Oppositional Imagination* limit its dramatization of engagement and openness to the intimate theater of sexuality. The aridities of stipulated masculinity and femininity are obviously as parching in social intercourse as in sexual intercourse. Well before the end of her book, Cocks turns her eye to the social stage; working again with concrete condensations of abstract ideas, she sketches out a series of stances vis-à-vis Masculine/feminine ranging from gross subservience through shrewdly gauged skepticism to outright resistance. Her exemplars of grossest subservience are the Marine and the Model:

> A theoretically exquisite pair: opposites inside the . . . order, comrades in their bond to it, both of them embracing — more, embodying in their very flesh — its claims to truth to the same exaggerated degree. The one strong and hard, the other slight or voluptuously soft, their bodies are the site of a unified system of meaning, a physicality ripe with intimations of aggression and allurement, vitality and vanity, brute command and an invitation to invasion. The Marine and the Model have been crafted out of rougher material into refined specimens of the Masculine/feminine idea through analogous disciplinary processes, the one located in the barracks and the bootcamp, the other in the modelling school and the photographer's stable. While the first purpose of neither the political/military nor

the commercial/communicative apparatus of power is to manufacture masculinity and femininity, they each readily would acknowledge that precipitating out respective, "unmanly" qualities and qualities "undesirable in a woman" was something that they regularly did. . . . Through their simple presence in the public world, the Marine and the Model help sustain the given order of sex and gender.

At a slight distance from these touchstone figures we briefly meet several types whose subservience to the regime is marked by thoughtlessness or deceit or cynicism, and whose failings stir near-repugnance in the author. ("They are so predictable, so ordinary in their vices and virtues, so stolid, unimaginative, and resigned.") Cocks moves quickly on to profile genuine resisters—critics, rebels, and others whose stances in daily life constitute molecular action of a kind against the Masculine/feminine regime.

Some of the resisters make "difficult company" because of their intransigent iconoclasm. Many are enlivening because of their "clear-sighted, hardheaded intelligence about and distaste for all the established order entails." All suggest ways of living in the contemporary world that challenge the gender-erasing tyranny and beckon toward "a new positive," an ampler freedom. The figure Cocks calls the Traitor is representative:

> In the simple course of being and living, [the traitor] betrays the interests at the heart of the sex/gender regime. . . . [He] lives out instinctively, so to speak, a renunciation of any right to mastery over women. His turns of phrase, bearing, sympathies, and desires are innocent of the phallocentric urge. This is not to intimate that he is someone whose urges do not draw him towards women at all, who out of mere apathy and boredom does not bother to tyrannize over them. . . . That the traitor renounces mastery over women . . . does not mean that he has no sharp edge, is incapable of a severity of mood or stubbornness of will, or takes no pleasure in exerting strength and force. It is rather that he sees no special prerogative for him in sharpness, severity, stubbornness — no exclusive right to strength and force invested in him by his biological sex.

The traitor finds other men quite disagreeable for what the conceit in their sex has worked in them. He often keeps the company of women. He need not exhibit or be enamored of the feminine vices, but vanity, triviality, a narrowness of vision and concern will strike him as being more tolerable than arrogance, emotional crudity, and the constant impulse to control. Thus he is happy to put up with the vices—or morbid symptoms—of femininity where he comes across them, in order to enjoy among women a comfortable flow of conversation, an easy play of personality, a jousting—not warring—of wits. The traitor in fact shares a whole range of sensibilities with women, or at least with women who have not acquired, through a change in their structural position, the classic sensibilities of men. His delights—for example, in the sensuous detail, the delicacy of character, the intimate connection—are frequently identical with theirs. So are his irritations. All in all, the traitor very naturally takes women's point of view, and, in their antagonisms with men, their side.

As her several profiles of resisters indicate, Joan Cocks shares with other spokespersons for gender flexibility a sense of the human story as, at this hour, closer to its beginning point than to its conclusion. Neither she nor the other resisters who remain committed to change have a sacred text in hand—or a detailed itinerary with clear destinations or a timetable more precise than "eventually" ("molecular details that begin to diverge in increasing numbers from the massive fact eventually will add up to a different massive fact, after all"). Although they speak often of transformations—transformed professions, recreations, methods of thought, patterns of feeling, terms of relationship—they seldom provide itemized specifications. Their vocabularies mix pride and impatience with self with anger at and envy of the other in ways that are often bewildering.

But the belief they have in common, an essential of classic feminism, has counterparts in some art, some religious aspiration, and in the rare politics that qualifies as courageous. It's a belief that humanity's horizon is currently too narrow and that imaginative action, social and individual, can bring into being higher levels of consciousness and nobler forms of life. Those nobler forms won't arise from attempts by the sexes at slavish imitation of stereotypes of each other—the masculine as pure vanquishing, pure toughness, the feminine as pure succumbing and pure tenderness. They'll originate in complex self-knowledge: knowledge generated by engagement and founded on reasoned hope.

9

A Community of Beings in a Single Self

F ROM THE FIRST, feminism raised aloft a compositively
imagined ideal of womanhood — an achieved wholeness arrived at through the commingling of qualities traditionally
classified as masculine (active ambition, courage, worldliness) with
qualities traditionally classified as feminine (compassion, generosity, innocence). As I have reiterated, the dream wasn't that
women would become men ("we more criticize what men have
made of themselves," as Catharine MacKinnon writes); the dream
was that, through the protracted engagement of the sexes with
each other, as equals, stereotypical narrowness would give way
to breadth and abundance. Activists differed about which element
of "the feminine" was most responsible for dulling women's feeling for their own many-sidedness. (The differences continue: for
Catharine MacKinnon the culprit is imposed docility, for Carol
Gilligan it's infatuation with selflessness, Joan Cocks excoriates intellectual naïveté, while other writers blame other defects.) Women
activists were also wary of explicitly identifying as male any estimable trait seen as withheld from females.

But the basic feminist point stands despite differences and evasions (and despite gender shift in course): the creation of richer,
more complex models of womanhood requires acceptance of gen-

der flexibility as a value—recognition, that is, that sealing off masculine and feminine "natures" in ways that render mutual teaching and reciprocal influence impossible impedes human progress toward wholeness.

Over the past decade, partly in reaction against the mania for women-becoming-men, a comparable position has found expression in the men's movement. Male activists have arrived, that is, at compositively imagined models of manhood that commingle qualities traditionally classified as feminine with qualities traditionally classified as masculine. Again the goal is range and richness, not slavish imitation of one sex by the other; again leaders aren't agreed on which elements of "the masculine" to blame for thinning out the gender; again there's no enthusiasm for explicitly identifying any estimable trait seen as lacking in *this* sex as naturally abundant in the other.

Nevertheless, the point stands as strongly in the men's movement as among women activists: the creation of more complex models of manhood requires acceptance of gender flexibility as a value—recognition that sealing off masculine and feminine "natures" in ways that prevent reciprocal influence impedes progress toward wholeness. The phenomenon of gender shift is as beleaguering to male advocates of gender flexibility as to females. Yet in the face of it some male spokespersons—historians, social critics, biographers, poets—have managed to win sizable audiences, and a few wield truly impressive influence.

An example: Robert Bly, author of *Iron John: A Book About Men* (1990). A work of cultural criticism, *Iron John* advances its thesis through commentary on a fairy tale thousands of years old. The story, best known in the Grimm Brothers' version, details a developing relationship between hairy Iron John, a mysterious Wild Man imprisoned in a cage in the King's courtyard, and the King's eight-year-old son, a lad whom Iron John persuades to free him. It's an initiation story, replete with cryptic narrative sequences, scenes, and images: hidden keys, clear pools, fingers that turn to gold at the touch of pure water, three-legged gift horses, garden encounters with a "God-woman." Bly retells the story charmingly, with extensive, persuasive commentary on the symbolic meanings of each episode; to read the story as this poet elucidates it is to marvel anew at the resonance of mythological modes of thought.

But Bly's purpose isn't to reawaken appreciation of fable and legend. His purpose is threefold: to anatomize some significant failings of contemporary men, both fathers and sons; to account for these failings; and to argue that ancient tales such as "Iron John" offer oblique but invaluable instruction about how to repair the failings.

The chief failing of the contemporary father comes down to this: he has allowed his male character to be drained of multifariousness, and has become, as a result, a "sanitized, hairless, shallow man." The man's workplace connections with other males are strained and artificial: "Contemporary business life allows competitive relationships only, in which the major emotions are anxiety, tension, loneliness, rivalry, and fear. After work what do men do? Collect in a bar and hold light conversations over light beer."

When the father comes home, he brings nothing with him except temperament, has no skills to teach:

> He is reluctant to tell his son what is really going on. The fragmentation of decision making in corporate life, the massive effort that produces the corporate willingness to destroy the environment for the sake of profit, the prudence, even cowardice, that one learns in bureaucracy—who wants to teach that? . . . What the father brings home today is usually a touchy mood, springing from powerlessness and despair mingled with longstanding shame and the numbness peculiar to those who hate their jobs. Fathers in earlier times could often break through their own humanly inadequate temperaments by teaching rope-making, fishing, posthole digging, grain cutting, drumming, harness making, animal care, even singing and storytelling. That teaching sweetened the effect of the temperament.

But there are no sweeteners in the contemporary father, this "enfeebled, dejected, paltry man." And the total absence of a teaching/initiating function deepens his withdrawal and passivity:

> The passive man [skips] over parenting. Parenting means feeling, but it also means doing all sorts of boring tasks, taking children to school, buying them jackets, attending band concerts, dealing with curfews, setting rules of behavior, deciding on responses when these rules are broken, checking on who a child's friends are, listening to the child's talk in an active way, et cetera. The passive man leaves his wife to do that.

His son, in consequence, is feminized. He learns feeling from his mother—is "pulled over onto the mother's side before he has stabilized himself as a man," and becomes merely another version of his "sanitized, hairless, shallow" father: soft, nice, "ecologically superior" to Dad but essentially energyless. Bly reports:

> When I look out at an audience, perhaps half the young males are . . . what I'd call soft. They're lovely, valuable people—I like them—they're not interested in harming the earth or starting wars. There's a gentle attitude toward life in their whole being and style of living. But many of these men are not happy. You quickly notice the lack of energy in them. They are life-preserving but not exactly life-giving. Ironically, you often see these men with strong women who positively radiate energy. . . . Young men for various reasons wanted their women harder, and women began to desire softer men. It seemed like a nice arrangement for a while, but we've lived with it long enough now to see that it isn't working out.

The reason it's not working out, as Bly sets it forth, is that, instead of living into their natural variousness, males and females alike are becoming imprisoned in regimes of self-simplification. Their ideas of the masculine and feminine are utterly out of touch with both the differences between the sexes and the likenesses. Putting the same point differently: they lack the schooled awareness of many-sidedness from which complex selfhood grows.

Men as well as women are natural nurturers, teachers, and protectors of the young, although they teach different subjects and nurture in different ways; ancients knew this, moderns don't. Men as well as women grow through lyric as well as practical experiences—grow by becoming lovers, for instance, by advancing from "raw sexuality" to idealizing passion; ancients knew this, moderns don't. Men as well as women need art and can and must make art—and need ferocity in their relationships—and need reflective space in which to resist their own insistence that their lives "belong to [their] work, [their] children, and [their] marriage"; ancients knew this, moderns don't.

Bly sometimes frames his account of linkage and difference within and between "the masculine" and "the feminine" in simple expository declarations:

> When a man possesses empathy, it does not mean that he has developed the feminine feeling only; of course he has, and it is good to develop the feminine. But when he learns to shudder [to shudder means feeling how frail human beings are], he is developing a part of the masculine emotional body as well.

> To live between [opposites] means that we not only recognize opposites, but rejoice that they exist. . . . Living in the opposites does not mean identifying with one side and then belittling the other. The aim is not that a man, for example, should choose the male role and then regard the female as the enemy. . . . Rejoicing in the opposites means . . . enjoying the fantastic music coming from each side.

> Our obligation—and I include in "our" all the women and men writing about gender—is to describe *masculine* in such a way that it does not exclude the masculine in women, and yet hits a resonant string in the man's heart. . . . Our obligation is to describe the *feminine* in a way that does not exclude the feminine in men but makes a large string resonate in the woman's heart.

Everywhere in *Iron John* the commentator speaks of multiplicities and unboundedness in men *and* women:

The European novel, a lovely phenomenon of the last two centuries, has taught more than one contemporary woman what a rich reservoir of impulses and longings she has in her soul that can be satisfied or remain unsatisfied. Few women say now, "The boundaries of my life are my husband's," or even think it.

The Wild Man is part of a company or a community in a man's psyche. . . . Just as the man in our story exists as a companion to feminine energy, sometimes following its lead, sometimes not, so the Wild Man lives in complicated interchanges with the other interior beings. A whole community of beings is what is called a grown man.

Bly's commentary on multifariousness invariably leads back into his story's insides. The Wild Man whom the King's son frees becomes the master of the lad's initiation; his job is "to teach the young man how abundant, various, and many-sided his manhood is." Toward that end the youngster passes through an experiential labyrinth in which he is by turns a destitute orphan, a lover, a thinker and poet, a trickster, a warrior, and much else besides. The youngster's learning commences only after he makes "a clean break from the mother"; yet a crucial moment in its progress is an instructive meeting with "the feminine in a nonmaternal form," a "powerful, blossoming, savvy, wild, instigating, erotic, playful" young woman.

The story makes plain through its sequences, Bly insists, that the ancients knew the stages marking the way up from shallowness. They knew that, early in life, the male youngster "has to overcome, at least for the moment, his fear of wildness, irrationality, hairiness, intuition, emotion, the body, and nature." They knew, further, that the young male needs to be "welcomed into the male world by older men," instructed by male nurturers, pointed toward risky experience and inevitable wounds, given chances to see deeply into nature as a consciousness wholly separate from his own. They knew that a son of privilege who hasn't spent an extended stretch down and out, poor, shamed, and despairing, won't grow up. They knew that there needs to be a lengthy period of inner cultivation and "soul concerns"—a period of thought, of bookishness, of "notic[ing] tiny desires," of learning poems by heart—and another period in which the youngster "develop[s] the lover in him from seed to flower." (In the Renaissance, says Bly, "it was not at all unusual for a young man . . . to take two or three years off, and spend it learning to be a lover. We spend those years in graduate school instead.") There must be yet another period in which the youngster does warrior service, physical or intellectual, to a transcendent cause. And in the fully initiated man, *all* this youthful experience remains alive and vital: "a whole community of beings is what is called a grown man."

Throughout the tale of Iron John the young man functions—unwittingly—as the nurturer of his nurturer. (He not only frees the Wild Man but also ultimately restores him to the throne from which he has been mysteriously deposed.) And throughout the tale Bly is at pains to dramatize the growing spirit of independence—the rapture in life and in self—that mounts in both the young male and the young female whom the story is celebrating. There's a splendidly energized spontaneity in voice and gesture:

> Once in summer, when [the boy] was working in the garden by himself, it got so hot that he pulled his head covering off, so that the breeze would cool his head. When the sun touched his head, his hair glowed and blazed out so brightly that beams of sunlight went all the way into the bedroom of the King's daughter, and she leapt up to see what that could be. She spied the boy outside, and called to him, "Boy, bring me a batch of flowers!"
>
> He quickly put his tarboosh back on, picked some wild flowers for her, and tied them in a bunch. As he started up the stairs with them, the gardener met him, and said, "What are you doing bringing the King's daughter such ordinary flowers? Get moving and pick another bouquet, the best we have and the most beautiful."
>
> "No, no," the boy answered, "the wild flowers have stronger fragrance and they will please her more."

When the boy walked into her room, the King's daughter said, "Take your headthing off; it isn't proper for you to wear it in my presence."

He replied, "I don't dare do that. I have the mange, you know."

She however grabbed the tarboosh and yanked it off; his golden hair tumbled down around his shoulders, and it was magnificent to look at. He started out the door at a run, but she held him by the arm and gave him a handful of gold coins. He took them and left, but put no stock in them; in fact he brought the coins to the gardener and said, "I'm giving these to your children—they can use them to play with."

Later, when the young man is called into the King's court to be thanked for a warrior deed that has saved his ruler, he's asked what he'd like as a reward:

"Well," the young man said, "I'd suggest that you give me your daughter as my wife."

Then the King's daughter laughed and said, "I like the way he doesn't beat around the bush; I already knew he was no gardener's boy from his golden hair." And so she walked over and kissed him.

Iron John is culture criticism in a poet's vein—meaning, it doesn't fret much about its own inner contradictions. (On some pages contemporary fathers *are* sanitized, hairless, and shallow, on others they're only *called* that by "uncompassionate" wives determined to misrepresent them to their sensitive sons.) As Christopher Lasch once observed, Bly "offers his reinterpretation of mythology not just as a metaphorical elaboration of enduring moral insights but as a program, an answer to the contemporary malaise . . . a cure for souls, a world-saving therapy for those who no longer believe in religion but appreciate the power and beauty of ancient myths."

But if *Iron John* has limits as therapy, as criticism of what men have made of themselves it's highly useful. Now you are becoming the men that the generation before you dreamed of marrying, said Gloria Steinem to the graduating class at Smith College, her tone communicating near-reverence for the model of the male achiever.

Iron John speaks directly to the pathos of lives shaped by delusions arising from that reverence. The diminution of those lives matches that of the life of Corporate Man; he taught them how to lose themselves.

And from beginning to end *Iron John* mocks the teaching, aiming its sharpest rhetoric not at "feminization" but at self-diminution. Like MacKinnon, Gilligan, Cocks, and many another feminist, Robert Bly at his best possesses a *balanced* feeling for gender flexibility—genuine joy in the music coming from either side—and a sense of human possibility nowhere met with in standard-brand gender shift minds. "Some say," says Bly, "well, let's just be human and not talk about masculine or feminine at all." And, he adds:

> People who say that imagine they are occupying the moral high ground. I say that we have to be a little gentle here, and allow the word *masculine* and the word *feminine* to be spoken, and not be afraid that some moral carpenter will make boxes of those words and imprison us in them. . . . All naming of qualities is dangerous, because the naming can be made into boxes. But we have to do better than in the past.

Precisely; and the conviction that, guided by the ideal of gender flexibility, we can do better has energized feminist thought from the start. The guidance the ideal provides takes the form of a psychological and moral frame of reference, not a set of daily rules to live by. The shaping principles, made vivid by writers and researchers like those just discussed, are that idolatry of either stereotypical "masculinity" or stereotypical "femininity" leads to self-victimization; that an imagination both of personal balance and of societal possibility is essential to the successful pursuit of individual development; and that immediacy—the here and now—demands also to be understood as an interim: the future in vital gestation.

In the real world, access to understanding of this sort isn't fairly distributed, and as a result, the majority copes with the Age of Gender Shift without benefit of useful, hopeful perspectives—without a positive frame of reference.

This doesn't mean, of course, that typical contemporary situations and feelings are identical with those of the killer woman tough guys who populate the opening chapters of this book— people who, having squeezed complication out of their being, proclaim with near-complete certitude that the act of "becoming men" is pure gain. To the contrary, the most common experience just now is that of being pulled in mutually exclusive directions, toward and away from extreme masculinization (or feminization), fighting interior wars for and against the mad imperatives of toughness, veering incoherently between regimes, possessing no sure point of balance. A teenaged female leader of an all-female gang is goaded into violence by male gang members yet clings improbably to a vision of herself as a maternal nurturer-protector of "her" people—until a tough male elected official shakes her grip on the vision . . . A successful fortyish businesswoman pushes herself unrelentingly to surpass competitors in her male world of work, and is simultaneously racked, as the parent of a young son, by mother-guilt and a sense of moral inferiority to non-working mothers . . . A sexual experimenter in her early twenties excitedly mimics the appetitive aggression of males her age, rejoicing in "liberation"— until, in an affair with a middle-aged male, she encounters a level of exploitative egomania that very nearly cripples her . . . Writers and artists ape male explorers of violent aberrancy and abuse and lose themselves in deviancy . . .

Confusion and disruption, shattering swerves and reversals, frustrating contradictions: these become the norm for many who are touched by the blight of women-becoming-men. Impossible to tell the story of gender shift culture without approaching closer to the insides of their disturbed, often pride-blinded, often moving experience.

THREE

Whiplash Injuries

10

Positivity Lost

MET WITH IN the elites, kickbutt extremists rouse indignation: How can well-educated, privileged folk glory in brutal egomania? Observed outside the elites, extremists stir graver response: a sharpened sense of the ironies of the American drive to rise—some call it ascensionism—and of the havoc wrought when myths of toughness merge with myths of probity.

Social historians and liberal-leaning public officials such as Robert Reich have usefully studied the background and effects of the merger on recent public policy. One important factor in the background is the fresh calumniation of the "undeserving poor"—echoes of and embroideries upon Ronald Reagan's tales of welfare queens riding in Cadillacs to pick up their government checks. More important—among the educated—in stimulating hostility to government "softness" was research establishing the devastating consequences to families of well-intended federal programs—Aid to Families with Dependent Children, for one.

But the rise of a politics of pitilessness is associated at every turn with the undernoticed high-fashion masculinizing promoted through gender shift. Life stories shaped by the interweaving of this politics with woman-becoming-man culture are among the most poignant in contemporary America. Sudden swerves at official levels from "concern" to hard-nosed pragmatism, abrupt rede-finitions of generosity and compassion as ignorance and cruelty: these can be truly heartbreaking. They issue not in semantic mazes but in crushing disillusion and resentment.

Consider the playing out of gender shift themes in the young life of Sandra Quintana, sometime student at West Side High (a New York City alternative school for troubled students), and in the lives of her teachers.

Sandra's education in toughness begins when she's a child (her heroin-addicted father beats her on his drop-in visits when he tires of beating her mother). For this child, as for others at the bottom, toughness is necessary armor, a basic survival resource. But in the new cultural production, toughness isn't presented as a survival technique — isn't seen as a disadvantage, isn't cornered, isn't caught struggling minute-to-minute to hang on or hold out against bullies. Riot grrrl bravado is *glamorized*. Coercion and terror are promoted as routes to self-respect and street status. Stereotypical male standards of self-expression — even of animal ferocity — are held up as definitive.

In her subteens Sandra is thrilled by the bravado. Resilience helps her endure the parental assaults, and she goes on to build a neighborhood name for pugnacity and defiance through rage, boxing skills, and riot grrrl–inspired relish of bloodletting. (Courtney Love: "I punched some bitch in the mouth and her teeth got in the way.") Sandra burnishes her reputation when in junior high she "disappears for ten days with her grandmother's gun." At a prom, in a fight about a boy, this would-be killer woman sends a girl home "half-naked after scraping the girl's face against the wall, throwing her repeatedly on the floor and ripping her dress down to the waist."

She learns how to boast — how to recreate for audiences bouts that end with her opponents looking as though they've been matched with Mike Tyson. ("I pushed [one of her teeth] all the way back. . . . I put my fingers inside her eyes. I wanted to take her eyes out, so they were all bloody and scratched. Her nose was cracked. She ended up in the hospital.") Male gang spectators, rooting her on during a street fight in which a challenger tears off her shirt, yell at her to forget her sex—and she obeys:

> I'm still hitting her, but really I was trying to stop and put my shirt back on. The guys were like, "It doesn't matter if she fucking leaves you naked, kick her ass!" so I was like, "Fine." There I was hitting her blam! blam! blam! without my shirt: Boom!

She hungers for a place in a "real" gang but, lacking connections, settles for starting a gang from scratch, R3, all female, "colors" of its own. She works at elevating R3's standing, winning police notice as a potentially dangerous force and stirring the wrath of the city's real gangs for encroaching on their turf. R3 is destroyed in a gang raid, but Sandra herself is recruited—invited to become a member of El Asociacion Neta, a group founded twenty years before in Puerto Rican prisons and ranking in the late nineties among Manhattan's largest gangs. A wretched, apparently unalterable future beckons: more pointless violence, more "male" pugnacity and savagery, extending out to the blank horizon.

But a change occurs. Within months of making Neta, Sandra embraces—with little warning or preparation—idealistic activism. An astonishment: a riot grrrl gang member giving herself abruptly and wholeheartedly to volunteer service in community projects and pressing El Asociacion's thousand-plus members to follow where she's leading.

Youth gangs with a service side aren't unheard of. In ghettoes where most families are dysfunctional, gangs are substitutes for family; gang leaders often fight the drift in their membership toward criminality; hands-on aid to the homeless, to AIDS victims, to newly released prisoners are among typical gang projects. Before its demolition, R3, Quintana's group, took up a weekly collection from members "in order to distribute it again according to need";

one of R3's purposes, according to an observer who tracked the group month by month, was to assist kids without families to call on and in desperate need of some means of organizing their lives.

But more than tribal rites and precedents is involved in Quintana's swerve toward "positivity" (her word). Grown-up helpers and allies are involved—teachers, counselors, youth workers at West Side High whose example brings alive the idea of nurturing and the possibility of learning and leading. The teachers in question operate under handicaps: poverty of resources, political feebleness, the symbiotic relations between gender shift culture and gang culture's violent wing. Few teachers fantasize about launching another Colin Powell or "saving" a mute inglorious Milton. The hope is simply to talk back to codes of barbarism and violence long enough—minus piety and via example—to seed doubt about them in tough-guy heads. The reward for teachers who manage to open a door is the sight of adolescent hardness questioning itself, beginning to grasp its own limits. The depressing blow is the sight of that same door slammed shut by budgets and platforms shaped by Giuliani-style politics of pitilessness—politics that has its roots in the hard-nosed masculinism from which Sandra Quintana's teachers are trying to save her.

The school principal at West Side runs a "Family Group" (first class of the day, discussion, confession, whatever) for the fifty or so hardest cases in the school: ex-cons, kicking-it addicts, the last-stop expelled and suspended, the parentless, jobless, prospectless "urban disadvantaged"—the Sandra Quintanas. The man's other jobs include fending off the bureaucracy, keeping classrooms humming and attendance high, trying to reverse downward trends in academic performance, persuading students that they're known and that they matter (he's constantly in the corridors, shooing students into classrooms, kiddingly shouting their names), playing Santa to kids who need subway tokens, teaching an American history class, coping with staff morale problems and a collapsing physical plant . . .

Sandra knows the principal well. She also knows a special education teacher whose evident trustworthiness and concern enable the insecure to dare to think and speak ... She knows a gifted youth worker who gambles that with Sandra in charge, a Neta chapter can be trusted to provide nighttime security for a public school that performs service tasks for old people, toddlers, "nonaligned teenagers" (the gamble pays off) ... She knows and leans heavily on Miriam, a youth counselor with a drug and alcohol prevention program who cheers when Sandra proposes intergang meetings in the schools and cheers again (and liberates paper and a copier for her) when Sandra becomes gang communications coordinator ...

Miriam believes that bottom dogs immensely value chances to initiate—to conceive and carry through group ventures that earn respect. She and others like her also believe that alternative schools can "develop a curriculum that incorporates the school into the community and gets the community into the schools":

> We can make positive rites of passage available to students [writes one teacher] through various programs at school that draw them away from the hazardous rites of passage they now seek out. The connections ... provide students with a sense of belonging to society [and] also, significantly, impress upon the community that these kids are not villains, but their kids, our kids.

Teachers who share these beliefs have an immediate impact on Sandra Quintana's emerging self. The girl remains a formidable scrapper: when the Neta hierarchies pull back from "service," she stands up to them, jut-jawed. "If being a Neta is really a way of life, if it's really about more than a string of beads and an attitude, then what's to stop me?" What's to stop her and her girls from leg-pressing 385 pounds in the weight room *and* scrubbing graffiti off lavatory walls *and*—with Miriam urging her on—organizing feed-the-homeless drives and clean-up-the-school campaigns, opening lines of communication among chapters (dreaming of a united political voice), starting an intergang newspaper (a column called "Positivity" focuses on bad situations that the young resolve "by keeping cool and thinking well")? What's to stop her from starting to take school itself seriously? Supported to the limit by the school elders—survivor idealists from the sixties—Sandra is finding a way forward, traveling the good works road, learning to lead. It's absurd to idealize the gang she's "reforming," but it's easy to imagine her, down the good works road, knocking at a community college door with an equivalency certificate in hand, even daring—in time—a transfer to Baruch. You go, girl!

Only as it happens West Side High *is* politically beleaguered: the chill wind of the New Urban Austerity is blowing. The nurturers in the building can invent curricular rites of passage that lay out multiple options to riot grrrls—but they can't buck toughness in high office. Toughness is the majority will, the *national* voice of gender shift. And toughness has been voted in. Uttering panegyrics on "historic opportunities . . . to scale back poverty programs," announcing that the city of New York has been "too generous for too long," toughness indicts sentimental liberalism for infecting the entire metropolitan service sector (schools, welfare, hospitals) with weakness and corruption. Toughness erases after-school programs, developmental workshops, school-based group activities, slashes day care centers, youth jobs programs, and enrollments in City University, ends city funding for soup kitchens and teenagers' sports leagues, cuts the Board of Education's capital budget in half.

And toughness isn't mere budget cuts. Toughness is a conviction among the powerful that the answer to the bottom sector's so-called needs is intimidation—an end to coddling and pampering. According to this reasoning, it is coddling that causes parentless urban teenagers to believe that they need the safety, protection, respect, and identity gangs provide. Coddling equals Family Groups in schools. Coddling equals teachers and administrators talking with gang members. Coddling is what a Board of Education conference on gangs agrees to deal with by following a "clearcut scenario of threat and counterthreat." Coddling is weak, soft, *feminine*.

Feeling the heat, Sandra steps up her gang members' efforts to prove their bona fides—their commitment to school and readiness to work with authorities. But the line on people like herself—and her counselor Miriam and the rest—is that they're insurrectionists. A school dean catches some gang girls scrubbing a bathroom wall, screams at them, "confiscates the brushes and buckets and marches the perpetrators" off to punishment. Rulings come down: A ban on clean-up-the-school projects. A ban on Quintana's newspaper. No more feed-the-homeless campaigns. "All gang meetings, special programs, group counseling, and work incentives [come] to an abrupt end."

Macho in command.

Toughness as virtue (flexibility as vice) is, needless to say, fully embedded in the American grain. Indian fighters, self-made entre-preneurs, Rough Riders, Hemingway heroes, cold warriors, crime-fighting district attorneys: the players change over the generations. So, too, do fashions in the expression of contempt for weakness. Mayor Giuliani's grinning jokes about cowing cabdrivers feature a mode of ironical winking that's standard among nighttime talk show comics. ("I'm late," says the mayor to a waiting commence-ment audience. "I couldn't get a cab.") Tough Teddy Roosevelt pre-ferred flat-out denunciations of "emasculated, milk-and-water moralities" and flat-out praise of cowboys like himself. ("A cowboy will not submit tamely to an insult [nor] has he an overwrought fear of shedding blood.")

But in those times, pre–gender shift, a voice—first "feminine," then feminist—still spoke against the cults that battled one an-other for place as champion baiters of the so-called coddled. "So-cial agencies" and "aid societies" labored humanely to open up ave-nues of development for people lost at the urban bottom. They and the professionals who succeeded them deposited invaluable capital in the bank: achievements in broadening trust between schools and communities justifiably hostile to schools ... achievements at creating classrooms in which civic illiteracy not only learns lessons of empowerment but also acts on the learning ... achievements in transforming "remediation" in math and English into serious intellectual labor for teachers and students alike. Ground existed for useful debate on how to build on such achievements.

But when women are hailed for becoming men, this capital is depleted. Today's kickbutt culture is as adept as any gang at intimidating; call it mean and its spokespersons answer that "mean" is girlish talk. No debate allowed. And the perfectly predictable consequence for Ms. Quintana, a particular nineteen-year-old briefly on her way up, is a downward spiral. In the Netas, Quintana has been "courageous enough to try to reshape the organization—to battle against the odds."

But the structures she leans on are fragile. The alternative school won't last another season. Her counselor Miriam thinks there's no future and can't "see the point in staying if she [isn't] going to be allowed to do her job." Three weeks after the banning of Quintana's newspaper the city announces it will cut costs by buying out some teachers' contracts. Miriam takes the offer and leaves. With nobody behind Quintana, and with the schools suddenly off-limits, her relations with the gangs she's harrying toward "positivity" disintegrate; there's a flare-up of street fighting and she takes a knife wound. "Once so determined to change the world," she "backs away from her idealism."

A familiar narrative, no subtleties. From experience a beaten child learns she won't survive unless she defends herself. From riot grrrl and gang extravaganzas she learns that aggressive violence can earn her a street name—a presence and self-worth. But in school, caring grownups speak obliquely, by example, of another kind of distinction. Not in *my* range, the girl surmises. Best not to listen. How can anybody in her place afford to? How can anybody like herself risk losing the little she has in the way of respect?

Her teachers persist, gently. They speak and act as if their world and hers actually coexisted. They appear to take for granted—puzzlingly, in time excitingly—that access to the courage of tenderness is as open to her as to them: that nothing in the past cuts her off from understanding the good of all as the good of each, or from imagining herself as capable of serving those in need. Confused, troubled, she tries to take hold of the situation in her mind, tries framing it as a kind of dare, a near-physical challenge. She resolves to go for it, gambling all on the promise of a different self, new air.

But there's a betrayal. At least partly because of gender shift—the advent of a culture preaching that the city has been too generous for too long—the promise Quintana's teachers implicitly made to her can't be kept. The gang girl feels stupid and used, torn between despising herself for being gulled into caring and despising those who persuaded her out of the unrelenting mistrust that gave her a life hitherto. The killer woman age demands that the youngster forget this conflict, but the scar will linger.

11

The Detachment Trap

S TRAINS VARY, UNSURPRISINGLY, with class level. Professionals, corporate executives, academicians, performance
and literary artists are among those drawn to stereo-typi-
cally masculine ways — seduced by self-simplifying manners and
language that promise added strength or an end to vulnerability. At
these levels strain materializes often as a shuttling between aware-
nesses: humorous self-consciousness at one moment about mimicking males, serious anxiety at the next about measuring up to
male-venerated standards. Difficult to chart in real-life dailiness,
the cross-currents of attitude and feeling come clearer in books —
works of research or argument or fiction wherein signs of ambivalence are harder to hide. The inner contention in such works — the
authors' nearly simultaneous embrace and rejection of male-asso-
ciated ways — is a subtle matter; it doesn't shout for notice. But the
aspirations and evasions that figure in the contention can be uncommonly poignant.

As they are in Sharon Hays's much-discussed *The Cultural Contradictions of Motherhood* (1996). The author, a sociology professor
at the University of Virginia, focuses her analytical gaze on what
she perceives as a conflict of ideologies, a contemporary war pitting
"the ideology of intensive mothering" against the ideology of mar-

ket America (the beliefs that organize attitudes in a capitalistic, bottom line–obsessed society). The book opens with an account of a job crisis reported by one of Hays's interview subjects, a businesswoman and mother named Rachel. When Rachel's two-year-old daughter was hospitalized, Rachel wanted to be at her bedside continually; although the sickness wasn't life-threatening, Rachel nevertheless insisted that the child needed her mother's presence and love. And this made Rachel's boss, a childless woman, angry. There was a crisis in the office and Rachel couldn't be spared. But Rachel was adamant: her daughter's sickness had to come first. A destructive conflict ensued.

Hays places the conflict as part of a "larger cultural contradiction," not as a narrowly local dispute. And she argues that neither Rachel nor her boss was right in any absolute sense. Both were driven by opposed cultural conceptions having to do with women's private sphere in the home and men's public sphere in the greater world. Rachel's sense of obligation derives from the imperatives of child care; her boss's sense of obligation derives from the imperatives of paid work. Both are serious people; neither of their ideologies is more rational, worthy, or valuable than the other. But to understand this conflict it's necessary to grasp the "content of the ideology of intensive mothering" — to "pry the ideology loose from its naturalized and sentimentalized moorings."

The tone and content of a work thus introduced would seem easy to predict. The writer opposes conflict-generating emotionalism and moralism that elevate this set of values over that; drawing on opinion-shaping mass cultural texts and pertinent passages of history—tracking intersections of accident, political interest, and sentiment—her book will show why the elevation of motherhood over entrepreneurship or vice versa is a mistake: why personal prejudices lack an objective, foundational basis (they're constituted by language and history, not by nature or divinity). A conventional deconstructionist attack, in other words, on irrational pecking orders among our myths.

In its general design *Cultural Contradictions* fulfills this expectation. Hays reviews the historical backgrounds of present-day parenting, spells out the messages delivered in multimillion-copy bestsellers on child care, and reports on particular interpretations both of the past and of the best-selling experts that now prevail among parents (stay-at-home mothers as well as mothers who work outside the home). The historical survey moves briskly from the middle ages to modernity, tracing a shift from ignoring the bad or frightening child to concentrating on the innocent child. There are accounts of Puritanism, with its preoccupation with overcoming the corrupt nature of the child, and of several ascendant anti-Puritan influences: Rousseau (the child as a noble being), Victorian sentimentalizations of the child, doctrines of child-centeredness, the ideal of the trained mother. Attention is paid to the increasingly popular image of the angel in the house.

With sentimentalization proceeding, Hays explains, women were coming to be seen as virtuous and pure, and children were seen as angelic innocents. As the new industrial economy reshaped family farms and family businesses, the separation of home and workplace became yet another building block for the ideology of intensive mothering. The world beyond the domestic hearth was increasingly portrayed as dog-eat-dog and brutally competitive—remote in every particular from the warm sanctuary of home wherein kindness and gentleness were cultivated. And home was women's world.

Finally, Hays offers analysis of three authorities who, responding to this immediate past, promulgated our current dogmas of intensive mothering: Benjamin Spock, T. Berry Brazelton, and Penelope Leach. Hays notes that nearly every American mother reads one child-rearing manual, and 75 percent of mothers read more than one. She establishes, through parallel excerpts from her interviews with mothers and from the pages of Spock et al. on the overwhelming significance of maternal love, that the triumvirate exercised direct influence on parental thinking straight through to the close of the twentieth century.

The tone and manner of the writing on these subjects is sometimes well tuned to the social-scientistic design—meaning it's detached, chilly, hard-nosed. Hays affects surprise, for example, that mothers don't approach child rearing in a businesslike fashion, but she also berates mothers who look for high rates of return with minimum investment of effort or in other ways follow capitalist logic. She's ironic about child-rearing manuals that descant on the universality of mother love: Hays enfolds parenting pieties in belittling quotation marks—" 'natural' love," " 'inherently sacred' child," " 'bad' mothers" and the like—and deals impatiently with homilies on the helplessness of babies. Her pages frequently restate the dry-eyed theme that only when "you are *inside* the logic of intensive mothering" does the thing make any sense. Viewed from outside, Hays writes, "asking parents to pump copious amounts of time, energy, and money into children" without thinking about efficiency or profitability "is surely bizarre."

But the voice of the no-nonsense social scientist who takes up these positions competes, in *Cultural Contradictions,* with another voice—a speaker whose attitudes seem markedly softer. It's as though the methodologically correct sociologist who is determined to maintain ironic distance, deriding "valorized motherhood," "valorized love," "Sacred Children, Sacred Mothering," can't fully control an impulse to step closer, to speak up for the view that the quality manifest in intensive mothering—selfless concern for others—has its own unique value, and may deserve higher standing than ambition, competition, acquisitiveness, bottom-line rationality in the large. Well before the end the book's two voices are caught up in a series of half-articulated, half-suppressed disagreements: differences about the strengths and limits of pseudo-masculine detachment, about the genuineness (or lack of it) of mother love, about whether an end to intensive mothering would or would not sharply diminish social cohesion and social hope.

And the differences surface not only from page to page but often within individual sentences as well. The book is chockablock with methodologically correct assertions that selflessness isn't a whit better than personal acquisitiveness *and* with immediately adjacent, methodologically *in*correct worries that the author's analysis will seem "coldhearted," that it "portray[s] mothers as too emotional, too gullible, or too sentimental," that it implies an intent to "attack mothers or the work they do." The writer shakes her finger in one passage at piety about sacred children, and in the next dwells on the possibility that the intensification of parental commitments to child rearing qualifies as human progress, and that "the ethic of maternal love" should be appreciated as usefully subversive of "rationalized market societies."

Everywhere there are attempts to interweave stiff, professionally correct gestures of neutrality with warm salutes to maternal character. A mother tells Hays—the passage is affecting—that she wanted children because "the more people you have to love you the better off you are." Threading her way past yea and nay, Hays frames the mother's point fairly in her own language, proposes in skeptical voice that the point is perhaps "overly sentimental," doubles back with a warning against undervaluing sincerity.

Reporting that her interviewees insist love is the basis of good child rearing, Hays reasserts her belief in their sincerity, but goes on to suggest that their insistence may signify nothing but the effect of child care propaganda on gullible minds. The layers multiply: mothers' talk, Hays avers, "mimics the talk of the experts," but this is not to say that the experts impose an ideology on passive mothers, but at the same time it's true that "what the experts say is what mothers want to hear."

At moments in *Cultural Contradictions* the writer's wonder at her interviewees' softness seems forced—a tough-guy mask meant to be seen through. Why, Hays asks coldly at one point, do mothers think shutting a colicky baby in a closet is cruel?

There are women, mothers told me in dismay, who leave their kids in day care from six in the morning until seven at night and hire someone else to pick them up at the end of the day . . . I was told the story of a mother who, faced with a fussy child suffering from colic, first strapped him into a car seat and then placed him in a closet. These are surely efficient methods of dealing with children, so why do many mothers consider them not only socially inappropriate but downright evil and unconscionable?

There are also occasions in the book when cold detachment seems about to reject itself—as when, in midcourse of demonstrating how Spock and others taught mothers that love is essential to child rearing, the writer pauses to insert a phrase declaring in effect that mothers needed no such instruction:

> Raising a child is therefore "naturally" (to use the term favored by Spock, Brazelton, and Leach) emotionally absorbing. Not only is this love thought to be the basis of the necessary commitment to parenting, it is also, as Brazelton advises, an absolutely "essential ingredient" for the proper rearing of a child. Mothers know this. They are well aware that children require loving attention, as Spock suggests, "as much as they need vitamins and calories."

Mothers know this . . . At these words—better: at this cry—the social science guard is once again dropped momentarily, together with the concept of experts as ventriloquists and mothers as dummies. *A mother's understanding of what it means to love a child and to be loved in return owes nothing to brainwashing—is no scripted contrivance or psycho-surgical implant. The understanding has roots as deep as those of human hope itself.* But the moment of unconditional solidarity that a reader senses—solidarity between the author at her work station and, say, a parent at the bedside of a hospitalized child—ends almost before it begins, with the intercession ("as Spock suggests") of authority.

Nor is this startling. For the writer to prolong the moment would be tantamount to criticizing her own assumption that it's actually feasible to formulate a compelling bottom-line version of mother love: an account of the value of "this love" arrived at by prying the phenomenon out of its embeddedness in sanctifying human, emotional, and moral contexts and setting it in a lab dish for analysis. The concept of such a pried-out value, separate from and independent of subjective feeling, belongs to the abstract, male-managed world of the marketplace, the academic discipline, the controlled experiment, not to the dense daily imprecisions of ordinary life. Yet the concept of pried-out value is, to repeat, central to *Cultural Contradictions*.

Precisely here lies the poignancy of the project. Sharon Hays is no rough-riding debunker of maternal love; she cares for her interviewees, finds (at intervals) intrinsic value in their responses, believes that those responses warrant respect from detached, pragmatic utilitarians. But she can't mount a challenge of the kind necessary to truly join the issue with bottom-line mentality— a challenge based on real distinctions between intrinsic and exchange values, or on fully comprehending assessments of the nature of sympathy. (Tawney's brilliant aphorism "Sympathy is a form of knowledge" again comes to mind.) The calculating, objectifying, prudence-worshipping regime that transforms abhorrence of sentiment into a master virtue is incapable of recognizing the existence of conduct that is supremely valuable for what it is in itself rather than for what it does, accomplishes, or gains, or even for the political influence it may exert as a force of resistance. In the eyes of this regime intrinsic value is weak, ridden with vague mysteries, "feminine." And it follows that a challenge to intellectual orthodoxy based on intrinsic value, and mounted by a woman sociologist, won't be taken seriously.

Yet although she mounts no challenge, Sharon Hays seems less than wholly at ease with the regime. Entrapped in a nowhere land of pseudo-detachment and pseudo-involvement, simultaneously evoking genuine feelings and denigrating them, she continues searching, page after page, for a language and a method that will confer bottom-line invulnerability on useless, profitless, loving vulnerability. No such language exists; no road out of the quandary can be found except through scrupulous valuing of what history has made of women prior to the tyranny of the bottom line—and gender shift is closing that road. Herein lies the pathos of the author's situation and of her book.

12

Self-Censorship and Double Binds

I N EDUCATED, RELATIVELY MONEYED classes, assumptions about male superiority often focus on presumed sexual sophistication rather than physical toughness or worldly power or methodological rigor. The position is that men are relaxed about their sexual needs (avoid idealizing lust, are wisely skeptical of the language of "love" and "fidelity"), and that women who adopt similarly straightforward attitudes thereby grow in strength and smarts. Arm yourself against sentimentality about sex, goes the counsel, and you improve your chances of finding and hewing to paths that assure ascent to equality.

Over the past few decades gender shift culture has translated this line of thinking into an array of institutions—singles bars, one-night stands, mass entertainments dramatizing sexual aggressiveness in women, and much more. A hundred late twentieth-century novels tell of heroines who, following the example of Isadora Wing in Erica Jong's *Fear of Flying* (1973), confront and explore their sexuality. Woman memoirists in number detail their experience as shoppers for porn. TV series study the adventures of career women learning how to treat men "as sex objects"—how to "just go out and have sex like a man," feelinglessly, in simple accord with need. In the series *Sex and the City* a young woman named Carrie is serviced at lunchtime by a man who, afterward, relaxes on his pillow and murmurs expectantly, "My turn." Carrie answers that she has to get back to work. A moment later, safely outside, she turns full-face to the camera, grinning in self-approval. "There," she says. "I've done it. I've just had sex like a man."

Modish commentary on Clinton-Lewinsky celebrated emulators of allegedly standard male sexual behavior. Talk show guests on cable channels and elsewhere affirmed solidarity with Monica the Promiscuous Woman—and, more generally, with women who "have sex like men." The *New York Observer* ran a front-page symposium in which ten well-known woman professionals—writers, editors, fashion designers, publicists—agreed that shock and hostility to the Oval Office affair were marks of benightedness. "Nobody is aggrieved here," opined Elizabeth Benedict. "It's like every girl's dream. You can be the President, and you can fuck the President, too." "All of my woman friends and I," said Patricia Marx, "would be happy to have sex with Clinton and not talk about it." "Oh," exclaimed Erica Jong, herself a participant, "imagine swallowing the President's come."

In Manhattan as elsewhere, in-your-face sexual bravura in this vein obviously isn't the life norm; it is, however, influential because it's backed by the chic period style described earlier—the basic stuff of killer woman fiction, ads, sitcoms, rock lyrics, and the rest. The messages come together as an advanced enlightenment for in vogue contemporary women. Point one of the enlightenment is that women who rise behave like men (i.e., they're free-spirited and bold, following their appetites wherever they lead). Point two is that women who don't conform to the enlightenment can be confidently dismissed as prudes.

It's the memory of repression that legitimizes the dismissal. Manners may indict as sluttish the sexually aggressive woman who alludes, publicly and relishingly, to the thrill of a power-swallow. But the memory of repression connects her with struggles that qualified in their day as heroic. Twentieth-century dramatizations of female sexuality threw open the windows of a sickroom hitherto shut for ages by insistence that the only womanly feelings are delicate feelings and that the only exceptional aptitudes found in womankind are moral aptitudes. Down-and-dirty sexual aggressiveness declared war on hypocrisy, intellectual dimness, and physical and emotional frustration; it was an alternative way of pressing claims to the right to compete; it criticized the cowardice of "nice" women who deferred to male creatures self-celebrated for their inability—also termed free-spiritedness—to honor solemn pledges of constancy. For these reasons, sexual aggressiveness is something more than a gesture of *épater le bourgeois;* it possesses an aura, an overbearing power.

Face to face with this power, sensitively conservative liberationists can't easily mount a criticism that reaches core issues. There are inhibitions to cope with, concern about sounding like a goody sermonizer: humorless, hysterical, unprofessionally judgmental, anti-feminist. There's doubt that anyone can actually chide, without sanctimony, the gleeful aping by females of "male" self-indulgence and cynicism. There's fear that one will appear to believe that the struggle against repression never was, or that one will seem to be secretly jealous of a sister's daring independence, or will sideline oneself in the major contests now determining women's future. The effect of such anxiety is to muffle the critical voice, sometimes in fact to turn it against itself.

An example: Not long after the *New York Observer* ran its symposium featuring enthusiasts of masculinizing aggression, the paper printed a column meant on its face to represent a different perspective. The writer was Molly Haskell, a film critic and columnist whose pieces treat non-celebrity Manhattan doings and past and present domestic life. (Haskell's husband is the pioneering film critic Andrew Sarris; on occasion her columns glance affectionately at his vagaries.)

The column in question opens with an account of a dinner party—the guests are woman professionals—during which discussion centers on Monica Lewinsky. "By the end of dinner," Haskell writes, she and a young friend she calls M. W. "were barely speaking, locked in fierce disagreement as to whether Monica was more sinned against than sinning." And this small war—"furious tongue-lashings and stony silences"—continues throughout the rest of the evening. "She kept accusing me of portraying Monica as villain, I charged her with 'victim feminism.'"

Given this start, the expectation is that the piece ahead will deal with core issues. Haskell's evident distaste for Lewinsky suggests impatience with people who refuse to respect marital and other commitments that fellow human beings make to one another; it also suggests readiness to challenge the fashionable orthodoxy holding that shedding "femininity" and adopting stereotypical male attitudes to sexual relationships speeds women's progress toward equality. How will M. W. meet the challenge? Can Haskell set this young woman straight? Bring on the fight, says the reader. Let the issues breathe.

It doesn't happen. Mounting her bicycle, the writer pedals backward, hunting an escape route. First she hides out in the *Rashomon* theme. Groups differ, we're told—the young from the old, men from women, and so on—in their perceptions of the young woman involved in Clinton's downfall; people "bring [their] own experience, fears [and] unconscious resistances" to the story, thereby determining its meaning. ("Women either swoon in approbation or forgive the schmoozingly lascivious good-on-the-issues President while men cry 'Stupido!' and call for his resignation.")

Next a digression on the resemblance between the Oval Office events and "the work of a particularly inept filmmaker whose tone remains unclear." ("No self-respecting screenwriter would leave the moral status of the characters so ambiguous, and even in the ads we would understand where Monica belonged—was she a star or a supporting player, a virgin or a whore, *femme fatale* or innocent victim?") Next, an abrupt change of subject—to the fad for dirty words. ("Taking sex into the public arena has opened the floodgates on dirty talk. Lit up by the rush of adrenaline and identification—who needs anti-depressants when we've got sexy disasters?—we're all degraded by the language we use.") And thereafter: podium sonorities. "[The] Clinton-Monica escapade is not hugely important in itself, but is part of a pattern of slippery, sleazy, quasi-illegal and grossly irresponsible behavior that has spread a thick layer of viscosity over the land."

There's one brief return to seriousness, one passage in which Haskell's relative isolation among the hipsters flashes back into sight. She remembers in her column a moment when she chided M. W. for being eager to bed Bill Clinton—actually cites both her shock at this eagerness and the words in which she expressed the shock. No sooner does she get out the words, though, than the fear of chiding resumes its assault. She withdraws once more into disavowal and self-accusation:

[M. W.] said the words I'd been hearing from all too many of my friends. "I'd have done it in a second!" [meaning had sex with Clinton]. I was shocked. "Then you'd have been a tart or a star-f—— r," I said. Was this bravado on her part, or straitlaced primness on mine? Am I jealous of her relative freedom as a young woman, and moralistically disapproving?

Haskell's initial insistence that she was fully engaged in the argument and her avowal of dismay at M. W.'s position and that of "all too many of my friends"—these are at obvious odds with the *Rashomon* turn and the "smart" shuttling among personae and tones. (There's quite a bit of shuttling: with "I was shocked" and "tart," Haskell plays the outsider, a socially sniffish lady looking down on coarse-spoken toughies; with "star-fucker," she's inside, knowledgeable about what groupies are and do; with the sanitizing dash in "f—— r," she conjoins hip and square.) But the risks of preceptorship are simply too high. *Better not to look anti-feminist— somebody droning on about constancy and other old lady obscurantisms. Better to join the general chuckling at judgmental types. Better to drop women-becoming-men and descant instead on multiple viewpoints and the large threat of viscosity.*

In one sector of the opinion-making classes, gender shift functions as a silencer, intimidating, self-censoring, inducing suspicion that the right place for strong moral convictions is the bottom of the deepest deep freeze. An internalized Big Brother, in short.

Elsewhere in the same classes gender shift produces a double-binding ambivalence in self-styled sex radicals—women stunned by the influence of their own aggressive sexual behavior. The radicals in question are pioneers who waged and won the struggle for sexual expression, including the right to "have sex like a man." Trailblazers all, they possess first-class bona fides—can't be attacked as closet puritans, would-be moralizers, enemies of the large cause of women-becoming-men. And their purpose clearly isn't to put down their sisters but rather to make sense of the unintended consequences of the victory they themselves won. But a sense of contradiction dogs their work; more than one concludes her effort to clarify the contemporary sexual scene not with a flourish of satisfaction but with a rueful acknowledgment that she herself is intensely—even hopelessly—confused.

An example: a *Vogue* article by Mary Gaitskill ("Ready, Able, and Unwilling: Why Men Say No to Sex") on negative male reaction to aggressive sexual behavior in women. The piece opens with an anecdote—told in conventionally hard-edged style—about an occasion when a woman said yes to sex and a man said no:

> At a festive all-girl brunch recently, I heard one friend ask another what had happened between her and the cute guy she'd gone home with the previous night. "Not much" was the answer. "I went down on him for about half an hour and then he wouldn't fuck me." "That sucks," said someone. "Literally," agreed the one for whom it was all too true. There were expressions of mild disdain for the bum who'd flaked, scattered laughter, and then the conversation moved on.

The conversation stuck with Gaitskill because, she says, she herself had had similar experiences, and so had several of her friends.

Much of her piece samples their stories. A great-looking thirty-year-old woman meets a charming man at a cocktail party and is seduced on their second date. "They get in bed, he gets her hot—and then he turns over and goes to sleep, although, as she puts it, 'it must have been hard to sleep with that raging hard-on.'" On a third date they get in bed, and this time he asks her to masturbate. "Assuming that his request is an interesting prelude, she complies. Afterward, he turns over to 'sleep.'"

Or there's the thirty-eight-year-old divorced woman in San Francisco who's interested in a thirty-five-year-old architect who lives in Los Angeles. He invites her down to visit him, whereupon "they make out, they talk endlessly, but he doesn't want to penetrate her—because, he says, he has problems with intimacy and involvement. They analyze this until she passes out. She goes home frustrated and hurt—and disgusted by his 'wimpiness.'"

Or there's a beautiful twenty-five-year-old medical student who meets a handsome Italian on an airplane and offers to show him New York City. "They, too, have a great time, which ends with them thrashing passionately in her bed. Only after he puts on a condom does he decide that he'd 'rather have a friend than a fling.'"

Trying to uncover the meaning of the syndrome, Gaitskill turns to friends and acquaintances for help. One possibility, she hears, is that men are becoming hostile to being perceived as sexual objects. "One 25-year-old man I talked to told me that he has on more than one occasion withheld sex at the last moment as an expression of irritation at female sexual hubris. 'I'm just sick of this whole feminist thing,' the man tells her. 'Let's have sex, sex is great.' I'm like, 'How dare you treat me like a sex object?'"

Another possibility is that aberrant, insensitive women who "identify with the pro-sex label" are reacting so strongly against the sexual restrictions placed on women that they're "stuck in the reactive position." Their sexuality becomes a polemic or role.

I have a friend in Chicago [Gaitskill writes] who constantly talks about sex. About half the time she talks about men like they're bitches. . . . There always seems to be some guy she's got to have, right now. She doesn't want to listen to his tedious conversation—he's not that smart, really—she just wants to fuck him. And if he's not available she'll call somebody else. . . . Sometimes, when she starts going on like that, I want to grab her and say, Where are you? Because she seems too insensitive and uncomplicated to be real.

Gaitskill's conclusion, however, is that the troubles she describes can't be traced to the influential excesses of aberrant Demi Moore or Sharon Stone characters, or to the neuroses of objectified men. The problem, she avers, is lost gentleness; women are losing "the ability to experience the tender feelings that make us aware of our own frailty. I mean the ability to be gentle."

After centuries of imprisonment in stereotypes of weakness, women-becoming-men break out of airless inhibition, self-protectiveness, cock-teasing disingenuousness. They enter a real world wherein down-to-earth acknowledgment of their sexual being becomes—not easy but possible. Effortfully following the male model, they teach themselves to enjoy sexual impulse and sexual experience. They school themselves in toughness and independence, break the craving for "commitments," stop exploiting the "superiority" two-facedly accorded the good and the pure and the non-appetitive. Through a hugely demanding exercise of will they become free spirits, able even to laugh off humiliation or rejection. ("I went down on him for about half an hour and then he wouldn't fuck me." . . . Scattered laughter.)

And now the voice of wisdom preaches against toughness. It tells women they must become gentle, need to study vulnerability—tells them to learn the lines they scorned as weakly feminine ("He said he wanted to get to know me before getting into the sex thing"), lectures them on "respect and basic kindness."

The original feminist voices spoke with a feeling for the complexity and ambivalence that Gaitskill seems now to express. They treated what history has made of women as a resource as well as a tragedy; they alluded regularly to the double truths created by centuries of conjoined hypocrisy and idealism; they acknowledged femininity at once as a locus of delicate feelings, "natural" tenderness, and reluctance to cause hurt, and as fantasy and deceit. Nor was early feminism undone by hard questions. (How is an independent woman's eagerness for equality to coexist with both her delight in her sexuality and her capacity for and interest in permanent human attachment?)

But the seismic shift toward the new culture wrecked the bridges connecting the present with thinkers capable of coping with irony-laced double truths. "Softness," "tender feelings," the gift of considerateness cannot now be grasped as elements of emotional and intellectual growth and distinction. For minds awakening to the limits of toughness, there's the disorientation associated with any sudden psychological step forward—a bewildering turnabout, a momentary unsettling of all assumptions about what should and should not be. "If men are confused about sex," cries Gaitskill at the close of her piece, "I don't blame them. I'm confused about sex." Admissions such as this open a view of gender shift "freedoms" as entailing, for some, imprisonment in injurious double binds.

13

Shades of Darkness

ATHER MORE TROUBLING are the situations of minds persuaded that the cause of equality demands not mere readiness to have sex like a man but proof of personal steeliness—a will unfazed by the severest physical, emotional, and psychological challenges, unmoved even in the presence of torture itself. At the turn of the millennium an increasing number of widely known women writers, performers, filmmakers, and novelists have commenced modeling iron imperviousness to horror—an imperviousness seemingly imagined as "masculine." In literary, relatively pretentious versions of the mode, heroines manifest an easy inwardness with males who savor brutality and commit madly perverse—cruelly unspeakable—crimes. The writers explore the dark interiors of demented protagonists' minds in a manner blending Faulknerian elements with the grotesquerie of Hubert Selby's story "Tra-La-La"; losing themselves in sadistic chaos, they sometimes merge their own authorial identities with those of killer male psychopaths.

Less pretentious explorations of this mode—pop explorations—avoid these extremes. Heroines of crime stories by women writers conjoin old-style omnicompetence (among numberless male forebears, Sherlock Holmes and James Bond) with new visions of female invulnerability; the heroines compulsively ridicule squea-mishness, and compete against and win out over males in demand-ing physical and psychological competitions. Always, though, the creators guard against alienating audiences; they provide frequent assurances that their hard-nosed heroines aren't without feeling. The multitalented heroine of Patricia Cornwell's crime novels, Kay Scarpetta, is a lawyer, physician, firearms expert, gifted cook and baker, surrogate mother to a troubled niece, and chief medical ex-aminer for the Commonwealth of Virginia; she's allowed to dwell caringly on the terror experienced by the victims of the crimes she undertakes to solve.

Yet Scarpetta is, nevertheless, highly contemptuous of "sensi-tivity." At work in the morgue, whether cutting open the dead ("up to [her] wrists in blood") or sewing them up ("suturing the last few inches of the Y incision, which ran in a wide seam from [the mur-der victim's] pubis to her sternum and forked over her chest"), she maintains postures of emotional detachment. Her reports of medi-cal findings in ghastly rape-murders are coolly ironic:

> The killer probably misfired. Most of the seminal fluid I collected was on the bedcovers and her legs. Or else the only instrument he successfully inserted was his knife. The sheets beneath her were stiff and dark with dried blood. Had he not strangled her, she probably would have bled to death.

When killers try to add Scarpetta to their victim list, she fights back effectively with a dissecting knife. There are moments in the Scarpetta series, in fact, when the heroine's joy in savage combat is depicted with vividness matching that of Spenser—Robert B. Parker's detective hero—crushing an opponent's face in one of the slugging matches that decorate Parker's pages: "[I] plunged the surgical blade into his upper thigh. With both hands I cut as much as I could as he shrieked. Arterial blood squirted across my face as I pulled the knife out and his transected femoral artery hemor-rhaged to the rhythm of his horrible heart."

And everywhere in Cornwell's mysteries attention is drawn to the difference between the medical examiner's firm matter-of-factness and her male co-workers' susceptibility to nausea and collapse. Morgue security guards won't touch the cold storage chamber that Kay opens and closes a half-dozen times daily—too terrified of corpses. ("Many guards and most cleaning crews did not work for [Scarpetta] long.") Wingo, Scarpetta's autopsy technician, strikes his boss as "much too sensitive for his own good and I sometimes worried about him. He so keenly identified with the victims it wasn't uncommon for him to cry over unusually heinous cases." When Scarpetta slices through a dead woman's skull with a Stryker saw, "bony dust unpleasantly drift[ing] on the air," male observers "retreat to the other end of the suite." When the stench of burning corpse in the crematorium room hits tough-guy detective Pete Marino and examiner Scarpetta simultaneously, she displays presence of mind, finds towels to wrap her hands so that she can shut down the furnace; weak-kneed Marino vomits ignominiously.

It bears emphasis that at no point in work of this sort—traditional having-it-both-ways pop—does the novelist-narrator represent herself or her heroine as immune to repugnance at the bestial and vile. Scarpetta rarely emotes, but her fans know that the reason isn't that she's heartless but that her sense of self-discipline forbids emoting. They understand, further, that she and her creator are humanely responsive, and they're comforted by signals that virtue alone is the ultimate cause her steeliness serves.

Less comforting for the reader is the rule in literary versions of this masculinist mode. Joyce Carol Oates's novel *Zombie* (1995) details loathsome crimes—and provides no reassuringly civilized point-of-view character or narrator to distance the audience from the horror. The book's narrator and protagonist is a thirty-one-year-old male psychopath named Quentin; Oates never ventures outside his mentality. A faculty brat (son of a physicist), this killer is obsessed with the notion of creating a personal slave or zombie: "A ZOMBIE . . . would say, 'Fuck me in the ass, Master, until I bleed blue guts.' . . . He would lick with his tongue as bidden. He would suck with his mouth as bidden."

Maddened by fantasy, Quentin studies medical texts that describe frontal lobotomies and other psychosurgical procedures by means of which (as he believes) a normal grown male can be transformed into a condition of total dependency. From one surgical text he learns about the leucotome, or ice pick, which is hammered through the bony orbit above the eyeball in the course of a lobotomy; his first purchase of tools for performing the procedures includes an ice pick. Once his surgical kit is complete, he launches on his appalling project. He drugs a succession of sexual partners, imprisons them in the basement of the building where he works as caretaker, subjects them to the hideous torture of back-alley lobotomy. And his creator—the novelist Joyce Oates—nowhere shudders, nowhere withdraws from the horror.

The sane adults who populate this psychopath's world are an incompetent lot. Quentin's overeducated parents don't suspect what he's up to; they're oblivious fools. The lawyer they hire to protect him is hopelessly gullible. The law enforcement authorities who try and fail to build a case against him are inept. Yet *Zombie* isn't a book about blindness; indeed, it doesn't have a clearly discernible theme. It stands forth rather as its own kind of demonstration project—evidence that a woman writer is perfectly equal to the challenge of living inside atrocities once thought of as material reserved to males.

Frightful atrocities they are, described at excruciating length. *Zombie*'s fifty-plus short chapters trace the particulars of its protagonist's feelings beginning with delirious anticipation as he imagines, in a dry run as surgeon, his upcoming triumph ("so EXCITED suddenly with no warning I COME IN MY PANTS before I can fucking unzip"). There are overviews of his frustrations with his first victims—youngsters he calls Bunnygloves, Raisineyes, Big Guy. Bunnygloves goes into convulsions when Quentin drives the ice pick into his head. He screams through the sponge tied in his mouth, snaps the baling wire lashing his ankles, and dies in twelve minutes.

"RAISINEYES" survives for seven hours in a tub. "BIG GUY . . . lived maybe fifteen hours I think dying as I was fucking him in the ass." At the book's midpoint Oates steps closer to the terrible interiors of the mayhem in progress. Her Quentin reports that, as he went to work on a fourth victim he calls NO-NAME, "my dick [was] hard as a club, & big as a club," and that this murder did in fact bring him to ejaculation:

> When I inserted [the ice pick] through the "bony orbit" NO-NAME freaked out struggling & screaming through the sponge & there was a gush of blood & I came, I lost control & I came, so hard I kept COMING . . . fucking ice pick rammed up to the hilt in NO-NAME's eye up into his brain & the black kid was dying, he was dead, blood gushing like from a giant nosebleed.

Subsequent accounts of Quentin's procedures stretch on for a half-dozen pages at a time, chronicling his ascent—via an alter ego he calls TODD CUTLER—to a quasi-heroic identity. The death of SQUIRREL runs to eight pages of abominations painful to sample:

> I squeezed [his penis] to rouse some life in him & his muscles jerked & he seemed to cry out inside the sponge. . . . A homely kid with blood-caked nostrils, I was getting pissed at him. His cock shriveled so tiny, like a ten-year-old's, & that look in his eyes. & thrashing his head, & trying again to fight—to fight *me!*—weak as a broken worm.

Joyce Carol Oates's impersonation of a psychopath isn't flawless; *Zombie*'s endless monologue often falls into idioms harder to connect with the character's background than with the author's. (Never a literature student, Quentin distractingly quotes—without attribution—phrases from obscure Eng Lit texts, for example, Swift's "Voyage to the Houyhnyms.")

But technical literary faults are beside the point. The prime issues raised by works such as *Zombie* concern non-aesthetic matters, chief among them the costs of unrelenting pursuit of freedom from stereotypical identity. Speaking as Quentin P. effects a release, for the author, from qualities and traits traditionally perceived as "feminine"; throughout its length the book carries overtones of pride. *Yesterday we were sealed off—prisoned in "natural" loving-kindness (delicacy of feeling, sensitivity, revulsion at the vile), frozen in "sensibility," denied the right to self-realization. But that past is over. Nothing now excludes us from the brutish, nothing locks our imagination in decorum and politesse. We're free to live inside Todd Cutler's vilest deeds, and we're under no obligation to render normative judgment—to indict his "horrible heart." We're free to work in-side—to straddle the terrified victim and to grasp his little pigtail, "banging his face against the floor & fucking him in the ass my cock enormous so the skin tore & bled, ONE TWO THREE thrusts piercing to his guts like a sword." Freedom is the right to transcend the normative. Women own the right.*

To this day tremors of surprise, even of shock, figure in the response to women acting, in life or art, as mad merciless killers, contemptuous of the normative. Ordinary humankind derives much of its intuition of the reality of goodness from numberless deeds of self-sacrifice, both observed and represented, that define historical womanhood—what the past has made of women. Bewilderment at a woman writer's seemingly exuberant embrace of barbarity in a sense saves books like *Zombie* from meaninglessness; readers talk back to the silence at the core of the work, chiding the refusal to judge, composing the appropriate indictment.

But as the assault on sensibility in fiction and elsewhere proceeds, and as scorn of historical models of gentleness and sympathy mounts, writers bend themselves more directly to ridicule of shocked responses, dismissing them as evasive, sentimental, and self-indulgent, shaming readers who yield to them. Both skin-deep hardness à la Cornwell and noncommittal masks à la Oates are rejected; heroines are required to prove not only that they're clean of revulsion at evil but also that they can endure—with heart-chilling impassivity to the very point of death—murderous levels of physical torture. In Susannah Moore's *In the Cut* (1995), a thirtyish woman professor of linguistics and creative writing (she's given no name) becomes entangled with two male police detectives: a murderer whose crimes the heroine is aware of and his partner. Her dread sharpens as the cops mock and insult her ("You're one of those broads, right? You know, man, one of those feminist broads"), but she learns to trade barbs with them, and comes to imitate their ice-cold deadpan styles of speech. (She jokes at one point that there are people "whom you can fuck only if you have permission to kill them immediately afterward.") At length, stirred by an impulse to draw close to the murderer's brutal partner, she has sex repeatedly with the man: "I was a little worried when I realized that it was more than wanting him to like me. I realized that I wanted to be like him."

The murderer's trademark in *In the Cut* is that he cuts off the nipples of his woman victims for "souvenirs"; at the book's climax he murders the heroine, first subjecting her to this torture. The torture scene—an unendurable image of gender shift savagery—veers between pity and inhuman detachment, and at the end the author invokes the heroine's defiant stoicism as admirable:

> My hand over my chest, the blood finding its way between my closed fingers, my ribs light in my warm hand, my breast lighter without the rose nipple to give it weight, to give it meaning.
> "Does it hurt?" he asked.
> It was difficult to move my head. "All right," I said. "It's all right."

Abhorrence of fearfulness—fury at stereotypical "feminine" fainthearts—lies close to the center of works such as *In the Cut;* in their pages innocence, gentleness, and other qualities conventionally associated with women's virtuous nature are redefined as vices, and "weakness" becomes the cardinal sin. And, at its most extreme, the passion to sever, once and for all, the connection between

"virtue" and the "weaker sex" drives authors to create sadistic heroines, characters who themselves become experimenters in perversion, abusers of children, or worse. Moments arrive in these works
when the authors—creators of women-becoming-men-becoming-
sadists—seem caught in truly impenetrable confusion, incapable
of commenting on, much less interpreting, the chaos into which,
presumably for the purpose of clarifying the directions of their own
lives, they plunge their characters. But even at those moments—
apogees of bafflement and fear of madness—the writers cling to
perversion as deliverance.

As in *The End of Alice* (1996), a work of fiction by the woman
novelist A. M. Homes. The book's unnamed heroine—a nineteen-
year-old sophomore at a women's college—identifies with a male
pedophile-murderer serving his twenty-fourth year in Sing Sing
for the gruesome murder of a subteen named Alice Somerfield.
The heroine engages the murderer in intimate correspondence—
encourages him to rehearse the details of his acts of cruelty and in
time imitates his ways, abusing and raping a twelve-year-old neighborhood boy.

Her obsession is explained as the result of geographical accident:
she lived on the same suburban street as Alice Somerfield, and her
elders' terror of the murderer—they wouldn't let her play outside
until he was caught—roused her scorn. Toward the close of the tale
the heroine approaches an expression of guilt about her relish of
"masculine" sadism. But retribution and atonement are remote
from the book's spirit (the jacket copy describes the work as "exhilaratingly perverse"). *The End of Alice* is, for most of its length, a
celebration of the onset of demented boldness. In her mid-teens
the heroine drives often to Sing Sing, observes the off-duty prison
guards, parks where she can hear the noise of the prisoners. She
spends a night in the motel room where Alice was murdered and
dismembered.

Conceiving a vision of herself as potential molester, she chooses
young Matthew, the subteen, and stalks him—writes the prisoner

about a planned project of molestation. She speaks of longing "to sample" the lad, of "drooling" in anticipation. Fully self-invented as a pervert, she turns her plans into deeds, not only foully abusing the boy but filling both her letters and her diaries with numberless moments of prideful glee in depravity:

> She leaves [the boy] laid out in the grass and moves over to the sprinkler. . . . Both breasts in hand, she tilts her hips back and forth, rocking, coming not just once but in a set, a small series of cataclysmic constructions. . . . Beneath her, as her hips continue to sway, the water automatically turns itself off. Nearly finished, she goes to her man [the twelve-year-old], stands above him, and lets go, sprinkling him with a steamy stream, pissing on his privates.

Interspersed with ecstatic recounting of her crimes are passages in which the male sadist-voyeur records his own delight in the techne of torture:

> For the procedure to commence, I sit between her legs, her mound faces fuzz up. . . .
> There is something to them watching me while I work the razor, stropping the blade before their eyes — letting them wonder where it will ultimately go. Before I sharpen, I sweep the dull end over their slits, their tits, and into their mouths, and sometimes if I'm feeling frank, I flip it over, cut off a hank of their hair, and tuck it into their mouths — girls like to suck on that, you see them doing it all the time.

"I'm not afraid of you anymore," says the heroine in her final address to the prisoner, "I'm more afraid of myself." And the book ends with the official account of the Somerfield murder, seemingly recited by the prisoner himself to the young initiate still wholly enraptured by the crime:

> Initial five [wounds] on upper torso, jagged, indicative of struggle; remaining fifty-nine, smooth cuts, most likely occurring after death. Victim decapitated, her head positioned between her legs, weapon

recovered at the scene—jammed in victim's vagina. Buck hunting knife. Fingerprints on handle match accused. Lab identifies menstrual blood and semen in vagina, anus, and mouth of deceased. Accused apparently continued relations with victim after her death. Victim's face and body covered in kisses. Accused dipped his lips in victim's blood and then kissed deceased repeatedly. Victim's blood found on accused's clothing, hair, fingernails, ears, painted over his lower torso and genitals.

Considered as a purely literary phenomenon, the emergence of transgressive heroines in serious fiction qualifies as a minor event in the continuing history of romanticism: to be placed, with care for the complexity of the relationships, in the line of Byron, Sade, Nietzsche, and others. But because of the hugely expanded cultural production in which gamy illicit negatives—"having sex like a man," liberation through violence and perversion—are identified as routes to growth and fulfillment for women, purely literary "placement" isn't adequate.

Neither is the brand of moralizing that is keener on indictment than on diagnosis. I believe—for reasons already stated—that the body of cultural material described in this and earlier chapters is of large political, social, and moral consequence and that the movements of thought and feeling it legitimizes need countering. But if there is to be any release from the maze in which thought and feeling are now confined, the resistance has to be canny. Resisters need to bear in mind, to begin with, that cultural influence works in complicated ways: books, films, commercials—media content in the large—provide new models for behavior, but excessively mechanical accounts of its impact can't be trusted. Human beings are not piano keys.

Other, more vexing problems arise from the embeddedness, in human history, of negatives in positives and vice versa—a thicket of contradictions. What the past has made of women has significantly stunted women's growth; gender shift (when assessed from a viewpoint different from mine) is among the factors encouraging fullness of development, strength, and the expression of assertive independence, and hence can't merely be derided.To put the same point differently, it is possible to believe both that what the past has made of women significantly fostered the moral development of the race, and that views of woman as the fount of all virtue (extremist feminism has often pushed these views) are preposterous and warrant vigorous correction. No exit from this labyrinth, in short, except through realism about contradictory elements both in history and in human nature.

Given the current climate and the intricacy of the pertinent problems, the right course is to combat at every possible juncture the forces now bent on oversimplifying issues of equality. This entails trying to shed light (as I have aimed to do) on what is wrong with the choices that the culture of gender shift presents as life-enhancing. And it also entails clarifying practical means of serving— and animating—the ideals of engagement and variousness dwelled on in Part II.

The early chapters of this book launched a study of the contemporary marketing of women-becoming-men—images and performances that present the progress or growth of the individual woman as a straight, untempered, unleavened movement into conformity with maleness misread as killer toughness and ruthlessness. The near-total obliviousness to history characteristic of this material is matched, as it happens, in other sectors of contemporary expression that are a step removed from mass audiences yet nevertheless influential. The same culture that produces panegyrics on adultery in *Cosmopolitan* and numberless movies about women murderers also produces, in ostensible reaction, outpourings of ahistorical gender *affirmation*—contrarian material depicting the progress of the individual as a movement into conformity with a cramping version of prerevolutionary woman. And the higher reaches of academe are producing an equally ahistorical mode of gender thought—abstract, remote from real lives, committed to treating gender as mere "performance."

I attempt, in the closing chapters of *Killer Woman Blues,* to come to terms with the simplicities and delusions found in this sector of the new culture—the sector committed to contrarian or reactionary affirmation of "traditional womankind." And, as was the case with the survey of theorists of variousness in Part II, my attempt to represent the contemporary school of reaction is based on personal conviction: I believe that the work of the writers chosen qualifies as paradigmatic in that it provides a view both of the themes now in general favor among self-styled traditionalists and of the forms in which—on the right and left—those themes currently find expression.

Time now to examine the themes and forms in question.

FOUR

Traducing History
vs. Growing Capital

14

Three Styles of Nostalgia

i. the modesty monger

THE APRIL 1996 issue of *Commentary,* the conservative monthly, contained an article titled "A Ladies Room of One's Own," a denunciation of coed bathrooms in the dormitories of Williams College. The piece was reprinted in *Reader's Digest,* swiftly launched a discussion in the newsmagazines and talk shows, and even—in time—stirred the college's administration to reverse itself and begin building single-sex bathrooms on campus. The author, a Williams sophomore named Wendy Shalit, reported herself overwhelmed with fan mail from females; upon graduating she began a journalistic career, writing for the *Wall Street Journal* and the *Weekly Standard* and establishing herself as an animated young voice on the right. In 1999 Shalit published her first book, *A Return to Modesty: Discovering the Lost Virtue.*

Keen on erudition, *A Return to Modesty* cites authors ranging from Maimonides to Mandeville, regularly bullies readers for their ignorance ("any cursory acquaintance with ancient Chinese sex manuals . . . will reveal," etc.), and glides within a page from high pedantry to senior-high platform platitude. ("What, then, will become of this generation? Is all lost for us? Should we give up and get depressed?") But the book nevertheless has cultural interest because of the light it casts on the role of falsifications of history in weakening the cause of gender flexibility and promoting the cause of gender shift.

As a counter-historian, Wendy Shalit isn't notably orderly or disciplined; she darts from showboat bibliolatry to autobiographical rumination to attacks on "extremist feminism" to mockery of whatever aspect of perceived liberal cant is in current public notice. But there's a unifying ambition—to persuade audiences that the movement for women's rights was and remains a unidimensional power grab—and there are recurring *a*historical themes. One is that feminism's main goal has been and remains to establish that the sexes are the same. Another is that the pattern of male-female relationships over the centuries has been shaped by the obsessive hunt, on the part of the weaker sex, for means of ending its weakness. Yet another theme is that the changes wrought by women's liberation, the sexual revolution, and allied events are largely hype and will shortly be rescinded.

The starting point of *A Return to Modesty* is that the troubles afflicting young women—from rape to stalking to "whirlpooling" (sexual assault by several men on a girl swimming)—reflect loss of respect for modesty. And the loss of respect is traced, throughout the book, to feminism's alleged fixation on sameness—its certainty that acceptance of the sameness of the sexes holds the key to equality between the sexes. Shalit's many targets—popular culture, weak-kneed college administrators, the federal government, highbrow academic theorists—are uniformly viewed as feminist toadies and surrogates, spreaders of the gospel that "to be equal to men, [women] must be the same in every respect."

Feminist-dominated college administrators preach mindless sex-blindness, and the cowed federal government insists that if women aren't as interested in sports as men, it must be a violation of Title IX. "What is sought is no longer equality, but sameness." Popular culture tirelessly propagandizes for the equal rights cause of promiscuity for all. (*A Return to Modesty* spends many pages on the equality-means-sameness messages delivered in movies and videos, and in magazines such as *Glamour*, filled with tributes to women who sweat and swagger.)

And theorists in elite universities expound the feminist-inspired doctrine of anti-essentialism: the position that woman is a "fictive category," and that significant biological differences between men and women don't exist. Shalit recounts a meeting of the philosophy course in which she was told she is an essentialist. What's that? she asked her classmates, and they explained that an essentialist is somebody who thinks the sexes aren't the same. But aren't they different? Shalit asks, and the classmates chortle. You're supposed to transcend essentialism, says a male seatmate. But how can I transcend, Shalit asks, if I don't know what I'm meant to transcend? More chortling. Once you mention differences—any differences—you're an essentialist and that's not allowed. Her classmates were as firm in their accusations and denunciations as they would have been in dealing with a racist. "No one entertained my view. . . . They just rolled their eyes."

Not just "anti-essentialism" but a whole congeries of social plagues issues from the obsession with abolishing difference. Worsening male violence to women: when you train men to assume women are exactly the same as they are, you can't teach them to be kind and gentle around women. The collapse of women's moral standards: the people who set the rules nowadays are committed to "sayings like 'Equality means equally bad as well as equally good.'" Also the "failure" of the sexual revolution and of women's liberation—two further results of vacuous feminist insistence that the sexes are the same, that differences are traceable solely to oppression, and that female modesty is unimportant.

The baleful influence of feminism is everywhere, in short—and the reason it's baleful is that, as indicated, feminists can't get beyond their fixation on sameness dogma.

Shalit's second theme—namely, that a preoccupation with balance-of-power issues drives all women's behavior, whether or not they're feminists—is developed in the book's account of the origins of modesty and immodesty. Modesty is seen as a shrewdly conceived strategy invented by a "cartel of virtue"; this single-sex cartel closely resembles male-managed monopolies in commerce and industry. "In the past," Shalit writes, "women secured the chances of lasting love by forming a kind of cartel: they had an implicit agreement not to engage in premarital or extramarital sex with men. This made it more likely that men would marry and stay married to them."

Whence came immodesty? In Wendy Shalit's account, slit skirts, obscenity, "promiscuity," husband-stealing, and the rest are, like modesty, realpolitical maneuvers. They're strategies meant to communicate strength and invulnerability—to trick men out of their condescension to the weaker sex and thereby ensure women's survival in the contest for short-term mates. The trick fails, partly because men know that women are physically weaker, partly because women really want long-term mates. "As with all cartels," Shalit writes, not excluding the cartel of virtue,

> there were incentives for individual women to cheat or "chisel" on the agreement and have affairs out of wedlock. But in chiseling, something unexpected happened to these women, too. Most of the women I know who are living with men hope that these men will marry them. And most of the women I know who have had affairs with married men hope that the men will ultimately leave their wives for *them*—and when they do, they don't want little adulteresses romping around their new husband. . . .
>
> This is why, if we are ever going to reduce the survival value there is in immodesty, there [must] be not five or six women following this or that arbitrary rule, but a real cultural shift. We must decide as women to look upon sex out of wedlock as not such a cool thing, after all, and recreate the cartel of virtue.

Male-female relationships over the centuries reflect, on this view, the impact of a succession of schemes by which the weaker sex tries to counter its weakness. The scheme called modesty works better than the scheme called immodesty, therefore best to return to it, embracing the pretenses of purity and remoteness from sexual desire which, in yesteryear, intimidated at least some men into permanent commitments.

And that return, Shalit claims, introducing her third theme, is well under way at the present time. Her parents' generation doesn't believe this, she admits. They don't think that the sexual and motherhood revolutions can be reversed. But, citing evidence of a resurgence of marriage, chaste courtship, and disillusionment among women about the work world, she avers that "romantic woman . . . is starting to make a huge comeback." The reason is once again realpolitical: "Those who are returning to virtue are doing so for precisely sensual reasons. They are often totally secular, but have found vice boring and insipid. . . . Modesty is the proof that morality is sexy."

The most obvious trashing of history in *A Return to Modesty* is the representation of feminism as totally absorbed from its inception with establishing the sameness of the sexes. Genius theorists, revolutionary humanists, thoughtful moderates, kooks, flamethrowers, and many others have contributed to the discourse of feminism over the years. Some among them, including some spokespersons for equality-means-sameness, fully deserve the scorn that the author of *A Return to Modesty* heaps on them.

But there's a difference between censuring an ideological extravagance associated with a multidimensional reform movement and claiming there's nothing to that movement except a single ideological extravagance. A major explicitly reiterated theme of leaders from Mary Wollstonecraft and John Stuart Mill to Catharine MacKinnon and Germaine Greer has been that feminism's project for women is precisely *not* that of becoming "the same as men." Yes! in thunder to campaigns for equal access to rights and power. No! in thunder to actions aping the ways of male power brokers. Yes! in thunder to challenging those ways with criticism bent on transforming values. No! in thunder to any allegedly feminist program, position, or theory that finds egocentricity and rapacity worthy of emulation by females. Shalit's willful disregard for these and other markers and anchors of the feminist cause cancels the past.

The same holds for her account of the origins of the behaviors on which her book is focused. The assertion that modesty was invented by an advantage-seeking, cynically motivated cartel of virtue is mathematically clear in outline but remote as the dimmest sitcom from the complex life circumstances that generate values and sustain them. Cartel-forming woman as Shalit describes her lacks footing in the contradictions and anomalies of pre-liberation social history and moral life; her modesty is detached both from humility, selflessness, and caregiving and from masculine oppression—reduced to a tool in the market competition for committed mates. And *im*modesty is similarly reduced; it's treated as a mere power play, utterly unconnected with struggles against servility and evasiveness, prudery and smugness.

With history thus revoked, women's past and present alike are rendered morally weightless, and so, too, is feminism itself. There are no links between the women's movement and the conditions of oppression and enforced generosity that developed women's capacity (and need) to imagine a better civil and domestic order. Nor is feminism connected with the courage and independence that, in more recent times, expanded women's capacity (and need) to imagine themselves as creatures of appetite, admiration for candor, and scorn for hypocrisy. Real change is unthinkable; hence the content of feminism as a criticism of an immoral society can be ignored. The only choices are those between "becoming a man" and "returning" to old-style femininity ("clearly modern woman still longs for courtship and romance")—between a morally empty modesty and a morally empty immodesty.

Real change is unthinkable: this, of course, is the point. Reducing past struggles for change to mere eruptions of manipulativeness and self-doubt casts a shadow over present and future struggles for change. It obscures continuities of moral aspiration. From the earliest days, the campaign for women's rights roused intense interest in the possibility of change. And that interest stimulated, in turn, far-ranging analyses of women's character and psychology (men's as well). Woman as caregiver, as incarnation of mercy, tenderness, and generosity: did she come into being because of her intrinsic nature or because male oppressors forced her into the mold? Does woman's progress toward wholeness require repudiation of the selfless, caregiving past and an embrace of the hard-nosed egocentricity associated with male "leaders"? Might both sexes advance if criticism were directed equally at what men had made of themselves during the centuries of women's subjection *and* at what the experience of subjection had made of women?

These questions led to the articulation of a series of seemingly contradictory understandings—such as, for example, that what women became partly as a result of male dominance constitutes both a social resource and a blight, and that the same holds for what male dominance (and the stunting of women's growth) obliged men to become. Exploring these understandings sharpened thinking about how to further the development of both sexes. It became clear that the best hope lies in rethinking the values of self-realization, family, and the social whole in ways that face up squarely to the complications of the past: seeing modesty and immodesty, for example, clear and whole in their historical contexts instead of taking flight from both into new myths.

Fatuity sometimes marked reflection on these matters, but, on balance, the gradually built-up body of thought qualifies as rich and suggestive; it forms part of the engrossing substance of gender history—the vital ideals, forced compromise, suffering, and poignant care that mark men's and women's past. When writers reduce the experience and behavior mirrored in this thought to mindless imitative veering, by both sexes, between power-grabbing strategies, they steal something irreplaceable: the capital that underwrites sane belief in purposeful social change.

ii. the macho-pastoralist

Similar depredation occurs when the stimulative power of serious thought about the sexes is unremittingly belittled — represented as trivial when compared with the influence exerted by push-pull biological drives, technological advance, shifts in economic structures. Commentary on gender issues can't ignore biogenetics, can't link behavioral change solely with intellectual trends; neither, though, can it shrug off the impact, on gender reality, of criticism, aesthetic images, and debate. Scorn intellection and determinism burgeons. The usable past and vital present are de-energized, rendered incapable of generating new goals, new lines of engagement, communication, and relationships, new selves.

Lionel Tiger's *Decline of Males* (1999), a book about the growth of women's power and the erosion of men's power, illustrates the problem. The author first came to fame for *Men in Groups* (1969), the study that introduced the concept of male bonding. *The Decline of Males* is an extended survey of justifications for treating contemporary males as objects of pity. Tiger argues that because of new modes of contraception and women's rise to socioeconomic power, men are increasingly "redundant and peripheral" and "profoundly alienated from the means of *reproduction* — women." He claims, further, that "the male is becoming so much trouble for everyone that in the future, in societies willing and able to control such matters, he will be lucky even to be born." A kinship system centered on males and females united in families is in process of being replaced by a basic mammalian system centered on mothers and children, "with ever more peripheral and confused males puzzled about their loneliness." And the trends pushing in this direction have little to do with ideas, nor can they be altered, the author implies, by thought.

Like *A Return to Modesty, The Decline of Males* is creditably hostile to doctrines of male-female sameness. Tiger is a loose-limbed writer, given to dactylic diddling ("What happens when people decide to accentuate the affectionate?") and repetitiveness (we're told time and again that Europe produced 13 million new jobs for women in one recent period as against 600,000 new jobs for men). But his biology-based attack on sameness doctrines is effective. Women are viewed as differing from men because the central biological events of life place women in a role men can't play. They inherit millions of years of practice at keeping life going. Their pregnancies, their milk, hormones, behavior, emotions—"positive, sullen, or varied"—are "astonishingly intricate legacies."

Differences between males and females arising from practice at keeping life going are plainly more consequential than differences between males and females arising from attitudes toward modesty; Tiger's defense of difference is far weightier than Wendy Shalit's.

But issues of sameness and difference are marginal in *The Decline of Males*. The key subject is, as I say, the already well advanced power grab by women—and that shift is presented throughout as the result of the operation of massive physical forces against which critical intellectual faculties are relatively powerless. Tiger is reverent toward geological time, physiological conditioning ("Destiny becomes anatomy"), and genetic codes; he is by turns exclamatory and lyrical about "species inheritance," "reproductive wiring," and the "human evolutionary legacy." But the human effort to create meaning and purpose—to imagine, through the languages of art or humanistic intellect or devotion, destinies unbounded by anatomy—seems not to impress him.

Only once in this work, in the closing pages, is mention made of the possibility of "fostering a set of ideas and styles of cordiality so that men and women have ways of mediating their real ancient and new differences as groups." And it's a gesture without follow-up. The bulk of *The Decline of Males* is belligerently impatient with suggestions that link the new differences with ideas or that offer non-biological explanations of the changes in social and family matters. Tiger holds that specific social, economic, and moral explanations, including feminist thought, "are comfortably simple but beside the point." He dismisses the body of temperate, informed feminist criticism of masculinist ways as though it amounted only to gender-boosting and had exerted no influence on the decline he is chronicling. Nowhere does he engage seriously with the work of women scholars and researchers who, eschewing insult and self-congratulation, probe differences between the sexes. (Carol Gilligan's research qualifies as a starting point for mediating new differences; Tiger mocks it as "Christian Science about human behavior . . . gratuitous stereotypes about maternalesque femininity.")

Everywhere he is pulled toward satiric disparagement of the human past. His grinning beast fables deprecate human life for its chaos and self-indulgence (animal life is saluted for calm, unpretentious order): "Foxes court and pair off . . . There appear to be no fox-priests, fox-psychiatrists, or fox–talk show hosts, inviting other foxes to describe their unhappy families."

And on the infrequent occasions when Tiger visits a moment in the human past for purposes other than ridicule, the terms of his approbation are laden with pastoralist poppycock, incommensurate with the history invoked; they obscure the nature of *non-biological* ancient and new differences that urgently need clarifying. An example: *The Decline of Males* alludes often to Mary and Joseph in Bethlehem and to the birth of Jesus; invariably the allusions stress two tendentious themes. The first is that "Christmas is a story about mammalian bedrock":

> Mary has to confront alone the central mammalian struggle for assistance at a crucial time. . . .
>
> She turns to the stable, where she is welcomed. Symbolically and in practice, this is where mammalian life is maintained. What could be more revealing? Bear in mind the importance of shepherds and other caretakers of animals in the pastoral and agricultural life of that part of the world at that time.

The second theme is that the Christmas story is about community generosity and conviviality—the giving of presents, "the equivalent of modern-day welfare":

> [The three wise men] arrive with gifts. . . . This is the character of the secular element of the holiday. People give gifts both to family members and others. They provide the highest level of hospitality during the whole year. . . . Birth and generosity unite at a glad and assertive party. Forty percent of all alcohol sales, the principal social drug, surround the Christmas and New Year fetes.

Tiger goes on to argue that "the brilliance of effective religious symbolism is at its most thrilling" in the handling of Joseph:

> Mary is a virgin. Therefore Joseph is not the father. . . . Therefore, he is not a "deadbeat dad" . . . required to pay child support. . . . No, the community is responsible. It accepts the responsibility with gifts, lights, and an extended hand.

From the wedding at Cana onward, enthusiasm for "a glad and assertive party" has an honored place in Scripture, and Tiger's delight in the season of gift giving isn't unattractive. The case is, however, that in reading the meaning of Mary, Joseph, and Jesus, history has focused not on "the community" but on the mother—on her selflessness, her refusal to seek relief from the harsh humiliations imposed by the obligations of care. Talk of mammalian bedrock and upticks in liquor sales and barnyard communitarianism conceals the profound truth: from generation to generation, in cell-by-cell increments, in passionate works of religious meditation and moving works of art, a large sector of humankind has interpreted the Nativity in ways that hallow the vision of one gender as transcendentally kind and caring. The figure of the helpless, suffering, inexpressibly poignant mother of Christ haunts the words of every activist, Christian or non-Christian, who speaks, like Catharine MacKinnon, of "embracing what we have become with a criticism of having become it," or who voices similar doubleness about her longings for "what we've never been allowed to be."

The point at stake here isn't simple. History, culture, and devotion created, over two millennia, a permanent ideal and a moral identity. For the last century and a half, some women—lately, *many* women—sought a language in which to declare, persuasively and unself-pityingly, their ambivalence about this identity: their conviction that sanctifying the courage of tenderness as women's courage alone finally injures both sexes. They have argued that cant about the "naturally selfless" sex lightens, for the other sex, the moral obligations that sanity insists must be equally shared, and that this same cant declares powerlessness to be the inevitable concomitant of virtue, and that belief in these absurdities divides the world into ruinously non-communicating moral and amoral realms.

The historical and cultural processes that produced this divided world are no less poorly understood than the biological processes that *The Decline of Males* presents as determinative. The same holds for the moral and intellectual dimensions of the economic and social crises Tiger sees as undermining the traditional family unit (wife-husband-child). And there are limits to what clear-headed education on these matters can accomplish; reconstructing relations between the genders in life-enhancing ways is no short-term project.

It can be worked at with some hope of success, however, provided the work is founded on solid knowledge of the history of the genders—history clarifying how the genders (as distinguished from the sexes) arrived at their present identities, where in those identities pliancy exists, and what social purposes can be served by an increase in pliancy. But historical knowledge is allowed no place in *The Decline of Males*. The genesis of curiosity about gender identity, breakthroughs in understanding how these identities were shaped, realism about the identities' flexibility (and about the limits of the flexibility): these are essential resources for anyone intent either on formulating "pro-biology, pro-family" initiatives or on evaluating attitudes perceived as anti-biology or anti-family.

But Tiger writes as though no such resources existed. His book betrays the same enthusiasm for one-dimensional explanations that marks Shalit's *Return to Modesty* (mammalian biology replaces realpolitical grabbiness as prime mover). It makes light of moral capital in a fashion exactly matching Shalit's. (Shalit allows female modesty no resonance as an affirmation of *individual*—not gender-determined—human dignity; Tiger allows maternal tenderness no resonance as an affirmation of *individual*—not gender-determined—capacity for selflessness.) And it's afflicted by the same blindness to the possibilities of contributions by the sexes to each other's moral growth, and by the same impulse to drain the genders of their lifeblood, namely, their intellectual and cultural past.

iii. the fantast

There are many "pasts," needless to say; history isn't an Open Book, speaking truth forthrightly to anyone who pauses to look into its pages. Erasure of the substance of gender history—one result of gender shift—can issue from arguments that ignore the pertinent past; it can also issue from arguments that less ignore the past than misread it, intentionally or otherwise, presenting, as though indisputable, interpretations of action, motive, and consequence that have no factual support. One of the most widely publicized treatises on the sexes in the nineties—Susan Faludi's *Stiffed* (1999)—is an example of history erased by obliviousness not of what has gone before but of the standards separating history from fantasy.

The book opens with a summary of promises allegedly made to the American men who served in World War II, namely, that the purposefulness marking wartime masculinity would continue in peacetime, that the space program would provide anonymous dutiful men with meaningful work, and that loyalty to employers, wives, and families and to the cold war spirit would be richly repaid. The promises weren't kept, and the country dwindled into a culture "constructed around celebrity and image, glamour and entertainment, marketing and consumerism." The new culture is all about appearances, Faludi asserts, not about inner resources; it's about vanity instead of manliness, style over strength.

The bulk of *Stiffed* presents material supporting this thesis drawn from Faludi's interviews with baby boomers across the nation: porn actors, Spur Posse "scorers," movie stars, shipyard workers, astronauts, militiamen, Promise Keeping evangelicals, football fans, ghetto gang members, and others. Almost without exception their highly readable life stories center on displacement, humiliation, and defeat. The interviewees speak no common language in accounting for their beleaguerment, but their interviewer paints them all as strugglers with "ornamental" masculinity, victims of "virulent voyeurism."

The gap between Faludi's language and that of her subjects is among the book's problems. But other, more troubling problems surface as the work advances. They stem partly from Faludi's heedlessness of the contradictions and inconsistencies in her explanations of events. At some moments *Stiffed* sees the advent of ornamental masculinity as the result of "the dictates of consumer and media culture," presumably corporate-managed. At other moments blame falls on the country as a whole for failing, after World War II, to give its returning soldiers a chance to cope with their experience as killers—for denying them "the opportunity to grapple publicly with their horrific secret burden" and to achieve "a moral knowledge to pass down to the sons."

Or again, at some moments *Stiffed* sees President John F. Kennedy as spokesman for a truly challenging virility, promising a space program that would "concentrate all of the masculine force and beauty of battle into one breathtaking explosion of exploratory power and muscle." At other moments the book approvingly quotes observers who view JFK as the founder of ornamental masculinity, the leader who "elevate[d] men into sex-object heaven."

Faludi often addresses subjects on which professional historians, liberal and conservative, have reached rough consensus; her opinions, invariably at odds with consensus, reveal no knowledge of its existence and present no factual ground for rejecting it. The description, in *Stiffed*, of the closing of the Long Beach, California, naval shipyard is couched in language suggesting that the demise of skilled workers' sense of useful productivity was, for the American work force, a post–World War II phenomenon; labor historians are in solid agreement that the demise was well advanced before the Great Depression. Faludi's allusions to the era of the Works Progress Administration invoke it as an age of golden opportunity irradiated by the "idea of a manhood embedded in and useful to an embattled society seeking to foster social welfare and equity." The period is remembered and described far differently—and more negatively—by those who lived through it. Her equally gushing appreciation of the "beauty of battle" is wholly repellent, and only a little less so is her certainty, maintained throughout this book, that the combat infantryman's experience was the norm for the U.S. armed forces in World War II. (Only a small minority of servicemen—fewer than ten percent of all those in uniform—actually saw combat of any kind.)

What's more, when Faludi seeks support of her conclusions in works by other writers, she often flat-out misrepresents those works. *Stiffed* argues that the second wave of the American women's movement was largely a protest against media images of "commercially packaged womanhood"; it avers that from the first mockery of the 1968 Miss America beauty pageant to the sit-in at the *Ladies' Home Journal* offices to the campus-wide hooting down of visiting *Playboy* scouts, a prime cause of modern women's crisis was identified as the mass media and mass merchandising culture. And the book asserts that Betty Friedan agrees with these claims.

But Friedan never backed such claims, never treated the "mass media and mass merchandising culture" as the origin of "the problem that has no name," never proposed that the anxiety, depression, and frustration of middle-class American women were caused by "the media." Friedan had a grasp of the psychological, social, and educational inequalities that lay at the heart of the problem—inequalities impossible to reach by altering media representations of housewives.

The defects just listed are scarcely trivial. But more troubling is Faludi's account of the nature of the American male just prior to World War II. Until the onset of the emasculating ornamental culture, the American male according to Faludi's reading was driven by a will to nurture, an instinct that placed the welfare of others high above that of the self and found its deepest reward in caring protectively and lovingly for others. He and the service-oriented society of the time held a fundamentally "maternal conception of manhood." This conception defined manhood by character—by "inner qualities of stoicism, integrity, reliability, the ability to protect and provide and sacrifice." And, Faludi insists,

> these are the same qualities, recoded as masculine, that society has long recognized in women as the essence of *motherhood*. Men were publicly useful insofar as they mastered skills associated with the private realm of maternal femininity. Like mothers tending selflessly to their babies, men were not only to take care of their families but also their society without complaint; that was, in fact, what made them men.

The apogee of the will to nurture was reached, Faludi writes, in "the men who had brought into being the Ernie Pyle ideal of heroically selfless manhood."

Faludi contends that nurturing, selfless caretaking instincts remained vital in men, for a time, in the postwar era. She notes that the commander of the Long Beach, California, naval shipyard declared in 1951 that the creed of the shipyard will be "not for us, but for others." ("The shipyard had devised a model of a father-and-son relationship based on work, skill, and usefulness, not on the monopoly and control of power.")

She reports, further, that male yearning for the nurturing experience is often expressed at meetings of domestic violence counseling groups, and even in classroom colloquies at military schools. But despite its survival in the odd venue here or there, maternal sensibility—former hallmark of masculinity—is, Faludi insists, in its death throes. And this "profound loss" marks the end of a "world where men cared for each other and for the workplace society in which they were embedded."

Maternal man would assuredly have seemed an *a*historical figment to the generation of Teddy Roosevelt and William James and Jane Addams—and to novelists from Wharton and Dreiser to Hemingway, Faulkner, and Fitzgerald—and to virtually every significant twentieth-century cultural observer, writers frequently benumbed by the spectacle of Success-driven male egocentricity. And only the extremely credulous can be at ease with Faludi's other trademark constructs: beautiful battles, heartening economic catastrophes, instant turnarounds for national beliefs and values, and male behavior, from generation to generation, as the paradigm of hope for the good society.

The concept of maternal man as casualty of "media culture" is, to be sure, functional for Faludi; it freshens her stance as spokesperson for the downtrodden. Her earlier book, *Backlash: America's Undeclared War Against Women* (1992), took up the cause of beleaguered women, victims of a "war" on their sex that followed second wave feminism's first breakthroughs to power. (*Backlash* claimed that "women never have been more miserable" than in the early 1990s.) In *Stiffed*, miserable men replace miserable women, "media culture" replaces men as the enemy, and the author reenergizes her posture as champion of the underdog.

At a cost, however. Not once in the nearly seven hundred pages of this book is Faludi's Pulitzer-prizewinning *Backlash* mentioned—and everywhere in *Stiffed*, as problems and issues disappear into the murk of pseudo-history populated by motherly men, the pity bestowed a half-dozen years ago on women is abruptly and inexplicably cut off. *Backlash* spoke angrily about "blows from men," about "men's opposition to equality," about men's "refusal to shoulder child care and domestic duties," about "sheer brutality." *Stiffed* sets quotation marks around "male domination" and "Patriarchy"—typographical gestures conveying skepticism about their very existence. It represents feminist criticism of masculinist values as a manipulative ploy and a product of envy and rage for personal elevation. Politically shrewd, women are said to have employed a "simple and personal adversarial model" by means of which to gain power. They took "advantage of a ready-made model for revolt," "unfurl[ing] a well-worn map and follow[ing] a reliable strategy." With little or no cause they blamed men for all their woes. ("Blaming a cabal of men has taken feminism about as far as it can go.") And as of the present moment, all their "most obvious enemies have been defeated outright."

There's a troubling disingenuousness in Susan Faludi's implicit disavowal of the quite recent work that brought her celebrity. But authorial opportunism isn't the failing in *Stiffed* that most matters. Everywhere in the book's length, now directly, now indirectly, in multiple passages representing nurture as the central preoccupation of males and in multiple passages representing power and appearance as central preoccupations of females, the author traduces the ideas and experience she purports to address. Well before the end, the major issue at stake in the historical struggle for liberation—how to achieve fullness of being—utterly disappears from sight.

As I indicated earlier, the strongest safeguard against falsifications of the past of the kind found in *Stiffed*—and in Shalit, Tiger, and writers of like temperament—is an unbending resolve not to seal off the history of the relations of the sexes from other historical changes. Broad patterns need to be kept in sight—the broad challenges to assumptions about rank and rectitude that have determined the direction of modern history. What has human excellence to do with physical power, property power, gender power? Why should power differences—economic, social, other—qualify as a just basis for hierarchies of value among human creatures? What besides superstition dictates that issues of equality and justice must be understood as subsidiary to and governed by the foundational realities of power, or that commonsense authority should be vested in the association of power with integrity and excellence?

Women's voices weren't the earliest to raise these questions and to announce the possibility that social and political arrangements—and the moral assumptions underwriting them—have come to be as they are without good reason. But women's role in pressing the questions—forcing attention to the status of revolutionary challenges—has grown steadily over the generations. And women's success in advancing understanding of moral hierarchy hasn't gone unnoticed; part of the reason why gender-bending sideshows, such as killer women, are promoted is that they distract attention from genuinely substantive challenges. Reductive, vulgar versions of the ends of change—canny diversions—have often before been espoused by interests opposed to change.

And the same holds for versions of change asserting, in another diversionary strategy, that the orders and systems now in place are wholly pliant, welcoming to serious challenge, eager to abet their own reversal. Pop gender shift materials both pro and con imply that social arrangements and structures of inner feeling are infinitely malleable. Claims of unlimited personal potency animate all performers regardless of whether their medium is the sitcom or the essay. *Whatever one wants one can have, whatever one wishes to be one can be* . . . Lewd gag lines about women-becoming-men set studio audiences shrieking with laughter—and trivialize the barriers to change; "neoconservative" espousals of a retreat to chastity do the same—by proclaiming the easy reversibility of things. The woman in the cartoon who introduces her male friend Harold with a sneer ("This is Harold. He's my core holding.") sums up the fantasy. Males are lesser (a fait accompli); individual ego rules.

Smiling assent to these and similarly loaded accounts of change in power ratios now weakens the sense of what, in its truly momentous aspects, the argument between the sexes was about from the beginning: what issues were and remain at stake, what kinds of activism are best gauged to keep those issues in full view, what interests in the contemporary world gain most when the issues are obscured. Saying it again: falsifications of history are deeply ingrained in cultural representations of women-becoming-men; the falsifications represent as completed a revolution that as yet has merely been contemplated; the resulting delusions devitalize aspirations to wholeness. Few can remember why the aspirations surfaced in the first place; few grasp the nature of the changes in self and society that those who battled stereotypes meant to foster.

It follows that serving the cause of substantive change just now demands complex political action, material as well as symbolic. The first component remains aggressive support for practical measures to correct residual, systemic inequities. The second component, scarcely less important, consists of work aimed at restoring the values of variousness and engagement to their place at the center of the struggle for equality.

The latter work is no mere rhetorical game, no simple matter of substituting one set of officially approved terms for another. The task is that of showing forth moment-to-moment realities of engagement in ways that illuminate the moral point of awakening "the community of beings within the single self." Because the sexes do not share the same starting line in the pursuit of wholeness, their experience of the pursuit cannot be the same. Yet some commonalities exist and can be set under purposeful examination. What does it feel like to press oneself, as a man or woman, toward true flexibility? What are the costs and benefits? Which challenges are hardest to meet, which temptations hardest to resist? The final chapter of this book aims to shed light on these matters.

15

Achievements in Variousness

A CONCLUSION

THE HERO OF the film *Mrs. Doubtfire*—feckless, jobless Daniel Hillard (Robin Williams)—looks to be in serious trouble at the start. "I'm addicted to my children," he says, but he's under sentence of life without them unless he sheds his old identity and arrives at a new self. His wife is divorcing him, and he has been granted only supervised visitation rights; the ploys and charms that once regularly saved his bacon appear to have lost their magic.

As it emerges, though, no problem. Drawing on professional skills and friends—Hillard earned his living, when employed, voicing animated cartoons—the hero transforms himself into a sixty-ish, heavy-breasted Englishwoman named Iphigenia Doubtfire; he then gulls his wife into hiring Doubtfire as her after-school housekeeper and babysitter. Feckless husband and father reinvents himself as an efficient caregiver, and the film proceeds to enchant audiences with a show biz version of the tests and challenges, costs and benefits of flexibility.

Predictably, the tests are undemanding and the costs minimal. Pre-divorce, Hillard as husband and dad performs according to stereotype, meaning he's a resolute slob: objects that slip to the floor from his hand, dirty socks, briefs, whatever, stay where they land unless his wife, Miranda, a harried interior designer, picks them up; Hillard never pulls an oar at housework. Post-divorce, the digs he moves into are pure grease and grime within weeks, furniture buried beneath soiled laundry, moldy towels, gnawed pizza slices, rancid half-empty Chinese takeout cartons. Hillard is a loving father—delights in joining his children's games, conspiring with the kids against chores and solemn elders. But can a person this slovenly and irresponsible really become—overnight— Iphigenia Doubtfire, impeccable housekeeper and quietly effective disciplinarian?

To repeat, no problem. Once on the job, Hillard/Doubtfire establishes—in a single afternoon—soft-spoken, no-nonsense authority with the children. (The kids—aged thirteen, ten, and five— dabble in rebellion but are set to housework and quickly tamed.) There's an awkward episode in the kitchen when a meal in preparation catches fire, but a call to a posh restaurant plus an outlay of $140 puts a respectable ready-to-serve meal on the table promptly; a night or two later (after watching Julia Child on TV) Hillard/ Doubtfire cooks a splendid lobster dinner for four. Housework is a breeze: the tyro housekeeper boogies joyously while vacuuming, wields a far-out broom as though it were a rock musician's guitar— no hint of weariness. No losses of virility, either: encumbered with skirts and heels, this new man-woman terrorizes street thieves and plays guileful soccer with the kids without misstep. Everybody's morale soars. Often in tears or rage before, owing to overwork, Miranda Hillard now relaxes and smiles, proud of her mannerly, happy brood, pleased with the shining order around her, aware of her huge indebtedness to the person she knows as "Mrs. Doubtfire." Hillard's own place is completely refurbished, as if by a miracle—interiors sparkling, closets neat, high standards the norm for at-home meals and cleanups.

Gender is weightless, says the tale. *Give a male an evening and he'll master the whole of the housekeeping repertory. Give him a day or two and he'll turn out tasty meals with ease. From the gitgo he implants dutiful cooperative attitudes and habits in the children, never raising his voice. No exhaustion, no hysteria, no hard tests or challenges—no problem. He can be whatever he wants.*

A movie version of flexibility.

The key, of course, is the concentration on externals. Danny Hillard annexes occupations, he doesn't engage states of mind. The events, actions, and jobs, even the pain (Hillard burns his finger once at the stove) that redefine this hero have to do with life surfaces. Nothing in the movie shows the man becoming inward even briefly with experience that's strange or repugnant or bewildering or life-enhancing or physically and emotionally draining. The boogieing cleaning woman puns unwittingly on the vacuum at the center of this Dad-as-SuperMom fantasy—on the absence, that is, of insight into the texture of engagement with a gender identity separate from one's own. To repeat: *Mrs. Doubtfire* teaches what flexibility is not.

And in the process casts oblique light on contemporary needs. Most human beings can recall an occasion when contingency installed them suddenly inside the feeling or thought of a member of "the other sex," but typically the moment of access lacks duration, can't be reflexively probed. A culture swamped with representations of killer women and clueless men needs practice at probing. It needs exposure to surprising movements of mind: men rising above standards of "prudence" and "justice" to grasp the moral peerlessness of maternal devotion, women fathoming the psychological impact of reverse discrimination against caregiving men. Above all, it needs chances to observe male and female minds reaching beyond stereotypical boundaries in pursuit of self-ripening and fullness of being—not scrapping gender identities but refining their understanding of what is and is not toxic in the nature of each gender.

One such chance comes in the study of the fighter Mike Tyson, *Fallen Champ,* produced by the gifted documentary filmmaker Barbara Kopple. The life story is familiar in outline. Tyson grows up in a desperately poor ghetto home (they had nothing, a neighbor recalls, not even soap), and his schoolmates call him "Dirty Mike"; while still a boy he loses his birth mother, commits a succession of street crimes, and is sent to a halfway house for delinquents; he dreams of becoming a prizefighter and catches the eye of a famous trainer-manager who takes him into his home, launches him as a boxer, nurses him into contention, works his corner the night he wins the championship. Fame and riches bring disasters: the trustworthy trainer-manager dies; the beauty pageant star whom the fighter marries files for divorce; sleazeball promoters move to take over the perceived money machine; a mediocrity strips Tyson of his championship; at age twenty-six the youngster who a little earlier earned $20 million for thirty-five seconds in the ring is back in jail, serving a sentence for rape.

Fallen Champ skips none of these essentials of the life (the film was made prior to the grotesque ear-chewing episode that led to Tyson's lengthy expulsion from boxing). And it's in touch from start to finish with the fury inside the fighter that relishes exploding other men's bones and brains: Tyson entertaining reporters after one bout with taunting claims that the opponent he just knocked out "cried" every time he was hit—"making woman sounds, shrieking like a woman." Tyson telling hangers-on after another knockout that he wanted to crush the loser's nose one more time—"I wanted the nose to go up into the brain." A parade of commentator-observers describing the champ as an "American pit bull," a "killer," a "crazy paranoid," worse.

But Kopple is also in touch with complicating elements in this nature. Her methods as an artist are partly those of collage; in *Fallen Champ* she works with conventional sportscast material, and with found footage of many kinds: home videos of Tyson as a youngster, reared by Cus D'Amato and Camille Ewald; cinéma vérité (Tyson at a Junior Olympics). She interviews defenders as well: Tyson-humanizing classmates, cornermen, fellow fighters, and others who insist he's extremely sensitive, an obsessive hugger of others, a pigeon fancier who loves to dance, is "weak," needs "confidence," needs "love," believes that "unless he performed nobody would accept him," has "such a sweet, sensitive voice."

And gradually, building on thoughtful juxtapositions and penetratingly ironic layerings, she shows forth a dynamic of feeling underlying superficial contradictions. Its elements include fear of humiliation, chaotically manipulative scrambling to fend off humiliation, intense shame at both the fear and the scrambling, brutal resolve to punish those perceived as shamers.

Time and again in *Fallen Champ*, Dirty Mike comes on as humble, wheedling, wispy-voiced, need-ridden, weak; time and again he repudiates this self in fury: beats up the sparring partner in the gym who's been persuaded to help him tune combinations and head moves, turns violent with the woman he's begged for a date. Time and again Kopple's camera records the fighter inventing ways of avoiding rejection, overdramatizing his vulnerability for the purpose of locking in, from someone else, at least nominal complaisance or pity. Dirty Mike learns to avoid mortification at dances and elsewhere by startling the potential mortifiers: "I figured out how to make it work, how to make the girls dance with me. You run up and you grab their hands and take them out on the floor and they can't say no. They're too embarrassed." Dirty Mike seems actually to force an undemonstrative cornerman, Teddy Atlas, into momentary tenderness: minutes before entering the ring, the fighter breaks down before Atlas, weeping uncontrollably, shoulders heaving, seemingly in terror of the battle ahead. Awkwardly the cornerman embraces him, murmuring, "Relax, Mike . . . You've done it already twenty times . . . Don't let your imagination get you . . . Let's go get ready for a fight." (Later Atlas asks in wonder, "How could a guy like that not think he's capable? He's a little weak. . . . He needs love.")

Dirty Mike blurts a confession of dependency and aloneness that binds his trainer-manager's wife closer to him. ("He asked me," says the frowning Camille Ewald, "he asked me would it be all right if I became his mother? If he calls me Mother?") When riches arrive, Dirty Mike adopts more conventional tactics, mingles displays of vulnerability with showers of diamonds and Porsches to persuade his beauty queen to love him unconditionally.

Kopple holds the chief elements of the dynamic in steady view throughout: pathos, cunning, real terror of humiliation. Her perspective is never unfeeling. She accepts that the woman Tyson was convicted of raping suffered genuine pain and that Tyson's wife, Robin Givens, was genuinely frightened of her husband. *Fallen Champ* achieves insight and breadth partly because it's as attentive to the star's female victims as to the star.

Yet Kopple is never heedless of the possibility that, with an eye on the main chance, the victims knowingly set themselves at risk. And she's clearly touched by her awareness that Tyson's scrambling strategies, driven by immeasurably ignorant longing, had zero chance of success. Shortly after acknowledging that the fighter needed love, Teddy Atlas held a pistol to Tyson's head, threatening to blow him away for behaving offensively to a girl. The surrogate mother Tyson clings to writes a letter denouncing him for "behaving like an animal." On national television, with Tyson at her side wincing at her words, Givens speaks of her husband (to a nervous Barbara Walters) as though he no longer existed, her coldly detached phrases striking like axe blows: "Michael is a manic depressive. He is. It's just awful. It's been pure hell. It's been worse than anything I could possibly imagine. . . . I don't know what Mike Tyson would be without my mother."

Arguably the resources figuring in the creation of Barbara Kopple's Tyson include "what history has made of women"; to judge from the movie, this filmmaker knows fear like the back of her hand, and knowledge of fear is among the legacies of historical powerlessness. One can speculate, further, that an age that lessens the pressure of fear fosters work such as *Fallen Champ*— work that breathes imaginative command and is exhilaratingly free of deference.

No one, though, can speak confidently about the origins of aesthetic achievement. What's indisputable is that the mind behind *Fallen Champ* has advanced well beyond stereotypes—"feminine" repugnance, "masculine" *Sports Illustrated* gush or indictment—to produce a model of unillusioned humanistic interpretation. Kopple's Tyson is a victim of poverty and prejudice—and also a sly, cocky victimizer of others. He's a huge ego, a desperado, a man racked by unslakable need who, trading in violence because he knows no other trade, gets better and worse than he deserves. Simultaneously seeing through his eyes and living along his nerves while assessing his conduct by standards remote from his own, the filmmaker arrives at clarity about some paradoxes of gender identity shaped by an inhumanly harsh social context. And, as though incidentally, without sentimentality or heartlessness, she reveals—in her own person as an artist—what flexibility is.

Flexible minds work in many mediums, obviously; the truths they develop can be carried in images or in argument, drawn from isolated extreme instances or from observation of "normal" practices and habits. Such minds lean heavily on the constructive imagination, the force that creates access, from inside, to thought and feeling not one's own. This bears emphasis: minds successful at reaching beyond stereotypical boundaries are acutely aware, almost invariably, of the interdependence of reasoning and imagining.

The interdependence is everywhere apparent in Natalie Angier's *Woman: An Intimate Geography* (1999). Described by the author as an attempt "to find a way to think about the biology of being female without falling into the sludge of biological determinism," *Woman* builds many of its arguments on parallels and contrasts between humans and other species. It doesn't minimize the problems issuing from the "dependence of women on men for their bacon and bread"; it stresses that "only among humans have males succeeded in stepping between a woman and a meal, in wresting control of the resources that she needs to feed herself and her children." And the book is strongly, although good-humoredly, critical of the rejection by women of "the idea of sisterhood and of female solidarity," and of the notion that all power issues between the sexes have been solved—that "we're all fine, we've fixed all the problems that feminism can fix."

But on page after page Angier complicates her account of the power relationships of men and women by evoking the insides of situations wherein conventional tottings-up of losses and gains for the relatively powerful and relatively powerless obscure rather than clarify the experiential facts. Her point isn't that power differentials are immaterial. It's that they function in tangled ways; the weak as well as the strong can close off the other's access to variousness and richness of being, thereby injuring the interests of both.

An example: Angier's discussion of the "sensory embellishments," for mothers and fathers, of love for a child. The discussion opens with objective comments on the infrequency with which fathers experience physical intimacy with their young. Just like mothers, the author notes, fathers can "love their babies madly . . . the more they sit and smell and clutch their babies against them." The problem is that the average father doesn't "sit and rock his baby against his naked breast . . . nearly as often as the average mother does." More often than not he's handed the baby when the mother is tired and wants a break, and holding the child becomes a chore and a duty. "He keeps his shirt on. He's buttoned up. The nerve endings of his flesh detect the baby's frequency only faintly."

But there are other problems, and as the writer probes them, speaking within the mother's sensibility, she summons feelings on both sides: possessive pride and dismissive impatience here, frustration and defensive, mildly resentful resignation there. Mothers tend to monopolize their babies, she argues, which at one level is perfectly understandable: they have to hold them to breast-feed. But neither this practicality nor habit quite explains the reluctance to let go—or the stony, preceptorial, even sometimes insulting line taken toward the mate when his turn comes:

The mother watches the father to make sure he is doing everything properly. She is the baby expert after all, and he is forever callow, a babe in the woods. Women chortle about men's clumsiness in holding babies, their fumblings, their bafflement. The nursery is still the mother's domain. There, she is poobah.

What follows in *Woman* isn't solemn, parents' manual–style instruction but rather a passage of self-critical reflection arising from a moment during which, smilingly and unpedantically, contrasting feelings have been brought to life:

> If we want men to do their share and shine at it, it's unfair to give them the handicap of our doubt, to practice a reverse form of discrimination: "We suckle; you suck." If women expect men to dive into the warm, rich waters of body love and to feel the tug of baby bondage, we must give over the infant again and again. Between feedings, between breasts, play touch football, baby as pigskin—pass it along.

Here and repeatedly elsewhere in *Woman,* the author's way of working creates a model, for her reader, of variousness in action—a various mind exploring male-female, maternal-paternal interaction, maneuvering easily between supposedly fixed gender identities. The costs aren't negligible: yielding a measure of sovereignty over a domain is easy only for poobahs awash in domains. The benefits include increased conversancy with the causes of paternal bumblings and bafflement, increased optimism that the ideal of shared baby care needn't forever be a figment, a firmer grasp of the alternatives to women-becoming-men.

No representation of the possibilities of imaginative engagement can cure the ailments of the Age of Gender Shift. But each such representation suggests ways of living in this age that could eventually renew it as a time of promise. Both Natalie Angier and Barbara Kopple speak for what is abstract until presented and palpable beyond erasure once brought to life. *I hear a man seemingly turned off, because "masculine," by baby care,* says the undervoice of

Woman. I also hear a woman speaking patronizingly in his ear, teaching him to stay turned off, saying implicitly: this isn't for you, you can't excel at this, don't even think of trying. I hear a man boasting about relishing cruelty, says the undervoice of *Fallen Champ. But I also hear the fear and shame-at-fear that he's driven to beat down: I sense a pitiable, soul-deranging entrapment.*

The audience these artists introduce to close imagining engages in its own pursuit of wholeness as it listens and observes—and the experience of engagement can drive home the moral point of awakening the community of beings within the single self. It's true, however, that even with an artist's shaping hand directing us to essentials, moments of engagement remain—like life—hard to read. Knotted in a snarl of ordinary human preening, political squabbles, and "objective" expertise, they can slip past unnoticed, failing to achieve their rightful power to instruct.

Equally true is that people who are talented at evoking in other minds, through words or deeds, the nature and uses of variousness are often forgetful of their own gifts, slow to draw on them in creating fresh contexts for reflecting on familiar problems and families. Men with an intuitive sense of the pertinence of maternal/feminine ways of feeling to an issue, women with a parallel sense of the pertinence of paternal/masculine ways of feeling to that issue, fail to speak from the center of their own complex being, fail to break the bonds of the strict constructionists' gender world. Too often legislative debates, public meetings, classrooms—discussions of education, medical care, inequality of opportunity—have a daunting quality of airlessness. There seems zero chance that an enlivening, revelatory moment can occur—an opening through which fresh light can fall on underexamined assumptions.

This was the situation for a time at a recent assembly in a Dublin, Ohio, public hall, a "town meeting" on the condition of American schools. Participants and attendees included citizens in number, mainly black and Hispanic, a half-dozen state and federal legislators plus other elected and appointed officials, representatives of the PTA, PTT (Parents and Teachers Together), the Association of American School Superintendents and other organizations, and a sprinkling of public school students and their teachers.

The audience was first shown a documentary contrasting conditions in poorly financed inner-city and rural schools with those in well-financed suburban schools. The film (it was produced by Bill Moyers and based on Jonathan Kozol's *Savage Inequalities*) showed powerful images of decay in the city schools: ceiling plaster coming down in chunks, mid-morning rain falling on pupils and their desks, dank dreary corridors, uninhabitable "gyms," shower rooms, classrooms, arts "spaces." It also showed suburban schools with strikingly cheerful, glossy, sun-filled interiors, limitless computer facilities, wide playing fields, beautifully combed grounds. When the film ended, feelings of outrage seemed to pervade the hall— anger at discrepancies worse even than those the students themselves or their parents had expected to be shown.

But the outrage subsided, displaced rather swiftly by wrangling, posturing, cliché. Speakers are now holding forth, to loud applause, on the Founding Fathers' commitment to the value of equality. A U.S. senator twice repeats her view that all American students must be able to "compete in the global economy." A well-known TV commentator and adviser to three White Houses notes that Roman Catholic schools with student bodies comparable to those found in inner-city schools perform better than public schools and spend less money. A schoolteacher and a researcher deny this claim. Experts on the positive results of voucher programs—in Milwaukee, Wisconsin, and elsewhere—are shouted down on the ground that Milwaukee isn't Cleveland or Dublin. A state legislator and Jonathan Kozol—the writer is in attendance—argue at bitter length about whether the school problem is a federal or state responsibility and whether public schools should continue to be financed largely by property taxes.

Parents enter the fray, denouncing tax abatements for corporations—sports teams among them. Legislators with a specialty in public finance defend the abatements on the ground that Ohio competes against states equally desperate to replace lost manufacturing jobs. (The United States is a war of all against all, says a voice.) An authority on the state's "incremental plan" for dealing with the physical condition of the schools asserts that, at the present rate of improvement, it will take 170 years to bring the schools up to standard. He's corrected by another authority: 220 years. A state legislator estimates the cost of upgrading at $100 billion— $4,000 for every man, woman, and child in the state. He, too, is corrected: $10 billion. Moyers asks an attendee if he has $4,000 to spare for school improvement. The attendee counters that politicians' "perks" should be cut. Speakers cite the "nationalized, socialized space program" as a model for action. Also the Marshall Plan. A Kentucky judge explains how, as a result of his rulings on behalf of the principle that the state is a unity, Kentucky has raised property and sales taxes and is spending a billion or so more a year on schools.

A student is called on: she weeps as she says she's worth a place that isn't falling apart. An angry minister is on his feet announcing that he's "boiling"; he shouts that "all the people with money don't want to share it!" Loud applause, rebel yells.

Abruptly Moyers calls on Kozol again, and this time the writer adopts a less combative tone. He expresses regret that "all of us, whether we're old liberal advocates like me or whatever—all of us talk about this in financial terms. All the discussion is financial." He suggests that such terms aren't appropriate. "When you see the situation . . . you sense the morbidity of daily life in a building that's so unpleasant—so squalid—"

Kozol breaks off, starts over, speaking more quietly now about the feelings and attitudes of the children actually attending the schools. Referring to them as "babies," he asks a series of questions on their behalf: "Shouldn't they be able to have twelve or thirteen years when they're surrounded by something beautiful even if it doesn't pay off, even if it's not good for [global competition] or General Motors or IBM? Shouldn't they have a chance to enjoy their lives? Why not give them a beautiful school *because* they're babies and deserve to have some fun before they die? Wouldn't that be a good reason for us to do this—as Americans who love children?"

More than once in the past the author of *Savage Inequalities* has been roughly treated, in print, for espousing holier-than-thou views and fashionably hopeless stances ("some fun before they die"). *The New Republic* among others fiercely mocked Kozol for declaring he fears for his soul when he comes to New York and lunches with a publisher at the Four Seasons. During tonight's town meeting the writer has seemed at moments opportunistic, eager to score points off Tory officialdom and win cheers from the left-leaning audience, slow to draw on his own best self in explaining how to advance beyond the financing issues his writing raises. It's a fact that few Americans can match his commitment, over a lifetime, to the cause of educational equity or his readiness, in a period when "old liberal advocates" are routinely singled out for abuse, to imagine and flesh out new arguments for that cause. And yet: granting that Kozol's is a valuable American life, is the kind of talk he just fell into genuinely useful? Returning to the themes of this book—the book in your hand—does talk about babies and fun and the beautiful actually contribute to the work of restoring variousness and engagement to their place at the center of the struggle for equality?

It does indeed, when and if it is heard: this is the only possible answer. It so functions because it directly contradicts the notion that utopia equals agreement, by both genders, that victory in the global competition is the big thing and the only thing. In one of his dimensions, Jonathan Kozol is a tough guy, not cowed by ridicule, strong in his cause. In another dimension he has access to the historically maternal, isn't buttoned up and impervious to the tug of baby bondage but is instead willing to *assume* there's a place at the most august policy table for lovingly protective behavior and ideas.

The hall is silent when Kozol finishes—no applause, no rebel yells; the place seems not so much impressed as mystified. (We were talking global competition here, right? abatements? equity? What did I miss?) In the age of killer women and clueless men, encounters with variousness tend, as I said, to mystify, with or without artists aboard. An old, male, liberal advocate who suddenly begins talking from within the heart of an "intensive mother"; a filmmaker who manages, without "becoming" the other, to breathe within a cruel rapist even as she judges him; a scientific writer who steps inside a new father's alienation and, as a woman, sorrows with the man: these are figures whom the architects of idealism assumed post-liberation culture would welcome with delight and immediately comprehend. But the meaning of such models, like the meaning of the richest passages in MacKinnon and Cocks and Gilligan and Bly, grows harder to make out amid the gender shift clamor.

Why not give them the beautiful because *they're babies?* Neither male nor female, not strong, not weak, simply sane: this is the only language with a prayer of straightening out twenty-first-century thought about gender and power. All that I've meant to say, from the opening page of *Killer Woman Blues,* is that losing our capacity to speak that language or to hear it will be catastrophic for the human essence.

NOTES

ACKNOWLEDGMENTS

Notes

Introduction

page

ix *humiliate men.* In a Jim Beam ad campaign a sheepishly subservient man paints a woman's toenails; in Cadillac commercials a woman driver taunts a man for ignorance of his car's power train. In Heineken commercials a woman at ease, comfortably aware of the male adjacent to her, pours a beer neatly and gracefully into a pilsener glass; the flustered male pours *his* beer incompetently, splashing it on the bar, as the title "The Premature Pour" is supered over him on the screen. In Coors Light commercials a woman beer truck driver pulls up in front of some men seated on boxes on a hot city street—the loafers look wilted—and hoists the truck's heavy door, revealing white curling mountain mists and a ton of beer. The loafers swarm toward this sight, and the woman truck driver comments contemptuously, "Men are sheep." Gatorade pairs Michael Jordan and Mia Hamm as competitors, with Mia shouting in derision, "Bring it on!" ("So how did we get to the idea of Michael and Mia?" Gatorade asks itself on the Internet. "The whole Gatorade 'Is It in You' campaign is based on the idea of having inside you not just Gatorade, but also the courage, the guts, the dedication, the desire, the will to win.")

xii *social organization.*" Joan Scott, *Gender and the Politics of History* (New York: Columbia University Press, 1988), p. 2.

xiv *it is."* Jim Windolf, "Little Men" (profile of Dian Hanson), *The Observer,* July 14, 1997, p. 21.

whole building!" Bob Blauner, "I Sold Out to Judith Regan," *Brill's Content,* March 2000, p. 86.

that woman." See *Esquire,* January 1999, p. 79.

Dow Jones." See *Vanity Fair,* August 1997, p. 160.

She's ballsy." See *Vanity Fair,* May 1998, p. 220.

from cowardice." See *The New Yorker,* October 13, 1997, p. 40.

Sharon Stones." Gerri Hirshey, "The Diva," *GQ,* November 1995, p. 155.

xv *us come."* Quoted by Joy Press in "Girl Power/The Selling of Softcore Feminism," *Village Voice,* September 23, 1997.

the office." See Maureen Dowd, "Pass the Midol," *New York Times,* April 15, 1998, p. A27.

mucked pigpens." See "Diane 'Got' Gore. But What Did We Get?" *Brill's Content,* September 1999, p. 59.

me first." Tucker Carlson, "Devil May Care," *Talk,* September 1999, p. 103.

xvi *social justice.* Most of the nation's metropolitan newspapers regularly carry news stories documenting officialdom's infatuation with hardness. One example from the *New York Times* ("New York Is Assailed for Welfare Delays," November 24, 1998, p. B4):

> While federal officials pursue their inquiry into New York City's welfare program, advocates for the poor testified before a City Council committee yesterday about the difficulties poor people encounter when seeking food stamp and Medicaid applications in city welfare offices.
>
> One mother of five, who told a city worker that she had no food, was referred to a food pantry, which was closed, one lawyer said. Another woman, who was six months pregnant and tried to apply for food stamps, Medicaid and welfare at 1 PM, was told to come back the next morning, the lawyer said.
>
> Neither woman got to apply for food stamps or Medicaid during their first visit to the welfare office, said the lawyer, Anne Callagy of the Legal Aid Society in Staten Island.
>
> Federal officials say the city's practice of delaying the distribution of food stamp and Medicaid applications may violate Federal law, which requires workers to distribute the forms without delay. Under the city's policy, a vast majority of people are refused applications on the first visit.
>
> All those who testified yesterday were critical of the city's tactics.
>
> City officials, who did not attend the Council hearing yesterday, say their policy of discouraging the poor from applying is intended to push people to rely on themselves, not on government. They say people who are truly needy will return for an application.

1. Women-Becoming-Men

3 *Any More.*" A 1996 *Newsweek* poll adds confirmation, reporting that "in the '90s . . . more of the cheaters are women." Jerry Adler, "Adultery/A New Furor over an Old Sin," *Newsweek*, September 30, 1996, p. 54.
the stronger. "Hey, let's talk about the F-word," says the copy in one milk mustache ad. See *Vanity Fair*, November 1996, p. 149.
4 *apron strings.*" *The New Yorker*, October 7, 1996, p. 46.
young lawyer." *The New Yorker*, November 20, 1995, p. 44.
Al Gore." *The New Yorker*, January, 19, 1998, p. 65.
touch prurient." *The New Yorker*, October 14, 1996, p. 74.
Let's hunt." *The New Yorker*, December 8, 1997, p. 78.
5 *bass-voiced.* A related voice prank comes from @rtwork, an artists' collective represented in the Whitney Biennial 2000. @rtwork switches the voice boxes of GI Joe and Barbie dolls on toy store shelves. See Janelle Brown, "The Net as Canvas," *Salon*, March 15, 2000, p. 3.
around you." Jean Lindamond, "Truckin' It," *New Woman*, November 1995, p. 126.
6 *for models.* See, e.g., *Harper's Bazaar*, September 1995, p. 335, and *Allure*, December 1996, pp. 134ff.
flight suits." Michael Roberts, "Craving Private Ryan," *The New Yorker*, March 22, 1999, p. 82.
Girl Style." *Teen*, September 1997, cover and pp. 106ff.
Got Screwed?" EOT ad in *Village Voice*, September 24, 1996, p. 7.
of desire." Tobey Hanlon, "Do You Need the Hormone of Desire?" *Prevention*, August 1997, pp. 73ff.
Planet campaign. Reebok ad, *Time*, May 6, 1966.
'em home." "Proust Questionnaire," *Vanity Fair*, August 1999, p. 100.
my hair." Hydro Clara, "On the Road to Becoming a Journeyman," *Moxie*, Fall 1999, pp. 31ff.
nervous wreck." Michael Schnayerson, "Life After Steve," *Vanity Fair*, November 1996, p. 236.
7 *blond hair.*" Susannah Hunnewell, "The Women Who Make or Break Male Supermodels," *Marie Claire*, December 1995, p. 34.
a living." Mark Kriegel, "Chyna Doll," *Talk*, June/July 2000, p. 92.
on him." William Plummer and Meg Grant, "Woman Warrior," *People*, June 24, 1996, p. 103.
ring careers. See Timothy W. Smith, "Frazier's Daughter Has Fast Debut," *New York Times*, February 7, 2000, p. B2.

Black," etc. Jean Strouse, "She Got Game," *The New Yorker,* August 16, 1999, p. 38.

Guys' Butts." Dana Silberger, "Playing with the Boys," *Jump,* October 1997, p. 62.

irreverent, aggressive." Fred Barnes, "Sometimes a Game Is Just a Game," *Weekly Standard,* July 26, 1999, pp. 22–24. Barnes's attitude to Chastain—and to her media adulators—is disapproving.

8 *role-playing adventures."* Nancy Malitz, "Invasion of the Girls Surprises Video-Game Makers," *New York Times,* December 21, 1995, p. C2.

a child. Amy Silverman, "The Virtual Bitch Slag," *Salon,* April 27, 2000, p. 2.

kick-butt dream?" Women who kick butt are now as conventional as women with balls. "Madam Secretary [admitted]," writes Nancy Franklin, "that she got a laugh out of the recent cartoon showing a woman trying on clothes in a store and being given this hard-line sales pitch: 'Madeleine Albright kicked butt in that suit.' " See "Talk of the Town," *The New Yorker,* December 15, 1997, p. 64.

the Sun. Lucy Lawless, who plays Xena, says, "Xena's agenda is just to get through the day without killing someone." See David Rensin, "The Woman Behind the Warrior," *TV Guide,* May 3, 1997, p. 22. On the movie and video history of tough women from *The Avenger* to *Thelma and Louise* and beyond, see Sherrie A. Inness, *Tough Girls: Women Warriors and Wonder Women in Popular Culture* (Philadelphia: University of Pennsylvania Press, 1998).

Reader's reviewer. "Babes with Blades," *Chicago Reader,* February 27, 1998, p. 28.

rageful things." See Margy Rochlin, "Beauty, Brains and a Knack for Giving the Censors Pause," *New York Times,* April 12, 1998, p. AR20.

of snow." Gina Belafonte, "Feminism/It's All About Me," *Time,* June 29, 1998, p. 61.

9 *to apologize."* Ann Powers, "The New Conscience of Pop Music," *New York Times,* September 19, 1999, Section 2, p 1.

a gangster." "Wise Girl," *Jane,* September 1999, p. 172.

people up." See "Frankly Admiring," *People,* December 14, 1995, p. 86.

your day." Lynne Russell, *How to Win Friends, Kick Ass and Influence People* (New York: St. Martin's, 2000), p. 28.

gonna watch." As always the cartoonists chuckle. In *The New Yorker* drawing by V. Twohy (March 11, 1996), one woman to another, both enjoying a box of chocolates and gazing at a vase of roses: "They're from David. He's been so much more considerate since I shot him."

dirty work." Elissa Schappell, "Why Bitches Get the Best Men," *Woman's Own,* August 1996, p. 11.

a Coke." Ibid., p. 11.

of thing." "He Spas/She Spas," *Jane,* September 1999, p. 116.

10 *a bit."* Daniel Frankel, "I've Had My Ass Kicked Before," *Men's Fitness,* December 1966, p. 107.

a guy." The dialogue in the key scene runs as follows:

> Dave: I'm leaving.
> Bobbi: You're leaving. Where? Why?
> Dave: You're why. Bobbie, you're never gonna change. It's just the way you are.
> Bobbi: What are you saying?
> Dave: I'm saying, look at yourself. You dress like a guy. You work like a guy. Hell, you even drink beer like a guy. I can't take it no more.
> Bobbi: You know what you can't take? You can't take me for who I am. You've never accepted me, Dave—and that really hurts.
> Dave: Accept? Lemme ask you a question. When we go out, what do you wear? Jeans and a blazer.
> Bobbi: Yeah, so what?
> Dave: So what? And then the waiter ends up bringing you the check. No, I don't think so. How can I accept it when people think you're more of a man in this fucking relationship than I am? . . .
> Bobbi: (Socks him on the jaw) You fucking bastard, you. (Stomping out) You make me sick.
> Dave: (Holding his chin) You even hit like a guy.

11 *making it."* Savings Bank Life Insurance ad, *New York Times,* April 30, 1996, p. A8.

forget that." Dave Eggers, *A Heartbreaking Work of Staggering Genius* (New York: Simon and Schuster, 2000), p. 103.

12 *really hot."* Late Night with Conan O'Brien, November 19, 1996.

be female." See James Wolcott, "Act I, Obscene Too," *Vanity Fair,* March 1999, p. 112.

give birth. "Vicki Shick and Tere O'Connor," *The New Yorker,* June 10, 1996, p. 15.

for children. TV Guide, April 26, 1997, pp. 30ff.

man-o-pause." Today, May 7, 1998.

and family. "Sex-Swap Cop Trades His Uniform for a Skirt," *National Enquirer,* September 24, 1996, p. 10.

the ass. Virginia Vitzhum, "Strap-on Epiphany," *Salon,* September 8, 1999, p. 2.

between us. Vicki Feaver, "Hemingway's Hat," *The New Yorker,* December 23, 1996, p. 108.

13 *much more.* Teasing show biz gender swaps, *The New Yorker's* W. Muller draws a man in shirtsleeves at his desk answering his wife's question (she's opening the mail): "No. I don't want to see an all-male production of *Little Women*" (November 23, 1998, p. 54).

and scrotum. Spy, October 1995.

totally energized." Graham Masterton, "The Sex Glow," *Woman's Own,* February 1966, p. 33.

Had One? Fiona Giles, ed., *Dick for a Day* (New York: Villard, 1996).

14 *Marcos–style closet.* For an account of the contradictory pleasures of boxing for women, see Rene Denfeld, *Kill the Body, the Head Will Fall* (New York: Warner, 1996).

to me." The New Yorker, March 16, 1998.

the woman." The New Yorker, August 19, 1996.

to him." In an August 1998 infomercial for Slam Man (a molded foam and plastic figure), Nancy Valen and other *Baywatch* actresses in boxing gloves throw jabs and right crosses at the figure. "I whack Slam Man pretty hard," says Valen.

15 *suffering terribly."* See Eleanor Clift, "A Terrible, Terrible Trauma," *Newsweek,* September 30, 1996, p. 57.

Environmental Medicine. AP dispatch, *Bradenton* (Fla.) *Herald,* January 30, 1996, p. 1.

an hour." Jon Nordheimer, "Gender Gap Not Worth Closing," *New York Times,* August 10, 1996, p. 37. A recent Mazda commercial opens on a car blasting "Rebel, Rebel" as it roars out of a parking garage. The driver is "a trim woman in her 30's" who's on her way to a PTA meeting. "Do not go gently into that PTA meeting," says the voiceover. See Patricia Winters Lauro, "New Campaigns Geared to Parents Replace Stodgy with Cool," *New York Times,* January 3, 2000, p. C1.

action-oriented." J. M. Twenge, "Changes in Masculine and Feminine Traits over Time," *Sex Roles* 36 (1997), pp. 305ff.

16 *to marry."* Gloria Steinem, "Learn to Trust Your Own Experience," *Hampshire Gazette* (Northampton, Mass.), May 24, 1995, p. 6.

of time." Betty Fussell, *My Kitchen Wars* (New York: North Point, 1999), pp. 100, 168.

2. Anatomy of Gender Shift (1)

20 *of detail.* A major debt is owed to Irving Babbitt, whose *Rousseau and Romanticism* (1947) ranks among the more powerful assaults on romanticism yet put in print.

grass huts." Camille Paglia, *Sexual Personae* (New York: Vintage, 1991), pp. 37–38.

21 *literary twits."* Camille Paglia, *Sex, Art, and American Culture* (New York: Vintage, 1992), p. 12.

affected dilettant[es]." Ibid., p. 128.

timorous nerds." Ibid. Quotations in this sentence are from pp. 216, 214, 219, and 210.

you belong!" Ibid., pp. 59–60.

in factories." Ibid., pp. 255–256.

22 *welcome flower."* Katie Roiphe, *The Morning After* (Boston: Little, Brown, 1993), pp. 101, 45, 135.

23 *of self.' "* Ibid., pp. 37, 38.

fantasies regulated. Ibid., pp. 102, 171.

25 *the world."* Harriet Rubin, *The Princessa: Machiavelli for Women* (New York: Doubleday, 1997), p. 4.

short hairs." Ibid., p. 40.

feed her." Ibid., p. 165. Quotes in this paragraph are from pp. 83 and 165.

to succeed." Ibid., p. 40. The theme of the irrelevance, to women of ambition, of rules—and of ordinary responses to those who break them—turns up often in books treating workplace strategies. "Women tend to feel guilty when they lie," writes Linda Obst, Hollywood production executive, "and angry when they are lied to. These emotions do not belong in the workplace." See Linda Obst, *Hello, He Lied, and Other Truths from the Hollywood Trenches* (Boston: Little, Brown, 1996).

26 *are themselves."* Rubin, *The Princessa*, pp. 68, 69, 104.

greatest desire. Ibid., pp. 130–131, 15–16.

a deal. Paglia, *Sex*, p. 63.

27 *wife relationships?* Ibid., p. 65. "I see with the eyes of the rapist," Paglia told the comedian Bill Maher on the latter's television program, *Politically Incorrect.* "We need more lust and aggression."

go on. Paglia, *Sex*, p. 63.

and submission." Roiphe, *Morning After*, p. 60.

the same." Ibid., pp. 37, 33.

28 *a killer."* D. M. Osborne, "The Devil Might Be an Angel," *Brill's Content*, November 1998, p. 100.

killer underneath." Patricia Sellers, "Don't Mess with Darla," *Fortune*, September 8, 1997, p. 64.

and how." John Lahr, "The Big Picture," *The New Yorker*, March 25, 1996, p. 77.

29 *with it." New York Post*, June 1997, p. 6.

hitting him." "Tonya Harding Arrested for Domestic Violence," Channel 6000, koin. com, February 24, 2000.

and shoulder." Bill Hoffman, "Soon-Yi Wooed Woody," New York Post.com, January 18, 2000. Hoffman's source is Marion Meade, *The Unruly Life of Woody Allen* (New York: Scribner, 2000).

amazing movies." Sarah Jacobson, review of "Grace Has Mace," *indieWire*, August 18, 1997, p. 3.

lust after." Jessica Hundley, "Where the Boys Are," *Salon*, March 20, 2000, p. 3.

could use." See "Kids These Days," *Spin*, November 1997, p. 40.

group's show. See Ann Powers, "Everything and the Girl," *Spin*, November 1997, p. 77.

in rage. See Alyssa Katz, "Postcards from the Edge," *Spin*, November 1997, p. 112.

30 *did it.*' "'Teen Beauty Queen Gives up Crown over Threats," Reuters dispatch, August 25, 1999, quoting the Lubbock *Avalanche Journal.*

14-year-old drowned." Ian Bailey, "Accused Drowned Virk While Smoking, Trial Told," National Post Online, March 15, 2000.

can find." Denis McCafferty, "Desperately Seeking Angry White Females," *Salon*, October 14, 1999.

3. Anatomy of Gender Shift (2)

32 *than bored.*" Unless otherwise noted, all comments by and about Esther Dyson are from Lesley Bennetts, "Wired at Heart," *Vanity Fair*, November 1997, pp. 158ff.

are stupid." See Jeri Clausing, "A Leader in Cyberspace, It Seems, Is No Politician," *New York Times*, April 10, 2000, p. C1.

33 *on that?*" Marcia Clark with Teresa Carpenter, *Without a Doubt* (New York: Viking, 1997), p. 180.

34 *that alone.*" Ibid., p. 179.

Davis–style. Ibid., p. 446.

a woman." Christopher Darden, *In Contempt* (New York: Harper-Collins, 1996), p. 231.

meaning gangster. Clark and Carpenter, *Without a Doubt*, p. 258.

fuck himself." Ibid., p. 148.

this—dresses." Ibid., pp. 263, 148.

their actions. Ibid., p. 179.

35 *a victim!*" Ibid.

its infancy." Ibid., p. 257.

36 *the prosecution.* See, e.g., Jeffrey Toobin, *The Run of His Life* (New York: Simon and Schuster, 1996), pp. 418–419. "Everything Darden

said [about domestic violence]," Toobin writes, "was probably true, but his opening could also be interpreted as a great edifice of rhetoric built on a foundation of little evidence." As Toobin observes, Darden's "burning fuse" summation was powerful but came too late to affect the trial's outcome.

scares us?" All comments by and about Ruthann Aron are drawn from Judy Oppenheimer, "Angry and Energetic," *Baltimore Sun,* June 22, 1997, pp. 1F, 6F.

39 *her bitch.*" All quotations in this section are drawn from Girlbaum, "The Girl Next Desk," *Bust,* Spring/Summer 1997, pp. 13-14. For more on *Bust'*s readership and content, see John Sanchez, "Freedom's Fallout," *Chicago Reader,* September 17, 1999, pp. 20ff.

42 *and "softly moan[ing]."* Maureen Dowd, "Hey Big Spender," *New York Times,* February 27, 2000.

for "coyness." Maureen Dowd, "Just Say Maybe," *New York Times,* August 22, 1999.

both ways." Ibid.

very long." Maureen Dowd, " 'Mr. Right' Becomes Mr. Rectitude," *New York Times,* March 8, 2000.

is propitious. Maureen Dowd, "Will You, Warren?" *New York Times,* August 15, 1999.

ice-dancing." Maureen Dowd, "Cowboy Feminism," *New York Times,* April 13, 1999.

43 *be debilitating."* Maureen Dowd, "Sure I Would," *New York Times,* September 12, 1999. The remainder of the quotations in this section are from the "Sure I Would" column.

44 *of risks."* All quotations in this section are drawn from the Federal News Service transcript of Dr. Marcia Angell's National Press Club speech on September 16, 1997.

46 *car keys."* All quotations in this section are drawn from Rebecca Mead, "The Good Old Days," *The New Yorker,* October 13, 1997, pp. 36–37.

4. The Media's Love-Hate Relationship with Women-Becoming-Men

50 *recurring themes.* Several historical factors figure in the background of the themes examined in this chapter and flourishing on the tube and at the multiplex. Oversimplified versions of maleness and femaleness arose in partial answer to the demands of a people engaged in nation-

building from scratch. The American individualist complex, which subordinates social and political commitments to the cause of self-realization, played a major role in thinning out "the American character." Twentieth-century and earlier heroicizations of isolates—characters intrigued by the phenomenon of their own indifference to others and persuaded that attachment, fellow feeling, and group outrage at injustice are marks of mediocrity—lent dignity to the ideal of the self as fearless scourge of sentiment.

Frontier myths and realities fostered the growth of the conviction that both men and women have simple, transparent natures determined by their sex. But the great American contributors to this faith over the years have included "feminized" ministers as well as Rough Riders, and an array of others: sentimental novelists, hard-assed evangelicals, Hemingway heroes, General George Patton, miscellaneous presidents, legislators, mass entertainers, CEOs, and labor leaders. Most of the contributors believed that significant human growth and development have everything to do with erasing within oneself thoughts, attitudes, and feelings associated with stereotypical versions of the other sex. Many contributors belonged to or led cults responsible for the nervy edge of American life: the cults of experience, of can-do practicality, of rugged virility, of learning-by-doing, the cults of team play, the common man, classlessness. Many were deeply committed not only to extreme oversimplifications of mankind and womankind but also to egalitarian gestures and mucker poses connecting the oversimplifications with "democracy." All the contributors defined real men as tough, real women as tender.

A few gifted artists and writers, Walt Whitman among them, battled the simplifiers and erasers, laboring to correct, through fully drawn, unsparing self-portraits, the national readiness to accept stereotypes. But with little success. Standard American versions of "the masculine" and "the feminine" continued to treat admixtures as depravity—continued to cram multidimensional humanity into molds fixing maleness as This (not that) and femaleness as That (not this). These simplified versions of the sexes were the bone and sinew of our national narrative, the structures without which bootstrapping and frontier myths would have been unthinkable.

Males who spoke for monolithic maleness, in accord with the latter myths, deprecated sensitivity and cultivation as weakness, and loved talking rough. Teddy Roosevelt separated real men (genuine males who hit the line hard) from "mollycoddles," "the weakling and

the coward," "the over-cultivated [and] over-refined," and other
"feminine" types "too fastidious, too sensitive to take part in the
rough hurly-burly of the actual work of the world." Billy Sunday
hailed Jesus as "the greatest scrapper that ever lived"—and deleted
memory of the courage of tenderness that refused to scorn Mary
Magdalen as a whore.

Females who spoke for monolithic femaleness were softly
effusive. Sara Clarke Lippincott, for example—a representative mid–
nineteenth-century writer and performer (pen name: Grace Green-
wood)—excluded all but the meek, weak, and "clingingly dependent" from the feminine essence.

Males or females who did not fit monolithic stereotypes were
considered to need explaining; the explanations usually cited traumas
resulting from natural or historical cataclysm. Thus Margaret
Mitchell presented Scarlett O'Hara aberrantly relishing an act of violence "with a joy deeper, more organic than any she finds in love,"
and made the reader of *Gone With the Wind* understand that Scarlett
had been masculinized by the Civil War.

Ten thousand opinion makers played roles in transforming human variousness into a diminished thing; many went at the work
with near-religious zeal; by the time of the women's movement—and
the birth of the ideal of gender flexibility—simplifiers and erasers had
whited-out nuance, indeterminacy, and ambiguity from the American psychological landscape. Only with the women's movement was
an effective resistance born. Spokespersons for gender flexibility
aimed at restoring color and complication to human innerness. They
imagined exchanges and interfusions shaped by choice and moder-
ated by a gradual sharing of roles. They believed that the pace of
women's advance from passivity and exclusion could be set by individual decisions regarding life opportunities and balances—individual selections from a once narrowly delimited inventory of ways of
being. Their expectation was that new characterological models
would emerge.

But, given the national past, the prospects weren't promising.
Generations had evaded truths of human variousness. Generations
had sacralized the macho bifurcations deemed functional to nation-
building in course. Four full decades before sixties feminism, a great
novelist and critic, D. H. Lawrence, observed in his *Studies in Classic
American Literature* (1923) that the nineteenth century had established "the essential American soul"—masculine, naturally—as
"hard, isolate, stoic, and a killer." Disagreement with that judgment

was conceivable, but there was no denying the difficulty of finding, on the crossover journey from female passivity to participation in the "male world," new characterological models. The dominant mindset had been erasing mystery from humanness for years, scoffing at claims that sexual difference was an imponderable *x*. Mass culture grew increasingly preoccupied with hardening the barriers—lace and gush here, can-do cowboys and linebackers there. The country needed a language capable of fostering development of the imagination of variousness. It needed ways of tempering the all-or-nothing climate of thought in which change couldn't be envisioned except as a veering between absolutes: abrupt shuttling from one reductive extreme to another (women-becoming-men). But history made it far less likely that the country would get what it needed than that it would get the gender myths sampled in this chapter.

Among the most stimulating recent contributions to an understanding of the narrowing of American character are Ann Douglas, *The "Feminization" of American Culture* (New York: Knopf, 1977); George Kateb, *Individualism and Democratic Culture* (Ithaca: Cornell University Press, 1992), and Thomas L. Dumm, *A Politics of the Ordinary* (New York: New York University Press, 1999).

to commercial. Entire sitcom segments are built on dramatized contrasts between physically aggressive women and their hopelessly pacific mates. Consider, for instance, a 1999 episode of *Ladies Man*. At the top of the show Grandma Mitzi Stiles remembers, from her school days, a prettier, more popular classmate named Barbara Bush: "I still daydream," says Grandma, "about smashing her face with a field hockey stick."

Her reverie is sparked by her daughter-in-law Donna's exhilaration at the prospect of violence nearer at hand. Donna has just swapped fighting words with Mavis, another mother, in a quarrel about whether Mavis's son stole Donna's daughter's Pokemon cards. During this verbal scrap, Donna grasped her crotch threateningly, as though she was holding the male genital package and could produce old-style male mayhem. Mavis answered with pepper spray that hit Donna's husband, Jimmy. (Jimmy at no point in the episode conveys an appetite for blood.)

Not so this couple's daughter Bonnie, however, alleged victim of the Pokemon theft. To identify the thief, Bonnie accompanied her mother, Donna, to the playground, where she was thrilled at her mom's performance. After a minute or so of adult patience, Donna collared a nine-year-old boy and—according to Bonnie's somewhat exaggerated version—socked him breathless with a blow to the wind-pipe. Recalling this assault, Bonnie glows.

It was of course Mavis's son who was "manhandled" by Donna, and it was this incident that brought on the pepper spray action in Donna's kitchen, and that leads to an effort by both wives to draw their mates into the female arena of bloodlust.

Jimmy meets Larry, Mavis's husband, in the park by appointment. Jimmy has never raised a hand against another in his life; Larry, equally pacific, brings coathangers for them so that they can hang their jackets on a jungle gym. "Have you met the wife?" Larry asks Jimmy twice, explaining why he can't go home without fisticuffs. Devoid of killer instincts, more fearful of their wives than of each other, disposed toward postponement of blows, the men exchange suggestions—tentatively—about which acts should be out of bounds. ("No gouging.") Larry proffers the card of an excellent ophthalmologist, and Jimmy's grateful. Seated at a table, they write official rules, gripped by the natural nonaggression of males.

But this truce has to end. The men must find a way to rip each other up. Brainstorming, working together on the problem, they trade insults, and at length roll off the screen to the ground as the sound-track plays catfight noise.

Post-commercial, Donna ministers to Jimmy's facial wounds, appearing solicitous. Bonnie volunteers that she owes an apology to Mavis's son since her Pokemon cards were merely misplaced. The audience roars with comic understanding. Donna and Bonnie caused a fight, harmed a loved one—to no end whatever. Old female burdens—sensitivity to moral wrong, sorrow at injustice and needless rows—are shed. Donna and Bonnie regard the blood spill nonchalantly, and Grandma displays her bravado (smash that face). Says the laugh track: *Delight in the* remorselessness *of these tough guys, these hard new American killers.*

5. Killer Women and Corporate Kindness

74 *a loan?* Diana B. Henriques with Lowell Bergman, "Profiting from Fine Print with Wall Street's Help," *New York Times On the Web,* March 15, 2000, pp. 1–16.

78 *circa 1830.* On women in revolutionary iconography, see Eric Hobs-bawm, *Workers: Worlds of Labor* (New York: Pantheon, 1984), chap. 6, "Man and Woman: Images on the Left."

79 *self-burnishing ploys.* The keenest contemporary anatomist of corporate self-praise is Jane Anne Morris, author of *Not in My Backyard: The Handbook* (San Diego: Silvercat, 1994), and a series of papers on the effects of corporate "donations" (published in *Progressive Populist* and elsewhere).

6. Gender Flexibility

85 *people's homes."* Catharine A. MacKinnon, *Feminism Unmodified/ Discourses on Life and Law* (Cambridge, Mass.: Harvard University Press, 1987), p. 76.
getting fucked." Ibid., p. 61.
to millennium. Joan Cocks puts the point clearly in her attack on MacKinnon, Susan Griffin, and Mary Daly: "That men are not merely the privileged beneficiaries of the sex/gender system but also its self-conscious authors and powerful agents; that the entire social world emanates from their desire, purpose, and will; that in all of history, women have been the blinded victims of male machinations; that in their true, unmystified, and uncontrolled state, women are essentially good—these are the core premises of radical feminist social critique." See Joan Cocks, *The Oppositional Imagination: Feminism, Critique, and Political Theory* (New York: Routledge, 1989), pp. 175–176.
86 *and men."* MacKinnon, *Feminism Unmodified,* p. 22.
male terms." Ibid.
as women." Ibid. Particularly obnoxious, in MacKinnon's view, is the domination, in legal thought about sexual discrimination and harassment, of the assumption that only the male standard qualifies as a standard: "In the guise of setting a single standard for persons, women are measured by the standards of men. Such a standard neither grasps the damage done to women nor values the products of women's social experience. Instead, the standard of men is seen as merely *the* standard. And in a sense, it is; or at least it has been. But to accept this standard reflects the very attitudes discrimination law exists to undermine: that the image of success, of potency, of what it means to do a job is the image of a man." Catharine MacKinnon, *Sexual Harassment of Working Women* (New Haven: Yale University Press, 1979), p. 144.
for change." MacKinnon, *Feminism Unmodified,* p. 22.
power itself." Ibid., p. 23.

87 *to be."* Ibid., p. 120.
88 *to women?"* Ibid., p. 121.
   been us." Ibid.
89 *our own."* Ibid.
   other people. Ibid., p. 123.
   value itself." Ibid., p. 122.
90 *the oppressor."* Ibid., p. 122.
   all women." Ibid., p. 75.
91 *a woman."* Ibid., p. 74.
92 *that way.* Ibid., p. 77.
   distorts it." See MacKinnon's essay "Feminism, Marxism, Method, and the State," in *Feminist Theory: A Critique of Ideology,* ed. Nannerl Keohane et al. (Chicago: University of Chicago Press, 1982), p. 3.
93 *that culture."* Arlie Hochschild, quoted in "Giving Women the Business," Harper's Forum, *Harper's,* December 1997, p. 57.
   and power. Mariah Burton Nelson, *The Stronger Women Get, the More Men Love Football* (New York: Avon, 1994), p. 51.

7. The Pursuit of Compositives

95 *the like.* The hard science model for difference research is, of course, the Harvard Nurses' Health Study, which, over the past generation, has produced more than two hundred published findings on relationships between women's diets and women's health.
96 *and intuition.* See Ann Douglas on the cult of motherhood in *The Feminization of American Culture* (New York: Knopf, 1977), chap. 2, "Feminine Disestablishment."
   sexual suppression." Sigmund Freud, "Civilized Sexual Morality and Modern Nervous Illness," in *The Complete Psychological Works of Sigmund Freud,* ed. James Strachey, Vol. 9 (London: Hogarth Press, 1961), p. 199. See also Freud's essay "Some Psychological Consequences of the Anatomical Distinctions Between the Sexes."
   population samples. The obvious example is the psychologist Lawrence Kohlberg; see below. In *The Psychology of Moral Development* (San Francisco: Harper, 1984), Kohlberg acknowledges that "the major part of my work on the development of moral judgment has been based upon longitudinal analysis of the follow-up data for my original cross-sectional male sample" (p. 340).
97 *don't exist."* Carol Gilligan, *In a Different Voice* (Cambridge, Mass.: Harvard University Press, 1982), p. 18.

universal applicability. The materials in question are assembled, together with Kohlberg's responses to criticism, in *The Psychology of Moral Development* and in his earlier book *The Philosophy of Moral Development* (San Francisco: Harper, 1981).

98 *5 reasoning.*" Kohlberg, *Psychology of Moral Development,* p. 340.

moral development." Gilligan, *In a Different Voice,* p. 18. Unless otherwise noted, the discussion that follows is drawn from pp. 18–35 of Gilligan's book.

103 *calmly on.* W. H. Auden, "Musée des Beaux Arts," *The English Auden* (New York: Random House, 1977).

104 *is experiencing.*" Ibid., p. 57.

105 *a right.*" Ibid., pp. 102, 103.

contextual relativism." Ibid., p. 166.

woman's care." Ibid., p. 74. Responding to attacks on her for romanticizing "pure womanhood" and "female care," Gilligan commented as follows: "I portray twentieth-century women choosing to have abortions, as well as women college students, lawyers, and physicians reconsidering what is meant by care in light of their recognition that acts inspired by conventions of selfless feminine care have led to hurt, betrayal and isolation. My critics equate care with feelings, which they oppose to thought, and imagine caring as passive or confined to some separate sphere. I describe care and justice as two moral perspectives that organize both thinking and feeling and empower the self to take different kinds of action in public as well as private life. Thus in contrast to the paralyzing image of 'the angel in the house,' I describe a critical ethical perspective that calls into question the traditional equation of care with self-sacrifice." See "An Interdisciplinary Forum on *In a Different Voice,*" ed. Linda K. Kerber et al., in *Signs: Journal of Women in Culture and Society* 2 (1986), 326–327.

106 *been made.* Gilligan, *In a Different Voice,* p. 67.

noncommunicating sectors. A like-minded critique of another academic discipline—economics—has lately been launched by Deidre McCloskey, who asserts: "No matter how you come at it mathematically, an economy takes place in a moral universe. That has been a big problem for economists to understand; they are so tied to prudence they don't regard other virtues as having anything to do with economics." See Louis Uchitelle, "A Transsexual Economist's 2d Transition," *New York Times,* June 19, 1999, p. B7. See also Julie A. Nelson, *Feminism, Objectivity, and Economics* (New York: Routledge, 1996).

107 *of knowledge.*" R. H. Tawney's Commonplace Book, ed. J. M. Winter

and D. M. Joslin (Cambridge: Cambridge University Press, 1972). Gilligan's implicit theme of complementarity has to do with political psychology—with postures and attitudes congruent with the culture of democracy. The quality of receptivity to others for which this author speaks up, through the character of Amy among others, matters civically as well as intellectually. Receptivity stands against the impulse abruptly to shun or exclude or reject; it stands for equal rights, democratic faith, inclusiveness of feeling, and identification. It is the tempering force that conjoins power with remorse, obliging it to a non-perfunctory, knowledgeably sympathetic address to otherness.

8. Spies in the House of Love

109 *sexed body."* Joan Cocks, *The Oppositional Imagination: Feminism, Critique, and Political Theory* (New York: Routledge, 1989), p. 13.
possible level." Ibid., pp. 219, 19.
110 *given order."* Ibid., pp. 46–47.
after all. Ibid., p. 49.
111 *not conflict."* Ibid., p. 10.
their own." Ibid.
112 *using it."* Ibid., p. 151. Unless otherwise noted, the remainder of this discussion is drawn from pp. 152–156 of *The Oppositional Imagination.*
116 *during his?* Not the least accomplishment of *The Oppositional Imagination* is its representation, in language, of the variousness of grown-up female sexuality. Other writers—Naomi Wolf, for one—are compelling on the sexual experience only of adolescents, not of adult women. See Naomi Wolf, *Promiscuities* (New York: Random House, 1997).
his body." Cocks, *The Oppositional Imagination,* p. 156.
118 *and gender.* Ibid., pp. 196–197.
and resigned." Ibid., p. 201.
119 *their side.* Ibid., p. 205.

9. A Community of Beings in a Single Self

123 *light beer."* Robert Bly, *Iron John/A Book About Men* (New York: Vintage, 1992), pp. 6, 33. The book was first published in 1990.

the temperament. Ibid., p. 97.
124 *do that.* Ibid., pp. 98, 62.
working out. Ibid., pp. 2–3.
125 *moderns don't.* Many of Bly's critics object that he believes young males alone need to recover their lost fierceness. The historian Gail Bederman, for example, argues that "frequently those who have criticized the 'civilized' present by invoking a lost 'primitive' past have strongly supported white supremacy, male dominance or both." See Gail Bederman, *Manliness and Civilization* (Chicago: University of Chicago Press, 1995), p. 239; a similar line of attack is taken by E. Anthony Rotundo in *American Manhood: Transformations in Masculinity from the Revolution to the Modern Era* (New York: Basic, Books, 1993), and Judith Stacey, *In the Name of the Family: Reflecting Family Values in the Postmodern Age* (Boston: Beacon, 1996). But there is no evidence of racism in *Iron John*, and Bly emphasizes often that occasional fierceness is functional for females as well as males. "In every relationship," he writes, "something *fierce* is needed once in a while: both the man and the woman need to have it" (p. 14).
woman's heart. Bly, *Iron John*, pp. 85, 174–175, 235-236. Themes of wholeness and emotional integration are developed at length in a more recent book by Robert Bly and Marion Woodman, *The Maiden King: The Reunion of Masculine and Feminine* (New York: Holt, 1998). The book lacks the sureness of voice and design that distinguish *Iron John*.
126 *grown man.* Bly, *Iron John*, pp. 186–227.
young woman. Ibid., pp. 55, 123.
127 *school instead."* Ibid., pp. 14, 132–133.
128 *play with."* Ibid., pp. 254–255.
kissed him. Ibid., p. 258.
ancient myths." Christopher Lasch, *Women and the Common Life,* ed. Elisabeth Lasch-Quinn (New York: Norton, 1997), pp. 150–151. Lasch criticizes Bly for believing that "aesthetic appreciation" can take the place of "an authoritative spiritual discipline." But he effectively defends Bly against attackers who misrepresent his work as a simplistic endorsement of "red-blooded manhood."
129 *the past.* Bly, *Iron John*, pp. 234–235. The sense of balance notable in *Iron John* is absent, apparently, from Bly's public performances as guru to young males. See Susan Faludi's scathing account of those performances in *Backlash* (New York: Anchor, 1992), pp. 304ff.

10. Positivity Lost

134 *her teachers.* The events in the life of Sandra Quintana summarized in this section are recounted at book length by Cristina Rathbone in *On the Outside Looking In* (New York: Atlantic Monthly Press, 1998). Except where noted, all quotations are drawn from this exceptionally full and touching reportorial narrative.

the way." See *The New Yorker,* June 8, 1998, p. 82.

the waist." Rathbone, *On the Outside,* p. 53.

135 *shirt: Boom!* Ibid., pp. 53.

137 *our kids.* Ibid., p. 250.

138 *thinking well."* Ibid., pp. 131, 305.

too long." Ibid., p. 236.

139 *abrupt end."* Ibid., p. 306.

shedding blood." Quoted by Kim Townsend in *Manliness at Harvard,* (New York: Norton, 1996), p. 243.

140 *students alike.* The best-known example is that of the late Mina Shaughnessy at the City University of New York. See her *Errors and Expectations* (New York: Oxford University Press, 1979), and my appreciation of her work, "Mina Shaughnessy: Meeting Challenges," *The Nation,* December 9, 1978, pp. 654ff.

the odds." Rathbone, *On the Outside,* p. 338.

her idealism." Ibid., pp. 306, 338.

11. The Detachment Trap

143 *sentimentalized moorings."* Sharon Hays, *The Cultural Contradictions of Capitalism* (New Haven: Yale University Press, 1996), pp. 1, 17.

144 *than one."* Ibid., p. 51.

145 *surely bizarre."* Ibid., pp. 129, 65. See also p. 64ff.

Sacred Mothering." Ibid., pp. 22, 32, 33, 122, and passim.

146 *market societies."* Ibid., pp. x, 173.

overly sentimental." Ibid., p. 127.

to hear." Ibid., p. 121.

147 *and unconscionable?* Ibid., p. 12. The intensive mothers would doubtless strongly object also to the new enthusiasm for Ferberizing, that is, using Dr. Richard Ferber's hard-nosed methods of "teaching" young children to go to sleep alone. The methods are outlined in Ferber's *Solve Your Children's Sleep Problems* (New York: Simon and Schuster, 1985). For critical views of the methods, see John Seabrook,

"Sleeping with the Baby," *The New Yorker*, November 8, 1999, pp. 56ff.
and calories." Hays, *Cultural Contradictions*, p. 110.

148 *mysteries, "feminine."* A fairer representation of the sound of a challenge based on intrinsic worth can be heard regularly in *Welcome Home*, a Virginia-based monthly journal published by and for so-called intensive mothers.

12. Self-Censorship and Double Binds

151 *President, too."* Elizabeth Benedict, quoted in "New York Supergals Love That Naughty Prez," *New York Observer*, February 9, 1998, p. 21.
about it." Patricia Marx, Ibid.
President's come." Erica Jong, Ibid.

153 *'victim feminism.'* " Molly Haskell, "We're All in Bed with Clinton," *New York Observer*, March 2, 1998. The quotations from Haskell are drawn from this column.

155 *in short.* Comparable moments in which men figure as the intimidators have become routine, of course. I still remember a summer morning in the mid-nineties when it fell to Elizabeth Vargas, substituting for the vacationing Katie Couric on the *Today* show, to interview Antonio Banderas—described by *Rolling Stone* as "the ultimate in sexy action cool." Vargas's questions fit the standard pattern of celebrity spots: queries about the tone of the violence in a recent film starring the actor, about his relationship with a famous actress, about the frenetic interest of fans in the couple's public appearances. Following a half-dozen bland exchanges and a commercial, the show returned to a two-shot: Matt Lauer fanning Vargas with a clump of copy, and commenting with feigned chuckling concern on the dishevelment presumably caused in her by adjacency to the "hunky hero" she had just interviewed.

During the protracted fanning Vargas, a tall, pleasant-voiced woman with a faintly tense manner and startled eyes, didn't speak; her fixed smile barely wavered. Lauer's loutish behavior amounted to an objectifying violation of private space and private feeling, and an insulting claim of close personal knowledge: *Like every male, I know what women find sexually arousing; I know that this hunk has just heated you up unbearably. My knowledge of this secret heat derives from my maleness—what I feel when I chat up Julia Roberts or whomever. My knowledge and our interchangeability place me in position to kid you amusingly. Because I understand that you wish to be seen as a regular guy (nice sense of humor, nothing prudish about Elizabeth despite the name, etc.), I prolong the kidding, certain both of its "entertainment value" and of its usefulness to your future.*

Vargas never turned away from her co-host—her equal. She didn't rebuke him, didn't tell him to speak for himself, uttered not a word about his behavior. The impression she left for the length of the fanning business was that she was reining in an impulse to protest, provisionally accepting objectification out of concern about appearing humorless or prissy or undemocratically aloof.

Just here lay traducing and betrayal. The ideal of gender flexibility envisaged self-respect that would not be based on mimicry of stereotypical masculinity. It implicitly rejected the notion that gender equality meant equal vulnerability to sex bombs. It held out the possibility, for men and women, of a candor about sexuality that rose above shared furtive giggling over dirty secrets.

But no more than the rest of us could Vargas claim this self-respect. She was incarcerated in gender shift manners—learning the ropes, the rules of good citizenship under the gender shift tyranny. The rules outlaw protest against sexual objectification because such protest reveals that the protester feels at a disadvantage, put upon, resourceless—in some way unequal. Gender shift tyranny despises the at-a-loss feeling because it's a telltale indicator that the insulted person actually is vulnerable to insult, i.e., isn't tough enough. Learning the gender shift ropes doesn't just mean learning to repress the capacity to recognize one's own humiliation; it means learning that the act of repressing the impulse to criticize masculinizing "liberation" is a vital step toward realization of equality. It means grasping that progress hasn't to do with challenging the oblivious and violative aspects of the other-sex regime one is joining through role exchange; progress has to do with understanding that the myth of toughness is here to be embraced and does not admit challenge by Vargas or Haskell or anyone else concerned about belonging.

moved on. Mary Gaitskill, "Ready, Able, and Unwilling," *Vogue,* August 1995, pp. 222-225. The quotations from Gaitskill are drawn from this article. Shortly after the piece appeared, Gaitskill published a short story on its themes in which an older woman (thirty-nine) and a younger man (twenty-six) have a sexual encounter marked by a series of penetrations and rejections. The woman's flashback memories recall previous similar encounters: "I recalled that my last boyfriend, who was also in his twenties, had told me that he sometimes liked to pull out of a kiss, so that the girl's tongue would be sticking out and looking funny." See Mary Gaitskill, "Turgor," *The New Yorker*, November 6, 1995, pp. 156ff.

13. Shades of Darkness

160 *to death.* Patricia Cornwell, *Postmortem* (New York: Scribner, 1990), pp. 200, 225.
     horrible heart." Patricia Cornwell, *From Potter's Field* (New York: Scribner, 1995), p. 411.

161 *the suite."* Cornwell, *Postmortem*, p. 155.

162 *as bidden."* Joyce Carol Oates, *Zombie* (New York: Dutton, 1995), pp. 49–50.
     fucking unzip." Ibid., p. 52.

163 *giant nosebleed.* Ibid., p. 82.
     broken worm. Ibid., pp. 145–152.

165 *like him."* Susanna Moore, *In the Cut* (New York: Knopf, 1995), pp. 51, 60, 46.
     all right." Ibid., p. 177.

167 *his privates.* Quotations are from A. M. Homes, *The End of Alice* (New York: Scribner, 1996), pp. 23, 140. See also *Appendix A: An Elaboration on the Novel "The End of Alice": Art and Text* (San Francisco Artspace, March 1996).
     the time. Ibid., p. 144.

168 *and genitals.* Ibid., pp. 248, 269.

14. Three Styles of Nostalgia

173 *from females.* Wendy Shalit, *A Return to Modesty: Discovering the Lost Virtue* (New York: Free Press, 1999), p. 233.

174 *get depressed?"* Ibid., pp. 114, 243.
     every respect." Ibid., p. 10.
     but sameness." Ibid., p 160.

175 *their eyes."* Ibid., p. 87.
     equally good.' " Ibid., p. 91.

176 *to them."* Ibid., p. 230.
     of virtue. Ibid., p. 231.

177 *is sexy."* Ibid., pp. 216, 192.

180 *their loneliness."* Lionel Tiger, *The Decline of Males* (New York:

Golden, 1999), pp. 27, 109, 27. That today's males are in a pathetic plight, "at risk of becoming 'tomorrow's second sex,'" is a theme increasingly attractive to right-wing foundations and the television producers and authors they finance: witness the three-part "gender wars series" presented in 1999 by PBS's *National Desk,* a public affairs program hosted by Laura Ingraham and Larry Elder. Partly Scaife-financed, this series dwelled at length on "Fem Fear" and "guys [becoming] the minority group." For an extended analysis, see Jennifer L. Pozner, "Rally 'Round the Boys," *Extra: The Magazine of Fair,* September–October 1999, pp. 20ff.

181 *intricate legacies."* Tiger, *The Decline of Males,* pp. 127, 137, 26.
evolutionary legacy." Ibid., pp. 103, 100, 75, 108.

182 *maternalesque femininity."* Ibid., pp. 260, 11–12, 82.
unhappy families." Ibid., pp. 101–102.

183 *that time."* Ibid., p. 199.
Year fetes. Ibid., p. 25.
extended hand. Ibid.

186 *and consumerism."* Susan Faludi, *Stiffed: The Betrayal of the American Man* (New York: Morrow, 1999), p. 19.
virulent voyeurism." Ibid., pp. 477, 505, 566, and passim. Stephen S. Hall reports on the impact of "ornamental culture" on teenage boys in "The Troubled Life of Boys: The Bully in the Mirror," *New York Times,* August 22, 1999, Section 6, p. 31.
the sons." Faludi, *Stiffed,* p. 378.

187 *sex-object heaven."* Ibid., p. 26.
of battle." Ibid., pp. 20, 26.
packaged womanhood." Ibid., p. 601.

188 *selfless manhood."* Ibid., p. 23.

189 *of power."* Ibid., p. 73.
were embedded." Ibid., p. 602.
more miserable." Susan Faludi, *Backlash* (New York: Anchor, 1992), p. ix.

190 *sheer brutality."* Ibid., pp. xiv, xv, xvi, xxi.
defeated outright." Faludi, *Stiffed,* p. 605.

15. Achievements in Variousness

194 *new self.* The nineties were awash, in song, story, and novel, with "child-addicted" males. Bob Carlisle's "Butterfly Kisses," a song about a father watching his daughter grow which sold 2 million al-

bums, became subsequently a children's book and a trade book. For a literary version of paternal devotion, see Stephen Dixon's novel *Gould* (New York: Holt, 1997).

196 *is not.* Not by intention, *Mrs. Doubtfire* provides a reminder of the defining element of *false* flexibility, namely, total absorption with personal acts, personal gratification. Hillard's sole purpose in seeking access to skills, feelings, and understandings associated with the other sex is to satisfy his own "child addiction"; no suggestion implicit or otherwise of an interest extending beyond that of the private self. Classic feminism's vision of variousness aimed beyond self-enclosure and connected release from rigid gender boundaries with broad-scale social transformation; it believed in the possibility that an activism-oriented gender consciousness could ultimately effect profound change in social and political structures.

A measure of the weakened condition of this belief is the insistence, by the powerfully influential school of theorists led by Judith Butler, that no significant alteration of existing masculinist structures is conceivable; the best one can do is to secure the gratification attainable by parodying gender stereotypes in ways that express personal awareness of the arbitrariness of gender norms and identities. "The critical task for feminism," Butler writes, "is not to establish a point of view outside of constructed identities. . . . The critical task is, rather, to locate strategies of subversive [parodic] repetition enabled by those constructions, to affirm the local possibilities of intervention through participating in precisely those practices of repetition that constitute identity and, therefore, present the immanent possibility of contesting them." See Judith Butler, *Gender Trouble: Feminism and the Subversion of Identity* (New York: Routledge, 1990), p. 147. For a critique of Butler's politics of "personal acts carried out by a small number of knowing actors," see Martha C. Nussbaum, "The Professor of Parody," *New Republic*, February 22, 1999, pp. 37ff.

200 *flexibility is.* No such revelation comes in the work of, say, Camille Paglia, because Paglia conceives of *her* variousness as entailing tolerance of rape ("not that big a deal").

201 *can fix."* Natalie Angier, *Woman: An Intimate Geography* (Boston: Houghton Mifflin, 1999), pp. 277, 276, 283.
only faintly." Ibid., p. 365.

202 *is poobah.* Ibid.
it along. Ibid.

206 *his cause.* A particularly memorable demonstration of the strength occurred during a 1991 *MacNeil-Lehrer* forum on a Department of

Education report recommending the establishment of a national examination system. Under fire from U.S. Education Secretary Lamar Alexander and three superintendents of major urban school systems, Kozol gave no ground and kept his point in clear sight of the national audience. One representative exchange:

MacNeil: They all seem to think that this trying to set a base line and national standards and assess performance is a useful exercise, and they're all very experienced educators. You don't agree with that?

Kozol: Nobody on this panel has disputed what I said, that Head Start is a blessing for pre-school children. . . . And yet we still deny it to three quarters of our kids and it would only take $5 billion to do it. . . . I'm not against the idea of national standards. I don't oppose that at all. It's good to know where everyone stands. But there's something a bit—a bit ungenerous about imposing national standards but refusing to provide any kind of national equity. In other words, kids in Mississippi will continue to get less than $3,000 a year for their schools. In Detroit maybe they're up to $5,000. Meanwhile, out on Long Island, Great Neck, outside New York, they're spending almost $16,000. But they're all going to be judged by the same standards. And it seems to me, with all respect to Secretary Alexander, that imposing equal standards but refusing to provide equal opportunity is the characteristic of a bully.

Acknowledgments

I owe many large debts. Richard Todd, Phyllis Westberg, Steve Fraser, and Elaine Pfefferblit provided invaluable counsel at various moments of crisis. Amanda Heller saved me from countless errors. Susan Edelberg, Margaret Groesbeck, and Michael Kasper at the Frost Library and Greg Gallagher at the Century Library were tirelessly patient and helpful. Jeff Kreines's massive knowledge of Movie (and Sitcom) America was an indispensable resource, as was Benj DeMott's knowledge both of popular music and of two centuries of American and European cultural criticism. I'm grateful to Martin McCaffrey for several inspired finds. Conversations with Tom De-Mott, Maria Prestinary, and Megan DeMott Quigley kept me alert to the impact of toughness dogma on urban schools and housing courts; David and Megan Quigley taught me—with exquisite inventiveness—much that I should have known but didn't about intensive parenting. (Together with Benj, David also pushed me—to my advantage—deeper into the book side of my argument.) Peggy Craig DeMott read version after version with a shrewd yet kind critical eye.

I owe my largest debt by far to Jo DeMott, who began forwarding ideas, possible texts, and interpretations to me when *Killer Woman Blues* was a four-page proposal and didn't stop until the finished manuscript was in the mail. Her belief in the venture, feeling for its themes, and exhilarating sense that wrestling with it was fun kept my faith high in the face of a miserable array of old folks' afflictions. We fought often—indeed are still at odds about many positions herein. But no matter: *We got there, kiddo. Measureless thanks.*